AUGUSTA DWYER

INTO THE AMAZON

THE STRUGGLE FOR
THE RAIN FOREST

SIERRA CLUB BOOKS
SAN FRANCISCO

Copyright © 1990 by Augusta Dwyer.
First published in Canada by Key Porter Books Ltd., Toronto.

Library of Congress Cataloging-in-Publication Data

Dwyer, Augusta, 1956–
  Into the Amazon : the struggle for the rain forest / by Augusta Dwyer.
    p.   cm.
  ISBN 0-87156-637-0
  1. Man—Influence on nature—Amazon River Region. 2. Rain forest ecology—Amazon River Region. 3. Amazon River Region—Social conditions. I. Title.
GF532.A4D88   1991
304.2'09811—dc20   90-40816
                                                      CIP

Cover design by Bonnie Smets
Cover photograph by Loren McIntyre
Book design by Scott Richardson
Map by James Loates

Printed in the United States of America on acid-free, recycled paper
10 9 8 7 6 5 4 3 2 1

"I am just one of many comrades who struggle against a political, economic, and social system that sustains itself in the exploitation of the environment and our people." — Chico Mendes

This book is dedicated to Chico and to those comrades

CONTENTS

PREFACE

I once spent a Sunday afternoon in the city of Belém browsing through an exhibit of rare watercolors, painted in the Amazon by three European artists, Taunay, Rugendas and Florence. All three had traveled the region in the 1820s as part of the Von Langsdorff expedition, a rather unusual undertaking in that Von Langsdorff, a German-born Russian officer and diplomat, went insane part way through it. Almost everyone caught malaria, and at one point the expedition was held up for two days, when the baron's elaborate frogged jacket was stolen by an Indian girl who ran off with it into the forest.

Like those long-ago travelers filling their notebooks, sketch pads and herbaria with data from the mysterious splendid jungle that covers 60 percent of Brazil, my original idea was to journey through Amazonia, just to see what it was like and describe the people who lived there. Like them, it was simple curiosity that impelled me; I would prod the great green body here and there, and come back with my own sketches of its reality.

It took one brief visit to the town of Xapuri, on a day I will never forget, with Chico Mendes and a group of rubber tappers in the midst of a struggle to save a tract of forest, to make me realize that, were I to merely sketch the jungle, I would be wasting my time entirely. The situation of the rubber tappers — and how they dealt with it — made it clear that this body I wished to prod was not only ecological but political. The rubber tappers put me on the right track, so to speak, a track I soon found threaded through the realities of Amazonia today as neatly as their tapping paths encircle the rubber trees.

I got the idea to write about the people of the Amazon while living in Rio de Janeiro, where I was working as a free-lance journalist. There was always plenty to write about. After various economic plans, inflation remained implacable, reaching a rate of 1000 percent in 1988. Crime and poverty were worsening all the time and we would ask ourselves how ordinary people, especially the poor, managed. Many Brazilians, for the first time in their history, simply wanted to go away.

After every weekend, the papers carried a new body count from the city's slums and shantytowns, as death squads — clandestine hired gangs, often of policemen — snuffed out small-time hoods or anyone considered to be a hood. As months went by, the number of homeless people, including young men, mothers with small children, and kids of every age, sleeping on the sidewalk on the block where I lived grew and grew. In fact, it was estimated that, in Brazil, there were about 5 million children sleeping rough, either partially or totally disconnected from their poverty-stricken parents in the miserable ghettos of despair that are now an accepted part of almost every Brazilian city.

Meanwhile, the nation's senate and congress were busy working on a new constitution, Brazil's seventh since it became a republic in 1889. In it, land reform died a slow death while the military retained a powerful influence. President José Sarney demanded and got a mandate of five years after handing out favors to the majority Brazilian Democratic Movement Party and other politicians, even though poll after poll showed his popularity rating dropping right off the graph. Strikes broke out among teachers, bank workers, petroleum workers and steelworkers who, in spite of heavy repression from the army, banded together and carried out the largest general strike in history in March 1989, with an estimated 35 million workers taking part. Negotiations on the foreign debt, the highest in the Third World at more than $120 billion, continued, with Brazil finally agreeing to resume payments in mid-1988. The country's exports were greater than ever, but with monthly payments of about $3 billion and no new investment, the economic picture remained bleak.

Since Brazil was first colonized, the Amazon has been seen as an El Dorado, a place of hidden riches and untold potential wealth. And as Brazil has modernized, hitting all the obstacles of modern capitalism, the Amazon is still held to be some kind of treasure chest, some kind of savior that will almost magically transform a Third World nation into another United States. Opened up with new technology and forced to reveal its treasures, the Amazon, everyone believes, will solve all those nasty problems in the south.

In fact, the Amazon does contain a great array of riches; it is a land of superlatives. Innumerable waterways thread the huge basin, an area the size of Western Europe. Its verdure is seemingly boundless. The second-longest river in the world, stretching almost from one end of a continent to another, the Amazon River produces one-fifth of the world's fresh water. In the equatorial valley that spreads through nine countries, there exist so many species of flora and fauna that only a fraction have been identified. The subsoil contains deposits of gold and precious stones, iron, nickel, tin and many other kinds of ore. Valuable hardwoods such as mahogany, teak and rosewood are part of the abundance of the forest, not to mention rubber, oils, nuts, fruit and medicinals. The Amazon is rich in promise, but so is the rest of Brazil, yet that has not made it a wealthy or equitable nation.

It may be that the region defies modern attitudes to development. After all, the Amazon is not easy to travel in; it is prey to rainstorms and flooding. Its soil, for all the lushness of the jungle that covers it, is poor in nutrients. But rather than the region, it may be the notion of development that is proving itself bankrupt.

The long flight from Rio to the north does not really lead away from the problems of the rest of Brazil. If anything, the Amazon is as seriously affected as the south by the debt, the necessity to export, the free-market-aided-by-government approach to economics that is popular in the capitalist world these days. Such pressures have turned the Amazon into a battleground and may eventually turn it into a desert.

The first Brazilian president to visit the Amazon was the dictator Getúlio Vargas, in 1940. Since his visit, repeated administrations, almost none of them democratically elected, have sought to conquer the Amazon through modern technology and rational planning. The greatest onslaught occurred during the military dictatorship (from 1964 until 1985, when Sarney took over), a series of governments headed by generals who encouraged Brazil's so-called economic miracle. Between 1965 and 1968, for example, Brazil's gross domestic product grew by 6 percent each year. From 1968 to 1971, it grew even more quickly, at 10 percent, reaching a record 11.6 percent in 1972. Such fantastic expansion caused the *New York Times*, in a 1971 article, to declare, quite correctly, that Brazil had shattered "all statistical records in business and industry." Changes were made to the mining code and investment requirements, encouraging foreign multinationals to come to Brazil. By 1972, for example, 158 of the country's top 500 companies were foreign owned.

With this growth came tremendous upheaval: about 24 million people left their home states in the 1970s. Land was taken over for mechanized farming of crops such as soya and wheat, but domestic food production could not keep pace. Studies done in São Paulo in the

1970s indicated that infant mortality rates grew during the first years of the economic boom, while another survey showed that 60 percent of adults in a São Paulo sample were undernourished. The Amazon was part of this expansion and its contradictions.

The region was used to siphon off the starving northeastern peasants and the newly displaced share croppers of the south, "a land without men," as one government bureaucrat put it, "for men without land." With tax incentives and subsidies from the government, big business was also encouraged to get into mining and ranching there.

Now those ranches are proving to be both uneconomical and unproductive. And while the world's largest iron mine, Carajás, is on stream and currently the source of a quarter of Europe's steel, Brazil's economic woes and debt payments are greater than ever. The state of Rondônia, which was supposed to harbor all those landless farmers, is a place of barren dusty towns and peasants barely keeping body and soul together as they battle poor soil, malaria and bank payments. Many of them have already moved on from the plots they were originally given. Even the hand-dug gold pit of Serra Pelada brought far more death and misery than its gold deposits could ever make up for. Meanwhile, the forest cover is being lost at a rate of between 9 million and 17 million acres (3.5 million to 7 million hectares) each year, depending on which of the equally devastating sets of statistics you look at.

I began the research for this book with a trip to Manaus, capital of the state of Amazonas, and to the state of Acre in March 1988. This was followed by another fairly short trip to the states of Rondônia and Acre in July. In late September, I flew to Belém, using it as a base for almost two months as I traveled to the town of Cametá, on the lower Tocantins River, and later to the towns of Conceição and São Felix on the Araguaia River. Sailing up the Amazon River from Belém took me about five days, and I arrived in Manaus again in November. In the last two months of 1988, I made two trips to Indian areas, to the Yanomami in the state of Roraima, and finally to the Tikuna Indians, along the far reaches of the Amazon (there called the Solimões) River, at the border with Colombia. The epilogue was researched in March 1989.

What the rubber tappers, and many others after them, showed me was that the Amazon cannot survive these repeated attempts to profit quickly from it, to militarize it and to cut it down. Nor can its people.

The river dwellers, fishermen, rubber tappers and other extractivists have been able to live in harmony with the Indians of the region and the environment, learning and surviving from both. They are the ones who should be making decisions about the Amazon. And that is what this journey is all about.

ACKNOWLEDGMENTS

Aside from most of those named in the text, I am extremely grateful to the following people:

My husband, Colin Mooers, Michael Small, and the staff at the Canadian Embassy in Brasilia, Peter May, Stephen Schwartzman, Edilson Martins, Dr. Emir Bemerguy, Dr. Napoleao Figuereido, Renan Antunes de Oliveira, Samuel Benchimol, Claire Lorrain, João Pacheco de Oliveira, Chico from the CIMI in Manaus, Philip Fearnside, Miriam Pereira, Ana de Souza Pinto, João Bosco Pereira Braga, Ideval Martins Alves, Maria Elena from IBASE, Felisberto Damasceno, Sister Carmem from the Bishop's Office, Boa Vista, Vadislau Ferraz Buhler, Jose Candido Viera, Paulo Vicente, Lucia de Andrade, and the Gaspar family of Itaituba.

Books by the following authors were also of invaluable help:

John Hemming, Sue Branford and Oriel Glock, and Shelton Davis.

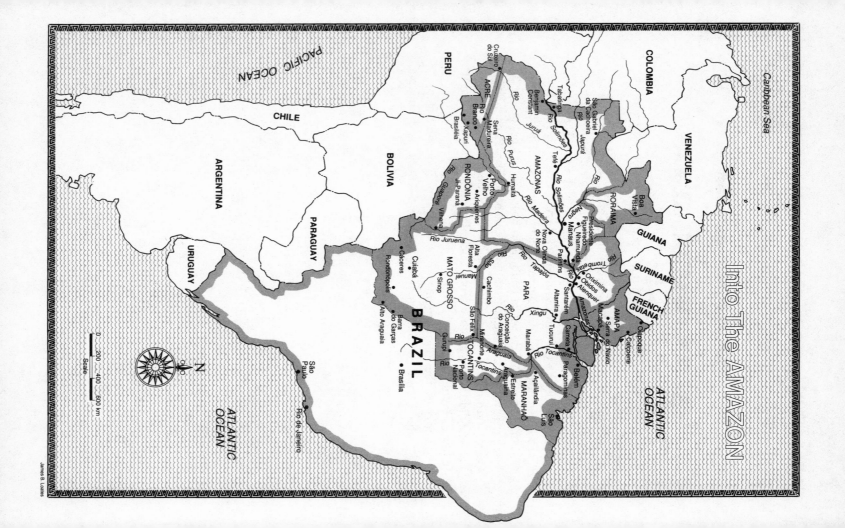

ONE

~~~~~~~~~~~~~

A THREAT TO THE FOREST

IF YOU ASK CLARICE FERREIRA Lima da Silva if she has far to go to visit her friend Cecilia Mendes, she'll raise her chin slightly as though pointing the direction and say, "Oh, no, it's right close by. Only about an hour."

It is only about an hour on foot, that is, a measure of time as distant from its urban meaning as the state of Acre is, it seems at first, from the rest of Brazil.

Mrs. da Silva and Mrs. Mendes, one in her fifties, the other sixty-two, live in Acre, on a rubber estate, or *seringal*, verging on the Bolivian border. To get to her neighbors, Dona Clarice will walk along one of the rubber tappers' paths, through the filtered rain forest light, along corridors of trees and hanging vines, cool under the infinite canopy of green. She will go accompanied by the sounds of forest life: the wind through the multishaped leaves, the cries of birds, perhaps the fall of a dying tree from its thin footing of soil, the persistent tapping of a monkey trying to break the shell of a Brazil nut against a tree trunk, like a man hammering a nail. Butterflies as bright as any carnival mulatta flash among the bushes.

Dona Clarice had been spending a lot of time at the Mendes place lately. Neat and tidy in her simple blue cotton dress, long black hair wound into a loose knot on her head, she was busy in the kitchen, making sure everyone had enough to eat. This has been her daily task. Dozens of rubber tappers were camping out there, three men from the Ministry of Agriculture, better known as INCRA, were doing a census, and Dona Clarice was helping with the preparing of food, with the endless washing up on the little platform of rough boards in the clear-running stream out back.

The kitchen was full of women that morning in mid-March; they sat on stools and chattered, they cradled small children, they carefully sliced and dried the meat in the big aluminum basin, brought in from town to feed the rubber tappers. A pressure cooker full of rice was bubbling on a flat clay stove, whose short metal pipe pierced the wall just beneath the eaves to let the wood smoke out.

The slats that formed the walls had spaces between them, through which the sunlight poured in long shafts, like the shingles of light the sky disperses through the leafy canopy of the forest. It glinted off the brilliantly scrubbed pots hanging from a crude shelf beside the back door and lit up the whole room with its bare furniture and basic kitchen utensils.

Cecilia Mendes, a tiny, still lovely old woman, was overseeing the goings-on in her kitchen. Owner of a raucous, gritty voice that seems to belie her diminutive size, she had long, straight hair, gone gray now, which she wound at the nape of her neck in a smooth knot. Often, she would wear an incongruous pair of black-rimmed glasses fastened around the back of her head with a piece of elastic. Her mother, she told me, was Bolivian, and as if to prove it, she began to rhyme off the days of the week in Spanish. She worked as she talked, leaning over a counter built out from the windowsill into the hard, bright sun, the soapy water dripping through the splits in the boards onto the ground beneath.

Many of Dona Cecilia's fifteen children, including five sons — Sebastião, Miguel, Francisco, Antonio and Nisomar — still live nearby in Seringal Cachoeira. A son and a daughter live in Bolivia, and another son, José, is a military policeman in the nearby town of Xapuri. By the time he was old enough to leave his rubber trees to Antonio to tap, her husband, Joaquim, had saved up enough money to buy a small house in Xapuri, but Dona Cecilia didn't like living in town. "I felt like a prisoner," she said, "all closed in. There was nowhere to go to, except out to the stores to go shopping. Then you have to spend the rest of the day in your house. Here I can be out as much as I want, visit my daughters, my girlfriends."

I met her daughters, neighbors, grandchildren and nieces; forgot, as I invariably do, their names. They offered me the ubiquitous glass of strong, sweet coffee that greets the visitor in any rural house in the Amazon. Slightly overwhelmed by all these people, yet evermore curious about them, I sat to join their chat.

What had brought these neighbors from the other clearings of the Cachoeira rubber estate to the Mendes house was not, however, a happy occasion. They were there out of fear, and only one topic took up their conversation. A neighboring rubber tapper named Jose Brito had sold his *colocação*, a tract of some six hundred rubber trees, to a local rancher, Darli Alves da Silva. They all knew, they were saying, that Darli would thus gain a toehold in the 90,000-acre (36 000-hectare) estate, and from there, force the remaining fifty-nine families to leave by whatever means necessary. He was going to use the land to increase his pasturage, making room for a few hundred head of cattle where once families had lived and earned a livelihood. The rubber tappers had talked of little else for the past ten days, Dona Cecilia told me. "No one is sleeping at night," she said, suddenly lowering her voice. "If we have to leave this place. . . . Well, I just can't think of anything that could be worse. We've lived here for nineteen years. Some families have been here for even longer, thirty, forty years." Jose Brito sold the land he occupied to da Silva in spite of an unwritten law among the rubber tappers of Acre that you never sell your land to a rancher.

It is a law born of the conflicts of the 1970s and early 1980s, when cattlemen from the south of Brazil, like Darli, forced hundreds of rubber tappers out of the forest to remake the landscape with grass and dewy-eyed Zebu cattle. Since those days of conflict and expulsion, at least twenty thousand families of rubber tappers have crossed the border into Bolivia to ply their trade. Thousands of others have joined the masses of unemployed or underpaid wage laborers in the slums of Rio Branco, the state capital about sixty miles (a hundred kilometers) north.

What both Darli Alves and Jose Brito had conveniently ignored when they closed their deal, however, was the latter's mother, a doughty old woman named Maria de Nazaré. Still living in the clearing with another son, Manoel, Dona Nazaré didn't even know about the sale, and when she did find out about it, refused to let it go through. Instead, she went to Xapuri and complained to Dona Cecília's nephew, Rural Workers Union president Francisco Alves Mendes Filho, better known as Chico Mendes.

I had first met Chico Mendes a few weeks earlier, in February, in Rio de Janeiro. Overweight, smoking heavily, friendly and talkative from the beginning, he seemed quite an ordinary sort of guy, reminding me of a small-town mayor, perhaps, from some rural backwater in Central America. He had come to Rio to talk to Peter May, from the Ford Foundation, about a grant for extractive reserves, and Peter, being a good friend, had invited me to join them for lunch. The restaurant Peter had chosen, at the Swiss consulate, seemed an incongruous setting; in his old cotton shirt and faded jeans, Chico contrasted with the rest of the clientele, tall, blond and soberly dressed in dark suits. The menu was in French and German, and Chico was disappointed but didn't bat an eyelash when the plate of roasted quails he ordered turned out to be tiny little birds with hardly any meat on them.

It was there that, for the first time, I realized that rubber tappers were not a quaint throwback to earlier times but a group of people suffering and exploited to this day. In my diary, I later wrote: "At lunch, I met one of the syndicate leaders, Chico Mendes, a priest, Gilson Pescador, and another fellow. Most rubber tappers, I learned, work an area for a boss and are constantly in debt to him for food, supplies, etc. Some never get away and never get any real money in hand. Mendes also gave me a little booklet of stories by rubber tappers, and their newsletter."

On the back of the newsletter was a drawing that seemed to sum up a situation with which I would soon become very familiar. A rubber tapper named Demir had crudely drawn a big man with a beard, captioned, "I am a rancher. The forest is mine. The rubber tapper doesn't even have clothes." Beside him was drawn a little man in ragged clothes, captioned, "I am a rubber tapper." A balloon above the little man's head said, in error-ridden Portuguese, but with a refreshing tone of challenge: "Hey there, big guy, there was a time when you shouted. The torn clothes are mine, it didn't cost your sweat. The forest is ours and your time has already finished. Now I have my rights and I step on your foot."

That afternoon, Chico also gave me a card. It said, quite simply, "Franciso Alves Mendes Filho, Unionist." That was the beginning of my friendship with him.

Feet bare, old cotton pants rolled up and spattered with mud, Chico Mendes looked about as far as he could get from the Waldorf Astoria in New York, where he had recently been presented with a medal from the Society for a Better World. He was also late. It was the day before my trip to Cachoeira, and I'd been expecting him all afternoon.

He walked into the spartan sawn-wood building that houses the Rural Workers Union office, and his already broad face broke into an even broader smile. "*Opa*," he said, extending his hand, "you're here." He told us how, traveling from the *seringal*, he'd happened across one of the Ministry of Agriculture men, mired in the deep red mud that comprises much of the road to Xapuri. "Yeah, and he was hurt, so I had to bring him to the hospital. And now there are two federal police following me. I think they're going to try to say I was responsible or something. Saba," he said, looking at the lanky mulatto sitting behind the office's only desk, "let me get in there to make a couple of phone calls."

Chico rang the local police first. A short, rotund man with a round, open face, a thick mustache and a swatch of curly dark hair, he had the sort of honest, unassuming modesty that made him seem familiar even if you didn't know him very well. His friendliness was warm and sincere; his tone of voice was always reasonable, yet his manner so forthright and determined, so grounded in the reality of Xapuri, that it didn't seem at all surprising that he could put his views across as comfortably to a group of international bankers as to a meeting of his comrades at the union hall. Behind him, rows of long shelves were cluttered with the paraphernalia of such places — stacks of pamphlets, rolled-up posters, old newspapers, a few books, a glass of coffee someone had abandoned. A framed certificate from the United Nations, awarding Francisco Alves Mendes Filho the Global 500 environment award for 1987, sat on the top shelf. The room's board walls were a faded blue, leaving exposed the building's mildewed inner beams and joists. Union posters and calendars covered much of this unprepossessing space. Outside, it had begun to rain.

"I'm just calling to say one of the INCRA men has had an accident and was hurt," Chico was saying. "I've brought him to the hospital."

The person at the other end was obviously wondering why Chico was telling him this. "It's just so you know what happened," said Chico, "to avoid any . . . Well, you know what I mean."

What he meant was that, once again, there was trouble for the rubber tappers living in the forests around Xapuri, a situation he was all too familiar with.

Our conversation at the union office was suddenly interrupted by the arrival of two young federal policemen, one tall and blond with a thin beard, the other, like Saba, mulatto. Both were stationed in Brasiléia, about thirty-five miles (fifty-five kilometers) south of Xapuri. They were dressed in plain clothes, and their manner was casual and rather friendly, as if to make it clear that they were above all this wrangling over land, or perhaps just above all these men in muddy trousers and beat-up rubber thongs. Chico, too, was calm and relaxed, talking to them in his usual reasonable way. After a lengthy conversation, it was decided that they would go out to Cachoeira the following morning. But just before leaving, they politely offered me a ride to my hotel. Driving slowly through the streets, they mentioned that they didn't know Xapuri very well. But I'd already seen the sights; it was not a big place. The bearded one told me his name was Marcos; the other mostly kept quiet. Both agreed that there was a lot of *confusão* — a euphemism for trouble — in the area.

An old town that sprang up during the rubber boom, Xapuri seemed quiet and unprepossessing. It is a small place of brick streets and wooden houses, lying along the Acre River, an effluent of the Purus, which flows into the Amazon. Yet violence was common. Both the mayor and the local police chief had a reputation for corruption as well as close ties with the nearby ranchers who enforced their own laws with hired gunmen.

As we drove along, we passed the municipal park. It contains a number of monuments, a bust of onetime dictator Getúlio Vargas on a plinth, and a balustraded, useless little stage, everything painted bright pink and inserted among the palms and mango trees. Near the river, across from the Banco de Amazonas, is another, smaller square, featuring a vividly painted statue of the town's heavenly patron, St. Sebastian, his plaster chest pierced by a clutch of arrows.

Behind the green branches of the tree-lined streets, the old rubber-trading houses expose their high ceilings and cavernous interiors through numerous narrow doors, a patchwork of fading color in the descending dusk. The town boasts only two hotels, none too clean and both busy with the flitting of giant flying ants. There is one restaurant, which serves only what the owner is cooking that day, and where patrons, frantically flapping their hands over their plates, must wage a constant battle against the flies.

The bus station sits in the middle of Xapuri's main square. The square's other focal point is an ancient boat propeller mounted on a white cement block. But the first thing you see when you get off the bus from the state capital, Rio Branco — a laborious journey of five hours during rainy season, past wide strips of pasture dotted with burned stumps and *babassu* palms — is the union hall, banked by trees on each side, a red star on its dark-green-and-white facade.

Sebastião Gomes, better known as Saba, a tall, skinny man with twisted teeth, looks after the place whenever Chico is away or busy with other matters. Saba was born in the state of Maranhão fifty-seven years ago and came to Acre with his parents when he was sixteen. "We came all the way to Xapuri itself in big boats in those days," he told us, pointing to the propeller mounted outside. "That there came from one those boats, just like the one we came on." A little farther down Benjamin Constant Street, a packed-earth track pitted with potholes, sits the yellow stucco Catholic church, an old-fashioned structure, its two-story spire only barely reaching toward heaven.

Early the following morning, we set out for Cachoeira, the sturdy Toyota truck donated by the Canadian government filled with men, women and children, all riding in the back with Chico. The trip was unexpected, since my original reason for coming to Acre was to write an article about a different rubber estate, called São Luis de Remanso. São Luis had just been designated the country's first extractive reserve, and I felt I could kill two birds with one stone there, doing research on the extractive reserve as well as the life of the rubber tapper.

But I had become intrigued by the situation in Cachoeira. Just before we embarked on our journey, Chico told me that the rancher, Darli Alves, had already threatened to clear the rubber tappers out of Cachoeira, vowing to kill them "one by one" if need be. But in a gesture of astounding hypocrisy, Darli had also complained to the police that the rubber tappers were occupying his land and arming themselves to prepare for a guerrilla war. This explained the presence of

Marcos and his colleague, who were following us in their jeep. They were charged with investigating the allegations.

Leaving Xapuri, we passed a fork in the road, just beyond which lay the Paraná Ranch, the 17,000-acre (6800-hectare) ranch of Darli Alves da Silva, named after the state from which he came. From there, it was more than twenty miles (thirty kilometers) of muddy and almost impassable road, through innumerable makeshift gates, to our destination.

We saw little traffic along the slippery dips and rises of our route: a solitary man on horseback, a pair of women, mother and daughter, cloth sacks in hand, heading into town to buy supplies. The sun was high and already hot, the road a red gash winding through acres of pasture, tall and green, on either side of us. About halfway to Cachoeira, the police jeep bogged down in the slick wet clay. Chico and the rubber tappers pulled it out finally with the Toyota, but it turned out that a pin connecting the jeep's four-wheel drive had broken, making the vehicle useless. It was abandoned at the side of the road, a modern monument to the intractability of the Amazonian landscape. Marcos and his partner had to clamber into the back of the Toyota with the others.

In spite of the delay, we arrived at the *seringal* in a couple of hours. The last leg of the trip took us through forest, where the air was cooler, the shade welcome and the track in better condition. There was a last barbed-wire gate to open and close, and a small wooden bridge to cross over a stream-fed pool, cloudy with mud. On the other side of the pool, we came to a stop in the first *colocação* of Cachoeira. *Colocação* means "the act of putting or placing" and refers to the placing of the rubber tapper in the middle of the forest. The clearing was larger than I expected, an extensive grassy area of about four acres (ten hectares), dotted with trees, grazing animals and a few small wooden shacks. In a far-off ring, its twisted branches reaching spiderlike into a clear blue sky, the jungle formed a dense palisade of gray trunks.

A few of the weathered shacks, surrounded by tall, sharp-bladed grass, were houses. One belonged to Chico's aunt and uncle, Cecilia and Joaquim Mendes, and two others to Sebastião and Miguel. There was a small wooden schoolhouse near Sebastião's, and a much larger school, still under construction, close to Miguel's. A stream ran through the forest behind the houses, and laundry was drying on the branches of a fallen tree.

The noise made by the approach of the Toyota pulled together a large knot of people in front of the Mendes house. Dogs barked; children descended from trees and ran around, occasionally stopping to stare. Antonio Mendes, a wiry young man with curly hair and a sunburned face round and red like an apple, told me to make myself at home in the little slat house. Antonio tapped the rubber trees on his father's tract of forest, and was one of two local union delegates. The other was Dona Clarice's husband, Manoel Custodio, a friendly-looking man, tall and heavy set, wearing glasses with thick green lenses and a big cowboy hat. Along with the neighboring rubber tappers, who were camping out there so that Darli and his notorious gunmen wouldn't try to get into the Brito place, I also met Gomercindo Rodrigues, a young union organizer from Xapuri. With his intense eyes, long hair and thick beard, Gomercindo struck me as the picture of a turn-of-the-century left-wing militant, an image he reinforced by telling me about all the time he spent walking from one rubber estate to another, days and days of walking, just to talk to people about the union and their rights. It was a difficult task, one Chico had done for years, but the only way to gather new members for the union from among the dozens of rubber estates that were cut off from the road.

Joaquim and Cecilia's small three-room house was as modest as the life of the rubber tapper and as simple as his aspirations. Constructed of slats cut from the soft wood of the *paxiuba*, a kind of palm tree, it squatted on low stilts to keep the heavy winter rains from flooding in. There was no electricity, no running water, no bathroom, and no locks on the Dutch-style half doors in front. The windows were merely the squares of wood that were missing, opening its interior to the blue bowl of the sky and the golds and greens of the forest clearing outside. "Enough to keep the rain off your head," as Miguel put it.

Like almost all the rural houses I was to visit in the Amazon, it contained hardly any furniture, only a couple of hard benches, and for the lucky, a faded hammock in which to relax. A few desks from the old school had been brought in for the Ministry of Agriculture men, and the room was full of people sitting on the floor and benches, talking about the resistance, going over local news.

The snooping around of the two young policemen was largely ignored. They were looking for guns, but everyone had hidden their old hunting rifles so they wouldn't be confiscated because of Darli's absurd accusations.

At lunchtime, the two men took a break and allowed the women to serve them. I asked the dark one whether they had stumbled across anything of interest yet. When he admitted that they hadn't, I asked him if they would now be going to the Alves ranch, to check for the presence of arms there. "Oh, no," he replied uncomfortably, hesitating before adding, "there's a lot of politics behind this, you know." Later that day, Chico told me that the lawmen had asked him if it was true that I was a journalist.

After lunch, a bunch of us stood around in the shade of an orange tree, watching Miguel vent his frustration on Marcos. They were seated at a couple of desks in front of the old schoolhouse, and from a distance we could hear Miguel. "We've never done anything to anyone," Miguel was saying. "This is the quietest place you could ever hope to find; there's never been any violence here, for God's sake. And suddenly you show up and start looking for weapons as though we were a bunch of criminals!"

I too couldn't help but feel indignant. Injustice is common in Brazil, but here it was so blatant. For the authorities, the evil intentions of Darli Alves were to be taken for granted, forcing the rubber tappers to go to great lengths to preserve what was justifiably theirs. As Miguel raged, however, we looked at one another and had to smile. Miguel was being so vehement that we almost felt sorry for Marcos. "Miguel really likes to say what's on his mind, all right," said Chico, laughing. "Yep, he's a good talker," agreed an old-timer.

Chico was busy that day, consulting with the rubber tappers for most of the morning. He also had to take Miguel's little girl into Xapuri to see a doctor in the late afternoon, but before going, he made time for an interview. We sat on a pile of lumber that was eventually going to support the roof of the new school. Dona Clarice brought us glasses of orange juice, and I asked Chico to tell me about the extractive reserve.

"You have already seen," he told me, "that until today our struggle has been to preserve the forest, because it is in this forest that we have our whole survival. There are centuries of existence in this jungle, this forest, in which the man of the forest lives and has never plundered.

"Until the 1970s, we lived peacefully in the forest, even though we were slaves of the bosses. We lived peacefully because we had the forest, and it wasn't threatened; it was part of our lives because it is our mother, we survived from her."

The presence of the ranchers in Acre posed a direct threat to the rubber tappers in two ways, he explained. First, the ranchers expelled families from the forest to clear a certain number of acres to set up a sizable ranch with which to make a good profit. But second, they needed a reservoir of available forest to clear as the first pastures began to degrade. As the years passed, those rubber tappers still working in the forest near the ranches eventually came under fire also.

The first response to the arrival of the ranchers was to organize into unions, said Chico. But in 1985, the rubber tappers had taken another step. Delegates from several unions all over the Amazon got together and formed the National Council of Rubber Tappers, of which Chico was named secretary. At their first meeting, they resolved to promote the idea of extractive reserves.

"The extractive reserve is a form of land reform," Chico explained, "discovered by ourselves." The idea is actually quite simple. The Ministry of Agriculture would be pressured to expropriate the rubber estates and designate them extractive reserves. That way, the land becomes the property of the nation, with the rubber tapper holding a title to use it. It would then be against the law to sell parts of it, to destroy it for ranching, in short to use it for anything but the gathering of rubber, Brazil nuts, medicinal plants, fruits and other products. The extractive reserve would also do away with estate owners and middlemen, leaving the rubber tappers free to market whatever forest products they liked to whomever they wanted.

This idea brought many new possibilities, new ideas that excited Chico and had him thinking about the future. With their livelihood guaranteed on extractive reserves, the rubber tappers could form co-operatives, look for new products to sell, even plant more rubber trees in the forest. Money would be requested from local governments to set up schools and medical posts. International organizations could help to finance these small projects and make extraction more practicable for the tapper than it had been in the days of the rubber barons. Profits, innovations and donations of technology would be spread equally among all the people of the forest.

"It is a way of using the forest rationally," said Chico, "and turning it economically viable. There is a lot of wealth in the forest. It is not necessary to destroy it."

Chico and the other members of the council had a list of rubber estates in hand, areas that ranchers were already threatening to deforest.

One of them was Cachoeira. But the state government, which must recommend areas for expropriation to the Ministry of Agriculture, chose São Luis de Remanso instead. This estate, about halfway between Rio Branco and Xapuri, had no owner, I was told, so it was cheaper and easier to expropriate. Furthermore, the rubber tappers there had a reputation for being far less radical than those in the municipality of Xapuri. With the first salvo of what could turn out to be a deadly battle fired that week by Darli, however, the first thing the people of Cachoeira did was produce a petition, signed by everyone, asking the governor of Acre, Flaviano Melo, to designate Cachoeira an extractive reserve.

The day crawled languorously into a late Amazonian afternoon. The two federal policemen had left. I was sitting in the new school, its roof beams open to the waning light of the immense descending sun. Dona Clarice, her daughter and a few other women were sitting with me, asking questions, talking about their lives on the *seringal*, chopping the hard surfaces off a few fresh Brazil nuts with a sharp knife. It was then that I noticed how quiet it was. I looked at Seu Joaquim's house. Of course, I thought: no radio, no television, no electric appliances of any kind. At the hour of the day when everyone in the cities or towns is watching the nightly soap opera, here there was total peace.

Sebastião, a dark, wiry man of forty-three, came to join us, followed by his eight-year-old son. While his father showed us what the various rooms in the school would be used for, the boy sat in the open doorway, making a toy car with an old tin can and four rubber wheels cut from a pair of sandals.

Over the half-finished walls, we could see a group of young men playing soccer with the Ministry of Agriculture surveyors in a large grassy field. It made for a strikingly beautiful, almost moving scene: the wide meadow, the shouts and exclamations, the forest shadowy and imposing in the distance, the whole picture bathed in the light of a vast sky slowly turning from pale gold to copper, already overlaid at its heights with a tenuous layer of dark blue.

We went into the house for dinner and were joined at the kitchen table by a journalist, Flaminio Araripe, who had come from Rio Branco to write an article about the conflict. Chico was back, and after the quiet lassitude of the afternoon, the little house was once again full of people.

Flaminio sat with his notebook in Dona Cecilia's kitchen, at the big rough board table, his only light the small lantern glowing in its center. He interviewed a fellow I'd seen hanging around all day, a timid, cross-eyed young man with a protruding brow like a monkey's. He turned out to be José Brito's younger brother, Manoel. He seemed rather awed by the whole thing, but didn't waver in answering the journalist's questions. "I really don't want to leave," he began. "We don't have anywhere to live outside of here. But," he added bravely, "I've talked to the union and now I'm going to stay in my place."

Then Flaminio asked to speak to his mother, the stoic Dona Maria Nazaré, who, leaning against the doorjamb, was slowly and carefully smoking a cigarette, as if she didn't usually do that sort of thing. She was wrinkled and bony, with dark eyes and a thin slash of a mouth. She was practically deaf and both her son and Flaminio had to yell in her ear to make her understand what was wanted. Then she nodded and, putting her hands on her hips, let out a rapid-fire stream of speech, nodding at the end of every second or third sentence. José Brito had sold their land without her authorization, she explained, looking the journalist straight in the eye. "He said he was leaving because he wasn't getting along with his neighbors, and that his wife was upset with me. He said he wasn't going to tap rubber anymore. Well, now that he's gone, the *colocação* is mine. And I have no intention," she stated flatly, "of leaving, ever."

Flaminio asked Dona Nazaré her age, and she answered promptly, "Fifty-eight." The rest of the people around the table began to snicker, saying, "Fifty-eight? She must be at least seventy-eight." But, of course, she couldn't hear them.

Flaminio posed the pair for a picture, cross-eyed Manoel touchingly impressed by such attention. They stood woodenly at the end of the table while the journalist focused. "Watch out the camera doesn't break," someone jested, but Manoel smiled anyway, suddenly straightening up and looking serious just before the flash. And that's the way he looked in the next day's paper.

At the end of the long day, the sky black and filled with stars, a meeting was held outside the house. The lights of the Toyota illuminated the scene. The main news was that the two young policemen had admitted to authorities in Rio Branco that there was nothing untoward going on in Cachoeira; they had classified Darli Alves' contention that the rubber tappers were arming themselves as "rumor."

So far, so good. Now, one by one, the rubber tappers stepped forward and declared that they would keep up the resistance, fighting Darli Alves da Silva to the end if need be. He would never push them out, never take over this forest. In the determination of their voices was the memory of the events of recent years, the killings by hired gunmen, the comrades forced into Bolivia as rubber estates were burned down, and the resistance strategies organized by Chico Mendes to save what they could.

Gomercindo talked about the police, still indignant about their visit. They had even questioned children, he said. "They went up to two little girls and asked them if their father had gotten a new gun recently," he recounted. "And the little one answered, 'No, but he has an old one at home.' This is absurd, a lack of respect for the rubber tapper."

"And what about the women?" asked Chico. "The *companheiras* should also have something to say about all this. Anyone? Dona Clarice, what about you?"

Dona Clarice looked down and shyly mumbled a few words. "Well, I agree with everything that's already been said, you know? I say it is all fine with me."

Marina, a striking young mulatta with long crinkly hair, a member of the local Workers' Party, said, "We must not forget that José Brito is a worker, too. He's as oppressed as all of us. But there is a law among the rubber tappers that you don't sell to a rancher. And now, we can see what happens when you do. We really have to make sure that our comrades on the other rubber estates know that this has happened."

The meeting over, the Toyota was loaded up and headed to Xapuri. I got a ride with Flaminio, who commented to his driver, "I was quite impressed with Marina. She's really something." "Yeah," enthused the young man, "she's really pretty." "Uh, I meant with her speech," said Flaminio uncomfortably. "I was impressed with her speech tonight."

We crossed the little wooden bridge and passed through the wire gate. Silence descended on the *colocação*, as it had on the rest of Cachoeira. All around us, the serene black forest that the rubber tappers had, for one more day at least, saved from destruction seemed to extend endlessly into the night.

TWO

CHICO MENDES

H E WAS BORN ON DECEMBER
15, 1944, on a *seringal* named, almost prophetically, Bom Futuro
("good future").

Chico was one of the oldest of Francisco Mendes' eighteen children. "All rubber tappers have big families," he remarked to me. Most
of the children died in childhood. To help the growing family survive,
Chico had to begin tapping rubber when he was just nine years old.

"All the sons of *seringueiros* did this," he said, referring to his
early start, "especially in those days, when the boss didn't allow
schools to be established in the *seringal*, because he always wanted to
avoid two things. The first was that people should learn to read, and
count, and discover that they were being robbed in their accounts with
the boss. And secondly, the problem of the children of a rubber tapper
going to school, this involved a decrease in production. So it was
preferable that the children of the rubber tapper not have a school, so
that way the boss could arrange bigger profits for himself, so his children could study in the best schools in the country, so he could buy
apartments in other places, go out gambling, spend money on liquor

and all the rest of it, guarantee the luxurious life of his family."

So Chico never went to school, though he soon became aware of the injustice of the system. When he was eighteen, his younger brother Zuza told me later, Chico wrote a letter of complaint to the president of Brazil, Juscelino Kubitschek, dictating its contents to his father, who knew some of the basics of writing. Shortly afterward, however, something happened that would change Chico's life completely.

Zuza, who was ten years old at the time, said that his father met a stranger at the boss's trading post, the place where all the rubber tappers would periodically emerge from the isolation of the forest and their daily labor to meet and catch up on the news. Francisco Senior invited the man to visit his home. One afternoon while Chico and his father were in the middle of smoking that day's latex, the stranger showed up. His manner of speech, the things he talked about, the newspapers he had brought with him — something Chico had never seen before — everything about this stranger fascinated the illiterate young man. And something about Chico Mendes must have caught the interest of the visitor. With Francisco's permission, the stranger undertook to teach Chico how to read and write.

"For more than four years, I would spend the weekends in the middle of the jungle at his shack," recalled Chico. "The neighbors would say that he didn't know how to write, didn't know anything. But he was very wise. This was in 1961 or so, and up until 1965 I maintained this contact with him. He was someone different from the rest of us; he came from another reality. Now, it was interesting how only I maintained this contact with him, and also learned there. My classes were on Saturdays and Sundays, at night, and were based on newspaper clippings that he received. He was very intelligent. I still don't know how he received those clippings; he must have had some sort of contacts who insured that he got them. He also set up a radio, right there in the middle of the forest, and we would listen. It was the first time I heard international programs in Portuguese. We began to listen to the Voice of America, Moscow Central and the BBC of London. Every night, I would hear the news from one of these channels, and afterward we'd discuss the political line of each one."

It took Chico almost a year to bring himself to ask the stranger about his past. Euclides Fernando Tavora was the scion of a wealthy and influential family from the south of Brazil. In 1935, as a young army officer, he had joined the ill-fated Prestes revolution, which, without taking the time to organize support from other sectors of Brazilian society, attempted to overthrow the Nazi-style New State of Getúlio Vargas. It was a revolt that ended in tragedy. Luiz Carlos Prestes, a figure of legend in Brazil, known as the Horseman of Hope after his incredible 14,000 mile (22 400-kilometer) long march in the 1920s, was soon caught and imprisoned. His wife, Olga, a German Jew who had joined the Communist Party in Munich when she was seventeen, was deported to Hitler's Germany and was eventually gassed in a concentration camp. Arthur Ewalt, who had worked with the Canadian Communist Party in the early 1920s before going to China and at length Brazil, was tortured so cruelly that he lost his mind. Many army officers involved in the revolt were shot, but Tavora was lucky: he was imprisoned on the island of Fernando de Noronha, 180 miles (300 kilometers) off the coast of Pernambuco state.

Through the influence of his uncle, Juarez Tavora, also a famous revolutionary officer, the young man managed to escape by boat to Belém. At some point, said Chico, Tavora headed for Bolivia, where he worked with the miners and other Bolivian workers. By the late fifties, he found himself in danger again, as the Bolivian revolution of 1952 began to suffer increasing attacks from the right. Tavora sought refuge this time in the endless forests of the Amazon. Crossing the border at Assis Brasil, he found a solitary home for himself in Seringal Cachoiera, to which the Mendes family had by then moved also, on a tract known as Colocação Ina.

In 1964, Brazil suffered a military coup and the event seemed to crystallize everything Chico had learned until then with Tavora. Chico explained this for me a few months after my first trip to Acre. In June I made a second trip and was visiting him at the little sawn-wood house in Xapuri he had recently managed to purchase. We had just finished a lunch of paca, a tasty forest rodent, shot by one of his Mendes cousins, and were seated on a couple of wooden stools in the front yard. Our conversation was punctuated by the typical sounds of the neighborhood: children shouting as they played, dogs barking, roosters crowing. Gomercindo Rodrigues had dropped by and told me about the fifteen gunmen who were now seen frequently driving around Xapuri, men living on the Darli Alves ranch but hired for him by the Democratic Ruralist Union, or UDR, an extreme right-wing landowners' organization to which many powerful men in Brazil belong.

I was fascinated by Chico's politics, and by the unusual education he had received at the hands of Tavora, about which he rarely spoke. "Oh, that. It's been a long time since I've talked about that," he'd told me with that thoughtful smile of his, when I specifically asked. Perhaps one of the reasons we got along so well, though, was just that: my curiosity about his political philosophy. Chico was a committed socialist; the lessons of 1964 and Fernando Tavora played a fundamental role in forming his vision.

"In 1964," said Chico, "after the coup, we listened to the Voice of America, and it ardently defended the coup, saying that it was the triumph of the forces of social democracy. Afterward, we listened to Moscow Central, and it was another vision. They said that it was a revolution organized by the CIA, based on the support of reactionaries and North American imperialism, and that this coup took place because progressive movements in Brazil were beginning to advance so much. The populist government of the time was making a few openings, but it did not have an organized base supporting it. And so it fell. So, they would say, many union leaders are dying in prisons, tortured, unions shut down, a whole series of things. The BBC gave a more general broadcast of what was happening in Brazil. And so Tavora began a discussion about what we had heard on the Voice of America and the other vision of Radio Moscow. Finally, he said: 'Well, the Voice of America defends the political interests of the American government. You can see that its programming always defends the interests of North American imperialism. On the other hand, Moscow, in spite of defending liberation movements all over the world, also ardently defends the interests of the Soviet line.'"

Tavora was making the point that neither system, capitalist or state capitalist, had anything to offer the workers of Brazil. And Tavora had seen that major changes in society cannot occur with only a small movement creating a revolution; they could occur only when the entire working class took and directed the initiative. Brazilians had no interest in defending the regime of João Goulart, deposed by the generals in 1964. Paternalistic and authoritarian, the Goulart regime had purported to speak for ordinary Brazilians, but in fact gave them no representation.

The military coup did indeed close down unions and imprison and torture their leaders. "We are going to pass long years before our movements recover," Tavora told Chico. Nonetheless, Tavora held out hope, convinced that liberation movements would always spring up again, because, said Chico, "they are bound to the reality of the people." Chico's job, said Tavora, was to enter such movements, as a worker, carrying with him the workers' struggle for justice. "He told me that someday I would be able to make my contribution, that perhaps in ten or fifteen years, new unions would emerge." It didn't matter if these unions were controlled by the dictatorship. "What is important is that you get inside and do your work," Tavora had told him.

Tavora had also made an uncanny prediction: "Who knows," he said to Chico, "but someday in your life you might succeed in leading a movement. You can never forget that."

Several months after the military coup, Tavora, then about fifty-eight, Chico reckons, suddenly disappeared. "It seems he got sick, from an ulcer or something, went into town and never came back," said Chico. Some people said that Tavora was picked up by the military. Whatever the man's fate, Chico said, "Once again I was alone, isolated in this whole question."

Nonetheless, he began what was to become his life's work, organizing people to resist the arbitrary rules imposed on them by the powerful. In 1968, one of the rubber tappers of Cachoeira incurred the anger of the boss by selling his rubber to a merchant. For this — for not selling to the boss, at the boss's prices — the man was threatened. Chico persuaded all the families of Cachoeira to sell to the merchant, leaving the boss frustrated and unable to do anything.

Chico left the rubber estate in his twenties and went to Xapuri to work for a merchant called José Azul, or Joe Blue. "He was *bem pretinho*," Saba told me later at the union office, "so black that people said he was blue," hence the nickname. Later Chico worked in the dry-goods store of Guilherme Zaire, a prosperous Syrian merchant, who acquired the rights to many rubber estates.

The picture changed in the 1970s, when Wanderley Dantas was elected governor of Acre. Dantas began to take trips to the south, in an attempt to attract ranchers and businessmen to his state. Like Brazil's military rulers, he felt that it was the wealthy entrepreneur who knew best how to exploit the enormous resources of the Amazon. Extraction of forest products, such as rubber, was a mark of the past. Credits for small farmers would be a waste of money that could be better spent on projects such as developing nuclear energy. At any rate, the generals felt that the landless wage laborer belonged in the big city slums, a cheap and docile work force to fuel Brazil's "economic miracle." In the Amazon, progress seemed to reside between the horns of a Zebu ox, or somewhere at the end of one of the expensive road projects, roads that, as many a cynic likes to say, go from nowhere to nothing at all.

In 1966, the Brazilian government set up the Superintendency for the Development of the Amazon, SUDAM, an organ whose basic and exclusive role was and still is to give money to the rich. While thousands of acres of forest were cleared, earning the owners their grants from SUDAM, the production of beef quickly fell. But that didn't matter, because the only reason to set up such ranches in the first place was to get the tax write-offs and the benefits of speculation. In some cases, the entrepreneurs didn't do anything with the land they acquired, in spite of their promises to SUDAM. They would clear a few acres, build a cabin and bribe the inspectors, who would return to Belém raving about the modern technology being installed at Ranch Such-and-such.

In Acre, however, the land was better than in other parts of the Amazon, and ranchers made good on their promises to SUDAM to start up their businesses. Most of the state was already divided into large rubber estates, so it was easy to buy or make false documents for huge tracts of land. Acre had gone through seven governments between 1899 and 1904, some Bolivian, some Brazilian, and it was very easy to forge tattered old documents and land deeds.

The rubber tappers in most cases did have rights to the land they worked. In Brazil, you can get title to the land you work after five years, if you are not paying anyone rent. After only one year and a day, you have the right to financial compensation for the work that has been done on the land. But as in other parts of the Amazon, there began a brisk business in land grabbing. Most rubber tappers didn't know they could go to court to try to win their deeds legally. The few who did try invariably lost.

The rubber tappers and their families were no match for the powerful businessmen from the south and their smooth-talking lawyers. Nor for their hired gunmen. Those who attempted to resist were brutally evicted. The Vale do Rio Acre, a wide valley curving south from Rio Branco, through Xapuri, down to Brasiléia and as far as Assis Brasil on the border, was the first and hardest-hit area in the state.

"From 1970 until 1975 or '76," Chico told me, "all our comrades who lived along the margin of the road to Brasiléia were expelled, using the most violent means possible. Their shacks were burned down, gunmen would show up on their land, their animals were killed. So a large number of these rubber tappers went to try it out in Bolivia, because there was no other job for them. Tapping rubber was all they knew how to do. Others tried their luck in the city. Today they live in a complete state of misery.

"Well, as these people were evicted from their posts, from their *colocaçãos* in the forest, these forests began to be destroyed by chain saws and by fire. There began the campaign to substitute the ox for man. With this, the very economy of the state began to fall. Just to give you an idea, from 1970 to 1976, more than 15 million acres (6 million hectares) of land in Acre were bought by landowners with the support of the fiscal incentives of SUDAM. They didn't have to spend a cent from their own pockets. This was a great disaster. From that point on, the forest began to fall."

The destruction was relentless and irreversible. In a survey made by the rubber tappers, they reckoned that about 180,000 rubber trees and 80,000 Brazil nut trees were destroyed in the area around Xapuri. This represented the livelihood of three hundred or more families. "And," said Chico, "that's not to mention all the hardwood trees, medicinal trees and wild animals. Wood deer, *cotia*, paca and monkey all disappeared. Also armadillos. The greatest feeling of desperation dominated the whole region. We had to organize ourselves, and that is how the first movement for the defense of the forest began."

In 1975, Chico participated in the formation of the first union, which sprang up in the nearby town of Brasiléia. Progressive sectors of the Catholic Church played a part in this. They had already been establishing ecumenical communities in some of the rubber estates and raising questions about the terrible evictions and devastation. Some priests were more advanced in their thinking than others. The movement began in Brasiléia because the priest there was encouraging, while the local priest in Xapuri was dead against it. Ex-priest Gilson Pescador, whom I had met with Chico in Rio, was sent to Xapuri to try to quiet the increasingly radical mood among the rubber tappers. He switched sides soon after meeting Chico, however, and so began a history of bad relations between Pescador and his cousin, the bishop in Rio Branco.

Chico was elected secretary of the nascent union, because, as he put it, "I had received a whole lesson in this from Tavora. Some people even wondered how I knew so much about it, but I never explained."

The first steps were precarious. The members of the union had to follow the guidelines laid out by the Ministry of Labor — the very government they opposed. And even though they obeyed the rules, the only safe place to hold their meetings was in the church in Brasiléia.

"Worst of all," said Chico, "the level of consciousness among the workers to resist the landowners with all the support of the authorities, police and judges was very low." Meanwhile the deforestation and violence continued unabated. At first, the union tried to stop them through legal means, but got nowhere. The local judges always ruled in favor of the ranchers. "So it was only then," said Chico, "that there arose the idea of organizing *empates*."

The Portuguese word *empate* means a standoff or stalemate, but in the north, it has come to mean "impeding." Many journalists and ecologists describe it as a sort of passive resistance, rather like the Gandhian protests against British rule in India after the First World War.

But the *empate* was more than that. It was, in many respects, a show of class force, a large group of people, often including entire families, descending on the ill-paid workers who were slaving away to destroy the forest. The *empate* was first an attempt to bring these fellow workers around to the other side, to make them understand that they were taking the food from the mouths of their comrades. It was also a statement, one that said to everyone: "You will have to kill us to get us out of here." Against all odds, it worked.

I asked Chico who had thought up the idea; it is usually credited to him.

"The idea came from the union in Brasiléia," he said, with his usual sense of fairness, "and I remember, in March 1976, we planned the first *empate* for Seringal Carmen, in Brasiléia. Sixty men organized themselves and spent three days entrenched there and stopped the destruction of 2500 acres (1000 hectares) of virgin forest. They put themselves in front of the chain saws, and the workmen retreated, they were afraid. There was an enormous pressure afterward from the authorities, but from there on, it proved to be the only way."

The acknowledged leader of the rubber tappers' movement at that time was Wilson Pinheiro, from Brasiléia, and much of the union activity was centered in that municipality. But the *empate* tactic spread. Chico described 1979, for example, as a year of "great agitation," not just in Brasiléia, but in Xapuri and in Assis Brasil as well. Wilson had talked to Chico about starting a union in Xapuri. But the ranchers of the region were working on what they hoped would be a solution to this unexpected problem, the liquidation of the movement's leader, Pinheiro.

Early on a July night in 1980, while Pinheiro was watching a police thriller on the old black-and-white television set in the union office, a gunman crept onto the roof, slid in through a window and, waiting for the covering sound of shots from the television program, pumped Pinheiro full of bullets.

At Pinheiro's funeral, fifteen hundred workers gathered around the coffin and demanded justice. They appealed to the authorities to punish the criminals — it was well known who they were. But justice crossed its arms. Seven days later, the rubber tappers resolved to kill a rancher known to be one of the instigators of Pinheiro's death.

They were true to their word. On July 27, two of them killed rancher Nilo Sergio de Oliveira. "This time," said Chico, "justice moved instantly. Twenty-four hours later, dozens of workers were in jail, tortured, their fingernails pulled out. There was an enormous torture session in the Brasiléia jail."

Chico hadn't been in Brasiléia at the time of Nilo's killing, but was traveling in other areas of the state trying to organize more workers. However, an order for his arrest was sent out, indicting him under the National Security Law of the military dictatorship. He spent three months sleeping in a different house every night, from fear of the ranchers' gunmen as much as from the police. "In 1981, I was caught and put on the defendant's bench in a military court in Manaus," said Chico. "I was lucky that I wasn't jailed, but we had a good lawyer. In 1984, at an appeal hearing, the case was thrown out for lack of evidence. But from then up until now, there began a very difficult life for me, persecuted by the federal police, the security forces and so on."

After the death of Wilson Pinheiro, some big changes took place in the union movement. Largely because of the influence of the Confederation of Agricultural Workers representative, João Maia, for example, the authorities began to negotiate with the Brasiléia union, offering them simple rubber processing equipment (called mini-factories) and concessions on deforestation. In return, the movement had to tone down its demands and let go of some areas where rubber tappers had legitimate rights to stay. Chico and a few of his comrades adamantly refused to go along with the compromise, believing that their rights were inviolable.

Inevitably, the main field of struggle moved to Xapuri. "With the death of Wilson Pinheiro," said Chico, "the movement suffered a certain fall, so we began to organize more in Xapuri. We devised a model of educational training for the rubber tappers to strengthen the movement — literacy classes and a bulletin, the *Poronga*, which was oriented toward the rubber tapper so he could learn to read and to organize. And this worked."

A new strategy of dispersing leadership in the union and strengthening participation by the rank and file also began in earnest. "I think that what I learned from Tavora was a great help here," said Chico. "He put it like this, that workers had to be organized and the principal leaderships should exist, but that they should have, besides, other leaders to strengthen the movement and make things more difficult for the enemy. And that experience we also learned with the death of Wilson Pinheiro. The union in Brasiléia only had Wilson, the chief of command. When he was killed, the movement emptied. It was a hard example for us; we had to learn from it, too."

This, Chico went on to explain, was one of the reasons they joined the Workers' Party, which had been formed in 1979. The Workers' Party, or PT, grew out of the dozens of strikes that swept through the industrial belt of São Paulo in the 1970s. It was made up of a wide variety of tendencies — including groups as disparate as members of the progressive Catholic Church, former guerrillas and former adherents of various Trotskyist, Maoist and Communist organizations.

At the same time, workers all over Brazil had grown sick and tired of what they derisively called *pelego* unions, which were undemocratic and not interested in advancing the workers' struggle for decent wages and working conditions. The Portuguese word *pelego* denotes a sheepskin blanket that is placed between the horse's back and the saddle to make the ride more comfortable for the rider. The *pelego* unions made the ride more comfortable for the bosses.

In 1983, workers formed a federation of trade unions called CUT, the Unique Workers' Central. It was, at first, made up primarily of union opposition groups within existing syndicates, and was extremely radical. Now it is somewhat divided between those who want a social democratic society, such as Sweden's, and those who want democratic socialism, a true workers' state. Chico belonged to this second group.

"I didn't see in any other party an option for the land, for the rubber tappers," he said. "And once we had news of the resistance of the workers, the struggle of the workers in São Paulo, we began organizing the PT here. João Maia (of the agricultural workers union) went to São Paulo and made contact with Lula," Chico added. Luis Ignacio da Silva, or Lula, was the president of the Workers' Party. "He brought us the proposals of the PT. It's incredible. João Maia had an important role in the beginning. Unfortunately, he let himself be led by personal interests and fell outside."

João Maia is now a state deputy in Acre for the ruling party, the Brazilian Democratic Movement Party, or PMDB, and is also head of the local Brazilian Forest Development Institute. Incredibly, as Chico said, Maia gave permission in 1987 for a logging company owned by two Japanese men from São Paulo, widely rumored to be partners of state governor Flaviano Melo, to cut down Seringal Ecuador, where Chico first tapped rubber. In July 1987 a group of rubber tappers who organized a sit-in at the institute's office in Xapuri were attacked by gunmen, one of whom was Darli Alves' son, Darci. Two teenagers were severely wounded.

The commitment of Chico and other leaders in the rubber tappers' movement becomes all the more remarkable considering how much they might have gained personally if they had sold out. As the movement grew and gained influence, the ranchers of Acre would probably have offered millions to get rid of Chico. Instead, they threatened his life.

By then, however, the movement had grown beyond the bounds of Acre, and indeed beyond Brazil. A national meeting of union delegates from all over the Amazon was set up in the nation's capital, Brasília. Chico told me that they chose Brasília because they wanted to prove to people, especially government officials, that Amazonia was not empty, "because people thought, or pretended, that there were no more rubber tappers, no more Indians in Amazonia. We proved that the forest was full of people, of human beings working in it, that what the ranchers said was lies."

In Brasília, the Rural Workers Union delegates formed the National Council of Rubber Tappers, electing Chico as its secretary. By this time Chico had also put some solid political experience behind him.

In 1978, what is now the middle-of-the-road PMDB was the MDB, the Brazilian Democratic Movement. It hadn't received permission from the military government to form, and thus was not allowed to call itself a party. It collected a number of people of all political stripes who agreed that the military government had to be done away with. Chico was asked to add his name to the list of MDB candidates running as town councillors in Xapuri. If the movement didn't have enough names, their candidates would not be allowed to run. Chico, with no money or expectations of winning, agreed to run out of solidarity. As he put it, "It was the only party in which the workers felt a certain confidence, for being against the dictatorship, in that black moment." To his great surprise, he won.

Chico later referred to this experience as one of the most bitter in his life. "I had hoped that my two other comrades in the MDB would also be able to follow a line more committed to the workers," said Chico. "This was my great deception. Aside from having taken these first steps without much experience, I soon perceived that the others didn't agree with my idea to use our mandate as an instrument of struggle in favor of the rubber tappers."

At the same time, intellectuals at the Federal University of Acre, in Rio Branco, had formed a clandestine new Communist Party (an older one having been in existence since the 1920s). Chico joined this party for a while, still trying to follow Tavora's advice to work at reforming such parties from within, making them more committed to the workers, but he soon felt that he had once again joined the wrong group. He finally found the party whose ideals matched his own in the PT, but ironically both times he ran as a candidate on their ticket for state deputy, he lost. The last time was in 1986, when the new civilian government's price freeze brought the government parties support throughout the country. In alliance with another pro-government party, the PMDB won twenty of twenty-three governorships in Brazil, and a large majority in both the senate and the chamber of deputies. The Workers' Party, on the other hand, won only 19 out of 427 seats.

As a result of these experiences, Chico could at least say that he had learned a great many things about politics. "I began to discover," he said, "how the party-political machine functions, such a tragic scheme, so ridiculous, how the workers are misled, and how they are maneuvered to the advantage of the politicians. The workers, unconsciously, do what not even a person who meets a wounded lion would do. He cures him and afterward is devoured. The workers strengthen the very politicians who defend their enemies. And many workers still don't realize this."

Articulate and committed, Chico became a national and international spokesman for the rubber tappers. Early in 1987, Stephen Schwartzman, a young American anthropologist working for the Environmental Defense Fund in Washington, got the idea of bringing Chico to Miami to talk to bankers at an international meeting of the Inter-American Development Bank (the IADB). The bank was planning to lend Brazil money for the paving of a road from Rondônia to Rio Branco.

Rondônia had been flooded by almost a million peasants during the seventies and eighties, encouraged by government offers of free 250-acre (100-hectare) lots of land. Most of these peasants had been sharecroppers in the fertile south and had been pushed off their small holdings by large landowners who began to produce heavily mechanized commodities such as soya and wheat. These products have made many a millionaire in the south of Brazil, and the country has become the world's largest exporter of soya. But the mass evictions caused havoc in the state of Rondônia.

The peasants came in buses and in the backs of flatbed trucks, taking the newly paved BR 364 highway. Yet the plots of land they were given could barely sustain them, and after a few years many left, selling the land to newcomers and striking off to look for new plots. The population of Rondônia rose from about a hundred thousand in 1970 to more than a million in 1989. More than 17 percent of its surface has been deforested.

The rubber tappers feared that if the BR 364 highway was extended to Rio Branco, Rondônia's fate would be repeated in Acre. Thanks, however, to the efforts of Chico in Miami, neatly dressed in suit and tie and only momentarily nonplussed by his audience of bankers, the IADB decided that they would lend Brazil the money for the paving only if ecological safeguards were put into place. Along the margins of the road, the government would have to set aside reserves for the Indians and rubber tappers who lived there, out of reach of potential invaders and land grabbers. Though all the studies of how to do this have been completed, Brazil has yet to execute the programs, and the road remains unpaved to this day.

Along with these results came international recognition. In 1987, Chico won a prize from the United Nations, the Global 500 award, for his fight to save the world's environment. He traveled to London, England, to pick it up and was interviewed by several newspapers. In September 1987, he flew to New York to receive a medal from the Society for a Better World at the Waldorf Astoria. "One of the most luxurious hotels in the world, it seems. I don't know," he said, laughing, as if in amusement at his presence there, "a very sophisticated place." Chico also began to receive some financial help in the form of grants from a couple of international foundations. The money, though, never lasted long. Chico told me that he used all his grant money in a matter of months to provide food for the hundreds of rubber tappers' families who protested in Cachoeira, in Seringal Ecuador and at the Forest Development Institute.

The international attention also brought Chico to the pages of the Brazilian press. After his return from Miami, he had found himself vilified in the Acre papers as someone who wanted to keep the Amazon in the Dark Ages. Now the recognition bestowed by these international awards brought the rubber tappers' struggle to the attention of other Brazilians for the first time.

When I asked Chico how his life had been affected by the travel and recognition, he said only that it was very difficult to be away so frequently from his wife, Ilza, and their two young children.

Chico had known Ilzamar Gadelha, a beautiful young woman with long curly hair and big dark eyes, since she was a little girl. Without a rubber stand of his own, he had found work in a *seringal* called Santa Fe. The owner of the tapping post, who gave Chico half the rubber in return for doing the tapping, was Ilza's father, José Moacir Gadelha. He shared his home with Chico and soon began to look upon him as a son.

Ilza told me about those days on Seringal Santa Fe. "I was small then," she recounted. "I was maybe ten or eleven when I met him. He lived with us for two or three years. After that time, Chico left. He went to Brasiléia and helped found the union there. And then there were the *empates* there in Brasiléia. I actually did hear speak of the strikes, of organizing, of the deforestation. But I was still very young, I didn't pay attention. Just what was all this?"

Then came the time when Chico was elected alderman for the MDB and later president of the newly formed Rural Workers Union in Xapuri. "He stayed in town," said Ilza, "but when he had time, he always came back to the *seringal* to tap rubber and break Brazil nuts for a couple of months, or a month, and with that, he would return again to town." Chico also liked to do some hunting in his spare time, especially for wood deer. "He never abandoned the work of the forest," said Ilza.

A number of years passed, during which Ilza didn't see Chico at all. But when the news came that he had been absolved at the military trial in Manaus, everyone on Seringal Santa Fe got together to walk into town and meet him. "We all came to town," said Ilza, "his brothers, us, his friends, a whole bunch of people came. So there we were waiting in Xapuri for him, and at the time of his arrival they put up banners and let off fireworks, that sort of thing. It was really great. And after, when I saw him, I began to fall in love. I already saw that he was a person who —" she paused for a moment, "was someone very special, you know? At that point we decided, that very same night, to meet at home and talk, and we started to go out together. I was seventeen. After a short time we became engaged. We were engaged for almost a year, and then we got married, in 1983."

Life with Chico Mendes was, however, far from easy for the young bride. For a year or so, they lived in Xapuri, said Ilza, "but this was without a house, without anything, because he didn't have any money to buy a house, dishes, pans, those sorts of things to put in a house. We stayed in a house with two friends of his, or in the house of a relative, or in the house of someone else. And the financial situation got worse all the time. I decided to go back to the *seringal*, to my parents' house. So we sat down and talked about it, how we didn't have any way of living in town. Him alone it was easier. With a family already, it was more difficult."

By then, a little girl had been born, Elenira, named after Elenira Rezende, the first woman combatant to die in the Araguaia Guerrilla War against the military dictatorship. Ilza stayed in Seringal Santa Fe, and Chico came to stay with the family as often as he could. A couple of years later, in 1986, another baby was born, a boy who was named

Sandino in honor of the Nicaraguan revolutionary. The little boy, playing in the front room of the house Chico had finally been able to buy, bore a remarkable resemblance to his father, with the same broad, round face, curly hair and slightly almond-shaped eyes.

More than three months after my visit to Cachoeira, the situation in Xapuri was still dangerous and tense. Chico continued to receive death threats and only barely escaped from a number of serious attempts. Mayor Wanderley Vianna, a member of the ruling PMDB, attacked the rubber tappers publicly at every opportunity. Then Darli Alves, in making his deadly move on Seringal Cachoeira, heralded an upswing in the violence.

Later I heard that the governor did finally designate Cachoeira an extractive reserve, thereby neutralizing Darli's attempts to take it over. The battle had been won, although not without great cost. "These first reserves are the fruit of our resistance," said Chico. "It didn't come free. The government only resolves to do something when a worker dies, when workers shed blood. We lose a comrade, two others are shot, and we make this one small conquest. But this struggle doesn't stop. We must continue to organize, with firepower and the support of up. The enemy is also organizing, always from the bottom the police."

The violence in Xapuri persisted throughout the year. Along with the shooting at the Forest Development Institute, a union delegate from Brasiléia, Higino de Almeida, was ambushed and killed by gunmen, leaving a wife and five small children. When Chico told me about it, how he had come back from a trip to the south only to have to go straight to the hospital and arrange burial, I was struck momentarily and almost subconsciously by a certain image. It was an image of Chico Mendes as the eternal older brother, the one who must see his comrades die and continue on in spite of the tragedy and injustice. I pictured him always being there, in spite of the fact that he too was marked by death threats that intensified as the year went on.

THREE

THE LIFE OF A RUBBER TAPPER

THE WELL-HEELED RANCHERS with their hired gunmen and big Ford trucks consider rubber gathering a primitive activity well on its way to deserved obsolescence. The rubber tapper is despised as a creature only slightly more intelligent than a forest animal. A landowner and state deputy named João Tezza told me that the rubber tapper was one of the most primitive beings in Brazil. "He doesn't know how to grow rice or raise a chicken. He has no idea how to even make a trap," Tezza affirmed. "The only way he can hunt for food is with a musket." I told him that I had seen rice fields and chickens and various other farm animals in two different rubber tracts in Acre. "That is impossible," he told me categorically. "Just take my word for it."

The lives of the rubber tappers I met seemed far better than those of people living in the wretched slums and shantytowns in Brazil's large cities. People had enough to eat, clean water to drink, lots of space; in short, a healthy environment. In too many cases, there were no schools or hospitals, but neither were there robberies, drug dealers or rapists. I made a second journey to Seringal Cachoeira, to take a closer look at the everyday life of the rubber tappers, and once again felt quite at home there.

I spent the night in a hammock in the front room of the Mendes house. It was colder than I had expected, and when Dona Cecilia put blankets over the windows, I took one down and used it to keep warm. Through the open window, a breathtakingly beautiful sky flaunted its indigo silk like an enormous tent, stippled with stars, the Milky Way a sheer sparkling veil running across the zenith. It was the kind of night sky I had seen as a child on my parents' farm. Perhaps it impressed me so much because I had once known but had forgotten that a sky could be so spectacular.

The world seemed perfectly still, the only sounds the regular coughing of Seu Joaquim from the other room and a chorus of frogs from the stream.

At dawn, the family was already up, and after a quick breakfast of coffee and hard biscuits, Antonio and I set out; the sky was changing from dark blue to pale gray, and a gossamer mist had settled around the cabin and the wall of trees in the distance.

We crossed the stream, passed through the barbed-wire gate and entered the forest. The track along which we walked wasn't wide, but well trodden and easy to travel. It made a rough loop around a tract of forest that contained maybe two hundred trees. A thick old rubber tree with a wide girth marked the beginning of the path. Antonio stopped and drew out a hooked knife, making the first cut of the day, a slant-wise incision with two or three firm, deft strokes across the pale gray bark. On the younger trees, he cut just one line — more than that would harm the tree — a delicate slash tinged red where the white milk comes up quickly and begins to flow. With his knife he cleaned out a strip of old rubber from the central canal down which the latex runs, the elastic stretching and snapping as he pulled it. With the knife's stout handle, he then tapped in a tiny metal chute, scissored from an old tin can, and placed a container on the ground to catch the flow. Just about any sort of thing will do: an old can, an empty Brazil nut pod, a plastic cup.

Since this first one was a wide tree, Antonio moved to the back and made another cut, adding another slash to the chevron-like pattern wrapped like a breastplate across the bark. Once the whole side of the tree has been cut, it is left to heal for maybe two years, while the tapper works the other half of the chevron. Then he cuts from the opposite direction, crossing over the old cuts rather than following them. The bark of this tree was stiff and mottled with such cuts, and a fine moss grew in the oldest tracks in the bark. We walked off to find the next tree.

It was not my first time in the forest, but it struck me again as not only beautiful and generous but also as really comfortable. It was cool and shady, with surprisingly few mosquitoes, and an incredible variety of sights and sounds.

Huge purple butterflies — I took them for morphos — lifted and dropped as they flew languidly from bush to bush, as if to imitate a shadow-dappled falling leaf. Phallic clay mounds, in which the larvae of the noisy cicada wait until the time to metamorphose and fly, sprouted around the roots of enormous trees. Rust-colored fungi raised concave surfaces to the light, like old-fashioned ashtrays. Alegaric mushrooms winged out from barklike old lace collars, and wispy, fine-spun vines twisted delicately up other trunks, their dark green leaves flat against the bark. As the sun came up, it shot through the canopy in long shafts of gold.

As we walked along, keeping an eye out for snakes, Antonio couldn't resist telling me about the trees we passed and the purpose they served. The rough bark of the *jutai* was good for coughs if you sliced off a ticket of bark and steeped it in boiling water. *Caneloa, comaru* and *taxi preto* were all good for dealing with a bout of diarrhea, and there was a *quina*, or quinine tree, for malaria. Another plant, with the curious name *orelha de anta*, tapir's ear, was used to treat asthma. "See that one up there," said Antonio, pointing to a palm. "That's a *patoa*. It makes a good wine." The most interesting tree was one he called a *cuaricuara*. According to Antonio, who scraped off some of its soft, spongy bark with his machete, you could squeeze a little liquid out of this bark and its drops would stop the bleeding of any large wound and heal it completely with no scar in just twenty-four hours. I was convinced that this tree presented the possibility of some incredible medical breakthrough until a Mexican friend told me later that the same thing happened with onions.

We made our way through a stand of wild banana, like a disintegrating circus tent, flaps falling everywhere. We trod narrow paths on the edges of steep ravines and crossed a couple of streams. At one point I stopped to drink some water, and Antonio interrupted me as I was awkwardly trying to palm some of the clear liquid to my mouth. Like a maître d' in some elegant French restaurant, he stooped and presented me with a neatly folded leaf, a perfect vegetal goblet. At every rubber tree, we stopped for Antonio to cut. "How long will it live if you use it like this?" I asked. "Thirty or forty years?" Antonio slapped the trunk proprietarily and said, "If you look after this tree, it will live longer than any of us Christians."

It took us about five hours — stopping to talk, Antonio frequently asking if I would be able to find my way home if he wasn't there, and I cheerfully replying no — to do just part of the track. We ended up at the place where we began, the large old rubber tree, its cup already beginning to fill with latex. Most rubber tappers would pause to eat at this point, then start back around, pouring the latex into a funnel-shaped can or a rubber-lined sack, to bring it home to smoke. Antonio, however, used another system. He left the rubber to coagulate, picked it up after a week, washed the yellow lumps in the stream, then pressed it into flexible blocks with a handpress.

In Sao Luis de Remanso, another reserve, I had watched a rubber tapper named Antonio de Souza coagulate rubber in the traditional way, by smoking it. Seated on a low wooden stool in a small hut behind his house, he poured the latex into a large shallow pan. Beside it, a fire was lit in a clay stove with a funnel-shaped chimney. The rubber, formed in a large ball on a long stick of wood, was swung from the pan and rolled around in the dense white fumes. Sometimes a little lemon juice is added to the latex to make it thicken faster. With constant coatings, like heavy cream over some giant skewered mushroom, the panful of latex is gradually emptied. When the ball is the right size — 110 pounds (50 kilograms) — it is ready to sell. It is arduous work, and the heavy smoke, apart from being truly unpleasant, is hazardous to the tapper's health.

To tap rubber the old way, the tapper must go out very early, usually when it is still dark. On his head he wears a metal helmetlike contraption that holds a candle or a kerosene-soaked wick, to light the way. The rubber runs better when it is cooler. Only by starting out so early can he get all the work — tapping, gathering and smoking — done in one day.

Antonio's father, Joaquim, was a tall old man who always looked as though he was about to break into a chuckle. Seu Joaquim was born in the northeastern state of Ceará, but the family left there in 1926, when he was eleven years old, and his brother, Chico's dad, was twelve. "And I remember it as if it were yesterday," he said, sitting on the cabin doorstep. "My father packed us up and we went by wagon to Dimoeira, up there on the coast of Ceará. Spent some time there, then took a boat to Belém. We stayed in Pará for about four years, farming, then we came by boat all the way to Acre. They said it was good tapping rubber up here." Then he laughed, a quiet, rather private laugh, perhaps in remembering, perhaps in irony.

Thousands of families like the Mendeses left the poverty and drought of Brazil's northeast during the rubber boom years, convinced that, in spite of the hardships, the snakes, jaguars, hostile Indians, the crushing isolation, they would strike it rich in the forests of Amazonia. Rubber: wasn't it making everyone rich? Didn't it build the opera house in Manaus and the municipal theater in Belém? Wasn't it one of the nation's greatest exports?

The system into which the Mendes family and others like them were placed was one that had existed since the beginning of the rubber boom, around 1870. The quest for rubber sent men throughout the river-threaded reaches of the Amazon. Along the way, Chico had told me, they often entered into conflict with the Indians. "The Indians were the legitimate owners of these regions, so the rubber tappers were used by the bosses to massacre them. Entire tribes of Indians, thousands of them, were massacred to meet the interests of those who exploited the slave labor of the rubber tapper."

The area with the best rubber trees, tall, thick and full of milk, was in Acre. During the first half of the rubber boom, Acre was not even part of Brazil but a territory belonging to Bolivia, although its non-Indian population was primarily Brazilian. Wars were fought over this strategic piece of land, and for a year it survived as an independent republic ruled by a man named Luis Galvez. With financial backing from Manaus, Galvez had succeeded in wresting Acre from Bolivia. That was in 1899, but foreign-relations strategies prevented the Brazilian government from recognizing the new republic. Galvez was deposed by the Brazilian navy less than a year after he took his precarious hold on power. But Manaus, eager for the rubber, continued to insist on the incorporation of Acre as a Brazilian territory. Three expeditionary forces were defeated before Placido de Castro, an immigrant from the south, finally won the territory. Brazil agreed to pay Bolivia £2 million and to build a railway from its border to the Madeira River in Rondônia as compensation.

Throughout the rubber boom, domestic and foreign banks lent money to merchants and entrepreneurs to establish rubber reserves throughout the Amazon. These credits were used to bring in workers, primarily from the northeast, and set them up in the forest with a shack, a few tools and some food. From then on, it was clear sailing for the bosses of the rubber estates. Forbidding the rubber tapper even to grow food in his forest clearing, they sold him all his supplies at inflated prices. They collected the balls of rubber at central posts, still known in Acre as "headquarters," and subtracted the price of provisions from the value of the rubber. In some areas of the Amazon, small, independent rubber producers could sell to the buyer who offered the most. But the overwhelming tendency in Acre and Western Amazonas was for the development of huge, privately run natural rubber estates. The rubber tapper who worked on such estates was called a *seringueiro cativo*, a "captive rubber tapper," forever in debt to the headquarters.

Chico told me that if a rubber tapper did manage a credit, he was often robbed or killed. "It happened many times that the bosses would order their gunmen to kill a rubber tapper who had a credit or was owed some money," he said. "Then the money was returned to the boss."

While the boom made a few people a lot of money, and opened up an otherwise isolated area, it did not last long. The rubber barons did nothing to invest in or improve their management of the industry, and one day in 1876, a bedful of seedlings slipped out from under their noses, in a British ship from the Inman Line, the *Amazonas*.

The seedlings were developed in Kew Gardens in London and eventually sent to Malaysia, where, with none of the species' usual predators around, they did well in plantations. Soon East Indian rubber was flooding the market at prices lower than those the Brazilians could afford to charge. By 1923, Asian rubber production of 370,000 tons (330 000 tonnes) had virtually swamped that of Brazil at just 18,000 tons (16 200 tonnes). Banks started calling in their credits, and many bosses abandoned their estates. Over the years, local merchants and river-bound peddlers took up some of the slack. They bought rubber as cheaply as possible and sold oil, salt, clothing, munitions and other dry goods from town expensively. But since it made a lot more sense to load up your boat with transistor radios and clothing and other such items, instead of rice and beans, the rubber tappers were free to grow foodstuffs in their clearings. In Acre, in spite of the loss of their monopoly, rubber remained the state's principal source of income. Most of the bosses kept their land rights, competing with the river peddlers and buying Brazil nuts for export from the rubber tappers as well.

After the arduous morning walk, I took a much-needed bath in the stream, in the shade of a tall *buriti* palm, the hard, dark purple fruit of which Dona Cecilia soaked in water before peeling and making a rich yellow drink. A stout wooden box on stilts stood nearby, containing a handkerchief-sized garden of fragrant herbs and hot peppers. Around the landing in the stream, dozens of multicolored butterflies flew up, as if a paintbox had opened and come alive. No matter what the temperature, the water in the stream was always cold, always running quickly over its bed of fine yellow sand, so that even though it was used for everything from laundry to scouring the pots, it would take only a few seconds for clean water to fill the shallow pool again.

Dona Cecilia's youngest son, eighteen-year-old Nisomar, had been doing quite a bit of hunting lately, and the kitchen was almost always full of game, mostly paca, but also *cuatipuru*, which resembles a reddish flying squirrel, and a large bird called an *iambu*. He received some help from the family dog, a tough little salt-and-pepper mongrel called Dangerous. Like most families in the forest, the Mendeses were pretty well self-sufficient in food. They had to be, since the money they received for their rubber and Brazil nuts — about $1,000 U.S. a year — was far from generous. Rice, beans, cassava, corn and fruit were grown in small meadows in the forest, and crops had to be rotated every year.

The rubber tappers hunt quite a bit, tending to prefer certain animals such as wood deer, paca, wild pigs, armadillos and a couple of the larger monkeys, called howlers and woolleys. Other animals are too small, or there exists a taboo against their consumption. A large reddish monkey called the *uakari*, for example, is so ugly that it has acquired a connection with the devil and is never hunted. Three-toed sloths are left to their solitary, languorous climbs among the crowns of the forest's tallest trees, because it is believed that eating them can cause leprosy. The meat of the anteater is said to have a very strong flavor of ants, while the *canastra* armadillo, the largest in the world, is left in peace because it is believed that something terrible will befall a hunter who kills one.

The rubber tapper has many ways of hunting. Often he takes his gun when he goes tapping, to kill an edible animal or bird should he see one. Sometimes he sets traps, usually by tying a loaded shotgun into a tree with vines and setting a trip wire across an animal's path. Nisomar had gotten all the paca in Dona Cecilia's kitchen by jacking them, hunting at night and shining a flashlight in their eyes.

People liked to drop by the Mendes house for a chat. Sebastião, the oldest Mendes son, asked me about the soccer teams in Rio, about which I regrettably had to admit the most profound ignorance. A simpleminded brother of Seu Joaquim, Raimundo Nonato, always joined us wordlessly for meals. After lessons, the house invariably filled up with children, but they stayed only for a moment to have a look at the visitors. The only child living in the house was Francisco's daughter, Neleide, whose mother had drowned in a shallow stream when she had a sudden fit while doing the laundry.

Seu Joaquim told us stories, how he had spent four years in Bolivia farming, about the rubber tracts he had been evicted from. His one dream, he told me, laughing shyly, was to have electricity in the house. "I'd really like to see that," he said, "lights on in the house at night. Although I have no idea how I will ever do it."

In a world without television or books or newspapers, and with only the stodgy programming of Radio Nacional from Brasília for those who have radios, sitting around talking and making jokes is the universal entertainment. Whether it was Dona Cecilia's bray while she was standing on her block of wood in front of the window counter, or Miguel's stories, or Seu Joaquim's frequent chuckles, laughter was always hovering in the air, like the thick smoke of the wood fires used to cure the rubber. One night while a neighbor was visiting and I was rather obviously, I suppose, keeping an eye on all the cockroaches skittering around the wall, Antonio told everyone about my reaction the night before to finding a large cockroach marching down the rope of my hammock toward my head. They all laughed out loud, except for Dona Cecilia, who defended me by announcing peremptorily, "She's not afraid of cockroaches, she's disgusted by them." And she went back to her window counter saying, "Ah, this crazy little house."

The next morning, I went out for a walk with Miguel, who resembles the Polish union leader Lech Walesa. This time, we entered the forest by a different route, over the stream in the back, through a dense, fantastically exuberant enclosure of bamboo and other growth. It was impossible to stop and look, however, as Miguel strode quickly ahead, his gun over his shoulder, his hunting dogs bounding around his feet. "You see," he was saying, turning corners and climbing and descending, while I scrambled to keep up, "I don't have to tap rubber today if I don't want to. I can take the time to show you around instead."

In spite of the arduous pace, Miguel talked almost constantly, telling me that he had lived in Xapuri for a while, where he had been a barber. "I had house with furniture, a television set, everything," he recounted. "But I began to realize that life in town was not for me, and sold the whole thing, lock, stock and barrel, so I could move back here." Miguel had only one small loop of rubber trees, which he left to a young man named Francisco to tap for half the money. Francisco, not yet twenty, was shy, with a craterous complexion and light fuzzy hair. He always wore a brown felt hat. Miguel had a small herd of cattle and did some buying and selling of rubber from the other tappers in Cachoeira. His wife, Francisca, taught at the little one-room school near Seu Joaquim's house.

We passed several piles of Brazil nut shells at the feet of the nut trees. Packed into a hard, woody shell like a cannonball, the nuts are usually harvested in December and January, during the rainy season, when it's impossible to tap rubber because rain gets into the containers of latex. Brazil nuts had gone up in price and were earning the tappers more money than rubber. "You have to be very careful harvesting the Brazil nuts," warned Miguel. "If you go out too early, before they have all fallen, one could fall on your head and kill you." Indeed, the majestic Brazil nut trees are among the tallest in the forest. Some ranchers try to keep them alive while burning forest around them, but the tree is delicate and can die from the heat.

No one seemed happier than Miguel about the fact that there was no boss around anymore; he could plan his days as he wished. He took me to the old headquarters, where he was making straw saddles and mats in an empty storehouse. At one point during our long walk through the forest, he suddenly stopped and looked at the roots of a large tree. "Aha, you see?" he asked. I didn't at first, but stooping over, I finally saw something: a bee crawling into a tiny hole in the upper roots. "And someone has already been here," he said, glancing at the trunk. Before I knew what was happening, Miguel had taken out his machete and started hacking at the trunk. Then I saw that a straight, neat cut had been made in the living wood, as a squarish piece fell off, like a cupboard door. Inside was a waxy brown mass of bulbous tubes, a honeycomb, crawling with bees. "Don't worry about the bees," said Miguel. "They're Italian. They never sting. You see, someone had already discovered the nest, taken out some honey and put it all back together again." He dashed off and started hacking at the foliage, returning in a minute with a narrow green reed. Poking it into one of the wax chambers, he said, "Go ahead, have a drink." I took a sip. It was very watery and tasted more like cough medicine than honey.

He also showed me an unusual vine. I had already been caught once by this prickly vine, which hooks into your clothes so securely you have to stop and undo it. Its name is perfect. It is called *Spera Aí*, or "Hold on, there." When it grows large and thick, it can be quite useful. If you slash it once, nothing happens, but if you slash it twice, a stream of cold, clear water comes running out to quench your thirst.

We walked down a wider path to the old headquarters and came across a pair of dark-skinned teenagers, brother and sister, walking toward Xapuri. The girl wore a pink dress and a camouflage cap and carried a plastic pail. Her brother told us that they lived in Bolivia, and Miguel said he recognized their father's name, once they said who they were. Theirs was just one of the many Brazilian families who had been forced to move to Bolivia to tap rubber. It would be another twenty-four hours before they made it to town. "Do you know where you will stay tonight?" asked Miguel. "Yes, we do," said the boy, "we have an aunt on a *colocação* that we'll reach this afternoon." "Well, then, goodbye," said Miguel. "Good luck."

Miguel took me around the old headquarters, a boarded-up shop and office and a few big empty storerooms, the whole thing on stilts to keep the produce dry. The boss had left some years before, said Miguel, and no one had taken his place, although there were rumors. Some said the old Syrian merchant Guilherme Zaire had bought it, others said Darli Alves had. There was a family living there, but they only rented the place and did some small-scale farming. Miguel made himself busy collecting oranges from the row of trees along the fence; bringing half a dozen with us, we started back to the family's *colocação*.

During the entire walk, through small fields and long, winding stretches of forest trails, Miguel talked passionately about the wonder of this world he lived in. "There is so much in here," he would say, "that we hardly even know about it all. And those ranchers just want to destroy it. Hundreds of families can make a living here, and if it's a ranch, then just one man can. He builds a beautiful big house, and we, we don't need that. We are used to having something that will just keep the rain off our heads and the animals out."

Miguel, a mean hand, I discovered later, with the ukulele, even sang a song while I walked around with him that day, an ode to the rubber tapper written by his wife, Francisca. It went like this:

Let's esteem the rubber tapper,
Let's esteem the nation,
Because it's with the work of this people,
That one makes tires for cars and even planes.
They made little sandals, and they made rubber thongs,
They invented little boots so the snake can never bite.
So many things that I don't know how to explain.
I even found a piece in the pressure cooker.

Later that afternoon, Gilson Pescador dropped by with a woman from the state Ministry of Education. He had left the priesthood and was running for mayor of Xapuri on the Workers' Party ticket. I gave him the books I had brought for the new school, modern Brazilian classics by writers such as Jorge Amado and Clarice Lispector. "They're wonderful," he said, "but I think maybe too advanced for the school here. But I had been hoping to start up a small library for the rubber tappers in the union hall and so now I can put them there."

This was also when I found out about the man's appetite. Announcing that he was hungry, he walked into Dona Cecilia's kitchen, emerging a few minutes later with Dona Cecilia behind him. She told me sadly, "Augusta, Gilson has eaten all the oranges you brought back."

Soon it was time to go. Chico arrived with a crew of foreigners — two British journalists, five American research students and a young Japanese woman. He introduced me to them in classic Chico style. Meant, I believe, partly as a joke, and partly as a compliment, he said, "And this is Augusta, the guerrilla."

Dona Cecilia, however, was slightly overwhelmed by the five new mouths to feed. "Oh, Augusta, what am I going to do?" she asked me quietly. "I just had all that fresh meat. Now I've put it in the sun to dry and I've only dry meat."

"Don't worry about it," I said. "Since they're from America, I'm sure they'll be just as happy with vegetables anyway."

A big group had climbed into the truck to return to Xapuri with Chico. Among them was Seu Joaquim, who, as I expected, just nodded and chuckled when I said goodbye. Before I got into the car that would take me to Rio Branco, Chico stopped me for a moment and said, "So, comrade, when are you coming back?"

They were the last words I would hear from Chico Mendes.

FOUR

A HOUSE ON THE RIVERBANK

FROM ACRE, IN THE WESTERN Amazon, I traveled to the other side of the continent, to the state of Pará in the east. From the modest house of the Mendes family in the middle of the forest, I went to another kind of rural home, this one high on stilts over the bank of a river. Like the rubber tappers, the river dwellers were suffering enormous changes in their lives because of a quest for progress over which they had no control.

Portents of the disaster on the Tocantins River began with a series of mysterious phenomena, almost like the biblical plagues of Egypt. The river almost disappeared for several weeks; cars and trucks began to use its smooth bed as a roadway, and islands were suddenly joined by great stretches of shallow mud.

Then one day the waters rose again, first salty, then black and fetid, unlike anything the river dwellers had seen before. People became ill, children began to suffer from diarrhea, and anyone who bathed in it for longer than about ten minutes noticed rashes on their skin. An enormous sheath of yellow scum made its way slowly down-river, coating the trailing branches and spears of *aninga* along the banks. The slime left an infestation of tiny insects, winged, water-borne creatures — also unlike anything the locals had seen before — milling in the thousands beneath the river surface.

Worst of all, the great schools of fish, the *curimata* and *mapara*, the shrimp and many other species that had once filled the river seemed to have vanished forever. Wild cacao trees growing in the floodplain forest stopped bearing fruit, slowly shriveled up and died. Upriver, the multibillion-dollar Tucuruí Dam had begun producing more than 2000 megawatts of electric power, and life for the people of the lower Tocantins River, an estimated 40,000 island- and riverbank-dwellers, was never to be the same.

Straddling the Tocantins River at the foot of the Carajás Ridge in the state of Pará, the Tucuruí Dam is the second-largest hydroelectric project in Brazil and one of the largest in the world. When all its turbines are installed, it will deliver 7000 megawatts of electricity. Much of this electricity goes, at subsidized rates, to aluminum and steel smelters in Pará and in the neighboring state of Maranhão, smelters that are wholly or partly owned by multinational companies, such as Alcoa in the United States.

What has caused the problems, however, is not so much the dam itself as the giant reservoir, some 910 square miles (2400 square kilo-meters), that feeds it. Where maps of Brazil once showed a wriggly blue line all the way from Itapiranga to Joanna Pires, a long, wide block the size of Luxembourg now fills in the green. In 1980, the state electric company, Eletronorte, accepted tenders from those who could clear the forest from the area. The winner was a joint-venture firm put together by a French investment bank, Lazard Frères, and a Brazilian pension investment company called CAPEMI. Other tenders estimated it would at least take ten to fifteen years to deforest the large tract of land; the winning consortium said they would do it in just three. They were able to do no such thing, of course, and with less than a third of the forest cover gone, the land was flooded. Acres and acres of vegeta-tion were inundated; entire villages, including their cemeteries, lay under water; and defoliants such as Agent Orange became part of the deadly mixture, because there was no time to cut down and haul out the trees to which it had been applied.

The result was a biologically complex soup that scientists in Brazil were just beginning to study. In Belém, I spoke to Anthony Anderson, an American biologist working at the city's Goeldi Museum. Anderson had carried out some preliminary studies before his funds were cut off by Eletronorte. He thought there might be three different but related causes of the frightening effects downriver from the dam. "One might be the presence of humic acids and tannins formed by the biomass at the bottom of the lake," he told me. "Another might be the lack of sediment trapped by the dam. A third might be toxins, and they would not have to be in very high concentrations to cause a lot of harm." The toxins and acids were not apparent in the upper layers of lake water, which were full of fish. The chemicals, it seemed, had pooled at the lake bottom. But they were not out of reach of the currents that impelled the water toward the dam then down the river.

I arrived in Cametá before dawn on an overnight boat from Belém, the capital city of Pará. On the dock a few men sat around on the boxes of their big two-wheeled carts, waiting for work. I walked to a nearby square and read for a while, until the sky grew pale gray and the few street lamps snapped off one by one. Soon, I saw a familiar face among the people who were beginning to fill the square: a young American graduate student named Penny Magee, whom I'd met in Belém. Penny was working on her doctoral degree for the University of Florida, studying the effects of the Tucuruí Dam on the lives of the people on the lower Tocantins. She had come in from the island of Paruru that morning to pick me up, as well as another young woman, a Brazilian researcher named Marília.

We set off for the market. Penny had a fairly lengthy shopping list to take care of. It included such exotica as jerked beef from São Paulo and floury white tapioca, a starchy by-product of cassava roots, used to make a sort of pancake called *beiju*. Then we went into the large covered shed that served as a fish market. There was plenty of fish for sale, all the usual freshwater species of the Amazon, but all of it from other regions. For local buyers, all of it was expensive.

We returned to the wharf, and Penny introduced me to Raimundo Gonçalves, head of the family with which she was boarding on Paruru Island. Serious and unsmiling, he was a tall, lean man with chiseled features and a pencil mustache. His piercing eyes, like those of a small animal, seemed strained with worry. But he was polite and invited me to stay a few days with his family.

As we waited for Raimundo's children to arrive, I noticed a stocky little woman with long gray hair and distinctly Indian features leaning against the shed wall in the shade. This was Dona Nair, I learned, Seu Raimundo's mother-in-law. Two of her grandchildren arrived, thirteen-year-old Elielson and sixteen-year-old Elezete, and they greeted her by asking for her blessing, pulling her hand in a rapid gesture toward their lips. The old woman granted the blessing by returning the gesture.

We moved down the steps and into a battered wooden boat, open and quite long, belonging to Mestre Jovico, an old man with a white beard. A number of other paying passengers were coming with us to the island: women laden with sacks of food or squat silver canisters of gas; a woman with a baby; a coppery-skinned man with an enormous sack of toasted tapioca rings. Like an ant bearing a huge white larva to its nest, he clambered skillfully over the raft of other boats with his light but cumbersome load, and deposited it matter-of-factly in the bow.

The double-tiered wooden wharf was busy that Saturday morning, with dozens of boats clustering around it like bees. Tiny skiffs called *cascos* swept in from across the bay, propelled by patched, homemade sails, which the boatmen took down and folded as the boats coasted neatly to a halt. Larger, motorized boats like Mestre Jovico's jammed the insufficient harbor area two or three rows deep. And there were also slightly bigger motorized boats, roofed and walled in, their white exteriors painted around the top with flags of blue, red and green.

Out in the bay, I could see large bits of metal pipe wafting on the waves. These, Penny told me, were the pieces of a dredge that the town's congressman, Gerson Pires, had won from the government in return for voting for a five-year term for President José Sarney. The congressional vote had given rise to a great deal of controversy in Brazil. Following on the heels of a military dictatorship, plagued by rising inflation, corruption and broken promises, most Brazilians had wanted to see Sarney given no more than a four-year term. But Sarney wanted five, and offered to pay for them. Shortly after the dredge had arrived, however, a big storm had broken it apart. The symbol of Pires' capitulation was left to float uselessly offshore, much like the Sarney government itself.

The last passenger, Seu Raimundo's twenty-year-old daughter, Elza, arrived, and we set off across the bay, which gleamed like broken glass in the midmorning sun. From far away, the tiny *cascos* looked like bright slivers of wood as they flashed over the waves. We headed toward a low island, a long, flat spill of green on the horizon. After about an hour, it loomed clearly, lush with thickets of slender young palms and leafy undergrowth. We skirted it and crossed another open expanse of river, then turned in to the maze of waterways that linked a huge knot of islands in the river's center.

The channel we took was fairly wide. Here and there, creepers of red brushlike flowers, called macaw's tail, wove carpets through the bracken. Black birds sat among the *aninga*, with its single spade-shaped leaf. Red-tile roofs poked through the feathery canopy of the forest, and we began to pass long sawn-wood houses washed in colors faded by the sun and rain. They rose imposingly on tall stilts. Each house, it seemed, was surrounded by groves of *açaí* palm, their sprays of fat berries sprouting from the upper trunks like enormous brooms. Penny told me that the custom was to throw the cleaned pits out the window after making a drink from the flesh, so new trees were always sprouting.

As we tacked along the mottled brown stream, water and forest combined to create a scene of lush exuberance, and the hollow, faded houses with their mossy roofs and narrow stilts an integral part of the scene. Through the open windows of the houses, I could see shimmering ribs of light reflected on walls and ceilings like brown watered silk. Small, naked children stared at us intently as we motored by. Laundry flapped in the breeze, and boxes of herbs and pots of flowers encircled the small docks and verandas high above us. Each house was made accessible by the smooth trunk of a *miriti* palm floating between wooden poles stuck in the mud.

One of the houses we passed was much more luxurious than all the others; it had electrical wiring, a TV antenna and panes of glass in the windows. This was the home of Orminda Barra, who was currently running for town councillor in Cametá. Her husband, Roberto, owned a sawmill, which sat in a great mound of sawdust beside the house and was connected to it by a long electrical cable.

A little later, we arrived at Seu Raimundo's. We stepped out of the swaying boat and lugged our bags up a ladder and over a precarious little dock, dangerous with loose and creaking boards, into the house.

The place was rife with small children, but only three were family: five-year-old Dinho, eight-year-old Dico, and eleven-year-old Ellison.

Although the same kind of structure as the Mendes family's shack in Cachoeira, Seu Raimundo's house was larger and more comfortable. The front room was furnished with a beat-up Leatherette couch, two old armchairs and a little table in the center. A shelf above the couch held two big old radios, one sitting on top of the other; a small shrine, decorated with paper triangles cut from a book of children's Bible stories, was built into a corner. Three holy pictures — St. George, the Blessed Virgin, and the Last Supper — graced the walls; there was also a pair of hand-colored photographic portraits of Seu Raimundo and his wife, Denair. The quality of the photos, the serious faces, the round, polished frames and beveled glass, made the pictures look quite old-fashioned. In fact, Dona Denair told me they were fairly recent, perhaps only eight years old, and I later noticed many such portraits in rural homes in the Amazon, always serious, always seeming to portray their subjects as elderly, however young they were.

I sat with my notebook at the big kitchen table, its rough board surface covered with a thick piece of transparent plastic. In front of me, the open window, its single shutter pulled up and tied to a beam with a length of blue nylon rope, was filled with the fringed jungle greenery of açaí palm trees. As she moved around me, making lunch, Dona Denair was singing a plaintive song.

Chora ribeirinho, sofre pescador,
Cadê nosso peixe que a Tucuruí levou?
Cry river dweller, suffer fisherman,
Where are our fish that the Tucuruí took away?

"What is that?" I asked her.

"Oh, it's a song we learned at church," she replied, and sang the whole thing through for me.

The kitchen was a dark, airy cavern of a room, its plank floor swept and smooth. There were two small gas stoves in different corners, and a hammock slung between a pair of beams. Down from the open window, a long, sloping counter topped with a sheet of beaten metal extended toward the back door. The wall above it was opened in a row of louvered slats, with a narrow gap at the bottom where the water from washing dishes could drain off. Dishes and utensils were piled into big wooden racks. Food was stored in a cabinet in the corner, tightly sealed in metal containers or jars to keep out rats and cockroaches.

The sawn-wood walls were mostly bare, but decorated here and there with pages cut from catalogs, displaying oddly out-of-place urban items like pocket calculators, sunglasses and bright summer clothing. A small shelf trimmed with red paper lace held a collection of cans and bottles and a jar of toothbrushes. A trio of square palm-fiber sieves hung from a single nail.

Dona Denair took down the sieves and went to a table on the back stoop to make a pot of the rich purple drink known everywhere as *açaí* wine, but which isn't really wine at all. She took several handfuls of palm berries from a basket and rubbed them briskly against the pitted surface of a large clay bowl, eventually amassing a mound of tough peel that resembled dark wet tea leaves. This mound she worked rapidly through each sieve, one by one, constantly adding scoops of water, until only a fine, creamy paste, like a thick soup, remained. Both the rubbings and the denuded berries were thrown over the stoop onto the ground for the chickens. "Do you like *açaí?*" Dona Denair asked me.

"Well, I've only had it once, in some ice cream," I admitted, "and didn't like it much. It didn't seem to have any flavor."

"Oh, no, you have to have *açaí* fresh," she admonished. "Even by the time it gets to Belém, it is not as good."

With her heavy, rounded body, curling black hair, olive skin and sloe eyes, Dona Denair reminded me of one of those languorously corpulent Tahitian women in a painting by Gauguin. She had just turned forty-three, and was the mother of ten children. A fervent Catholic, she participated actively in the church community on Paruru Island.

After a lunch of fried fish, rice and *açaí*, which the children mixed with cassava meal, we set out across the log bridge that spanned the stream behind the house to have a look at some of Seu Raimundo's cacao trees, his principal source of income. They were spaced beneath the forest cover on about fifty acres (twenty hectares) of land, a quite considerable holding by local standards. Seu Raimundo had earned the money to buy the land in the famous gold pit of Serra Pelada,

where his brother had acquired a square-yard plot that had surren-
dered about 650 pounds (300 kilos) of gold. The pit had not proven to
be the ticket to wealth they had hoped for, though, as falling rocks and
water made it impossible to get to the mother lode, even after more
than two years of digging. Seu Raimundo told me a number of stories
about those days in Serra Pelada, where at one time eighty thousand
men toiled and climbed, carrying endless sacks of dirt along precarious
pathways in a desperate search for gold.

The stream sliced our path in two places, and we had to cross a
second broad trunk, a prospect that made me nervous since my shoes
had become slippery with mud. Typical of cacao farmers in the
Amazon, Seu Raimundo had planted a variety of fruit trees—banana,
guava, papaya, cashew — among the cacao, as this was said to make
the cacao do better. Seu Raimundo had bought this piece of land with
a considerable grove of native cacao trees already on it, and since then
he had planted about seven thousand new trees.

At first the trees had done well, and production was good, more
than 2200 pounds (1000 kilos) of fruit a year, but since the closing of
the dam gates, the harvests had slowly diminished to less than half
that. Pointing out a twisted, unhealthy-looking tree, he said, "It's just
like a man who is not getting his vitamins. He loses his strength. With
this water, the land is not getting its vitamins."

In previous years, the only work involved in producing cacao was
gathering the football-shaped yellow fruit, then cutting out the seeds,
which eventually went to make chocolate. The floods that occurred
every year during the rainy season replenished the soil with rich loads
of silt. Now the dam was holding the crucial nutrients back. Seu
Raimundo had devised a natural fertilizer, made of açaí pits and other
refuse, and was finding an improvement. The newly planted trees
responded best, he said, just as they had suffered least from the lack of
silt. As we strolled along, he showed me what the polluted water had
done to the trunks of many young trees — the bark had actually been
eaten away.

Seu Raimundo was the delegate, on Paruru Island, for the Rural
Workers Union, which was based in Cametá. The previous delegate,
an old friend, had passed the position on to him. But in the last elections, when the union leaders had given him voting forms already
marked in their favor, he had refused to go along with their demands.
Instead he joined a growing opposition group within the union, which

was trying to democratize the organization, to put in a new leadership, honestly elected and ready to fight for them. "That's when I began to notice the situation the people were in," he told me later, "and I began to struggle, not only to defend myself but to defend people in general."

As we walked back to the house, tiny crabs skittered out of our way, and Seu Raimundo pointed out various trees native to the area. There were tall *virola* and *andiroba* trees, both sold frequently to sawmills. The *andiroba* was especially prized because of its resistance to termites. Rubber trees, quite different from the giants I had seen in Acre, squatted thick and gnarled among the ferns and other brush. These rubber trees were tapped in an unusual way. Rather than carving a line across the bark, the tapper made a series of little stabs, affixing large, pearly snail shells, and in one case an old corned beef tin, to the trunk with smudges of clay to catch the flow of latex.

We stopped to look at Seu Raimundo's small garden of black pepper plants, a spice usually grown inland, on *terra firma*, or what everyone referred to as "the center." The plants were doing well, he said, and might provide an alternative income for the people of the islands.

In the meantime, there seemed to be nothing anyone could do about the lack of fish that once abounded in the river and had provided the main source of income for the river dwellers.

We were up early on Sunday morning to take Mestre Jovico's boat, rented from him for the weekend, through the islands to visit people and talk about the changes that had occurred since the construction of the dam. Only Dinho and his older brother Elielson were supposed to come with us, but Dico sulked so much during breakfast that he was finally allowed to come, too.

We started off with a slight breeze blowing and the water calm and low. The air felt fresh and cool as we motored along, the old boat throbbing steadily beneath us. As we headed down a channel, we saw several places where fragile screens, made from slats of *jupatí* palm, had been strung across the shore. These were a kind of fish trap. We passed a pair of *tracajá* turtles, their scabrous heads crowned with dots of yellow, sunning themselves on a log. A young couple paddled by in a *casco*, their brightly painted paddles flashing in the sun, a frowning baby on the bow. It struck me that the *casco* was like a waterborne version of the bicycle. Cheap and easy to use, it is one of the first things a small child learns to manipulate and the main form of transport among the islands.

We did not go far on this first leg of our trip, only to the community center on the neighboring island of Maparaí. A large wooden platform had been built high over the shore and railed off like a promenade. On it were two pavilions, one for meetings and dances, another for drinking, and a small white church. We climbed onto the dock and met Dona Maria, a sturdy, motherly woman, looking like a school teacher, with short brown hair and a dark green dress. Maria da Conceição Aquime, was a volunteer in the Catholic base community, and worked in its health program, an underfunded project that could do little more than document the desperate conditions of the local river dwellers. (Base communities were formed by the Catholic Church in regions of Latin America where the number of priests was insufficient to serve the local population.) She and about a third of the population were trying to organize a campaign for compensation from Eletronorte for the effects of the Tucuruí Dam.

We walked into the largest pavilion, where a small group of people were chatting in the welcome shade. There was a raised platform built in the far corner, set with a table and two benches. As we sat down and began our interview with Dona Maria, the people came closer, pulling some benches away from the walls to sit and listen.

"Before this problem with dam," Dona Maria began, "life for us was good. It was abundant. Lots of fish, shrimp. The water was good and today it isn't. Today all that is left us is the consequences of the dam and hunger."

Previously, she told us, the water was clean and clear, a glassy blue that reflected the sky. The harvests of wild cacao were good. "And there was lots of fish," she said, "*curimata, mapara*. All kinds of it." It was enough to stand on the bank and catch a fish for that day's dinner, she said. "Now the only fish comes from above the dam down here for us to buy. What we had for free before, now we have only for money, and with a lot of sacrifice." The result, she added, was a growing incidence of malnutrition on the island, especially among children and pregnant women. "And what is that from? It's the lack of food, of money to buy the food we need," she said.

An old man in a ragged shirt also spoke up. He was a fisherman called Luceu Gonçalves, seventy years old, and, it turned out, the husband of Dona Maria.

"There was always plenty of fish here," he explained. "I was a fisherman and I know what fish is." In years past, he said, he would go out and make catches of eighty to a hundred pounds (forty to fifty kilos). "It was a lot of fish," he said, "but today, when you've got ten pounds, you've got a lot. You're only working for your meal. That's why I thought it better to sell my nets. The fisherman can only pay the people he needs to work with him when he's getting fish. If you spend a month and don't get fish, then you're only just fighting for your meal and that's all."

For everyone on Maparaí and the other islands, the situation was frustrating and ironic. The big refrigerated boats that once came to buy their catches now came to sell. "I feel sad about it," admitted Seu Luceu, "because the way things are, if they got better, I'd be happy. But it's only promises that they promise," he said, referring to the plethora of vague and unsubstantiated commitments from Electronorte.

Many people were leaving the island, said Dona Maria, but a few were trying to change the situation. They were getting together and demanding action from the government and compensation from Electronorte. "But it is very difficult," Dona Maria admitted. "People think the struggle isn't worth the trouble, that it won't accomplish anything, that there is no way if not by the will of God. Many people do not believe in our work."

I asked if they had had any inkling that such things might happen once the dam was completed.

"We knew that they were building the dam," Dona Maria replied, "only we didn't know what the consequences would be. After we did discover, it was too late. A few base communities did send petitions to try to stop the construction, asking that the gates not be closed, that this would harm us, but the voice of humble people is worth nothing. Perhaps if all the communities had gotten together when things were good, this would never have happened. Perhaps we would still have the abundance we had before."

We sailed on for a half hour or so before reaching another island and pulling up at a row of houses. One of them was a small general store run by Dona Denair's younger brother, José Maria Cardoso. He had the same eyes and broad face as his sister, although his longish, unkempt hair and curly sideburns made him look as though he should be playing in a country music band rather than selling dry goods on a tiny island in the middle of the Amazon. He spoke frankly and forcefully about the effects of Tucuruí, especially among the people he knew.

"Before, on this piece here," said José Maria, waving his arm toward the flat green shores to either side of his house, "just about everyone lived by fishing. After the dam was built, things changed. Now people are starting to leave for the pepper plantations to work for others. They'll go and work for two or three months, spend a week here, and when the money gives out, go back to the plantation.

"There's folks here," he said, leaning against the counter, "many heads of families, and that's their whole life, always moving. Often they stop over with their families one or two days and that's it. In fact, about a dozen families have already moved away for good from this piece here."

Many went to try their luck in Belém, José Maria said, looking for any kind of work they could find. But with nothing put by, usually only one person, the head of the household, could afford to go, leaving his family behind. Inevitably, many families, poor and dependent, began to feel the strain, and the once tightly knit fabric of relationships began to break down. It was possibly the most tragic effect of Tucuruí.

"When a couple is together with their family," said José Maria, "things always go better. And when one goes, sometimes the children start leaving, too, and don't even obey their parents anymore. Kids are starting to work very young here, doing something, anything at all to earn a little money. And then, they get that certain way about them, you know? They're gone for sure, and even their own fathers don't know where to find them anymore."

Children were being taken out of school to work in the pepper harvest, he told us, which took place from October to December. "The kids of today are becoming marginalized," he said, "because there's no way they can learn anything."

The only recourse left to some people was to harvest *açaí*. The production of palm berries had not been affected by the dam, but with nothing else to eat, people were cutting out the palm hearts, which killed the young tree. This was common during the rainy season. Even with a rise in the price paid for *açaí* berries and *açaí* wine, a lot of local families, especially those with only a little land, were caught in this no-win situation.

"You could see it in a harvest like this one, which is just ending," said José Maria. "There are people who have been cutting out the palm hearts all winter. They can't buy cassava. They can't buy coffee. They have no choice, so they go out and every day cut a hundred or more hearts. When summer comes, many don't have *açaí* berries to sell. The situation is obliging people to destroy the things that we've always kept up."

José Maria implied that only now were the rural poor beginning to realize that established politicians would do nothing to help them. The municipal government would gain a great deal, José Maria thought, if it would simply take the people's side and find some solution. But he was sarcastic about those who came campaigning now from door to door. "They come now just in this period before elections," he said. "After they've won, nothing. So we've decided to fight against these people, see if we can't work hard, struggle, and put some people from our class into power."

Like Maria da Conceição, he had found that this was not easy. "There are always some people who, even suffering, go around with their minds made up. But, at any rate," he added optimistically, "things are changing. The struggle is advancing; we're talking about things and making our own decisions. Otherwise, you can see, nothing today is done for the common people."

As we sat talking, customers came in from time to time. José Maria's conversation was punctuated with his calling out prices as people went behind the counter and picked out what they needed. The shelves offered no luxuries except a few bottles of a strong sugarcane brandy called *cachaça*. The shelves were filled instead with mundane merchandise such as cooking oil, matches and soap. The purchases weren't paid for, but the prices were toted up in a book. "Often people have every desire to pay their bills," said José Maria philosophically, "but they have nothing. It's really a pity."

We set off again, this time to see a fisherman called José Xavier Vianna, known to all as *Abacate*, or Avocado. In spite of his funny nickname, this wiry man of thirty-eight, who had eight children to clothe and feed, was facing one of the worst situations we were to see all day.

The house where we visited him — his brother's, he told us — was large and well-lit and made of *buriti* palm slats. There was little furniture in the front room — a bench, a hammock and a wardrobe with a broken door. Instead, the space was taken up by the tools of the fisherman's trade — shrimp nets and gill nets, cylindrical shrimp traps, larger cylindrical shrimp nurseries, Styrofoam floats and a long string hung with rather nasty-looking big hooks. They were tools of a trade Abacate could no longer practice.

He had fished all his life, Abacate told us, and every year the fish had swum up the river and filled his nets. He described the catches of *jussuara* and whitefish, the ubiquitous *curimata* and the island streams full of shrimp. Then came the dam.

"Not that it finished all at once," he said. "No, but we noticed, from one year to the next, the decline of fish. The migrations have decreased until we practically don't have any anymore."

It was as if a poison had clouded the once fruitful waters, Abacate said, and the poison kept the fish away. "They notice that the water is different," he said, "that it's contaminated. Because now we are seeing that the *mapara*, of which we always had lots, and *curimata* are being imported from the Amazonas River. And it was never like that before. In Cametá, they are unloading sixty tons of *curimata* at a time. That's the kind of fish we used to have here, and now we don't."

The family was just scraping by, gathering *açaí*, some rubber, whatever they could find. The previous winter they had spent days eating nothing but mangoes. Not just his family, but many others, too, Abacate told us. That he still felt game for a fight with Eletronorte was incredible, but he was, and he explained why in thoughtful terms, like someone with too much time on his hands.

"You know," he said, "it's like we look in every direction and can find no solution. We look toward the representatives of the people, or those who call themselves the representatives of the people, and they do nothing to resolve the problem. They don't even want to know.

"I see it this way," he went on. "Suffering as we are the consequences of the dam, and this inflation we have, well, it makes a person reflect on his life. From where does this suffering really come? Could it come from my family, or could the guilty ones be my neighbors? A person reflects, and he begins to see that this suffering comes from those in power, from this dam, from the big guys. And he says to himself, if I'm being hurt by these people, then why am I supporting them, voting for them? I should be putting my hand in for those who are fighting to tear down that power, to try to make things better for us."

Abacate had been a member of the union for ten years, he told us, and felt that the union was the only way the river dwellers of the Tocantins could gain compensation.

"I am reaching a very concrete conclusion from all this suffering, all this deception. I want to stay and fight, together with my comrades, to see if we can't make a better life for ourselves and for others, too. We're organizing in the union, in the fishing colonies and in the base communities, to see if we can't find a solution to this problem. Even by doing this interview, right? I'm hoping that people of goodwill will support this struggle, together with the workers, with those who suffer."

But like so many others, he understood how hard it was for people to find the force and the morale to resist. "Many times a guy passes the whole night with his net and doesn't even get a meal," said Abacate. "He comes home in the morning, unable to work, dropping with sleep and nothing to eat. So he prefers to go somewhere else. But we talk about this, me and my neighbors, about the situation and how we need to organize. You know there are some guys who work for others and earn no more than 200 *cruzados* a day. It's slavery. What can you do with 200 *cruzados*, these days? A pack of cigarettes isn't much less than that, is it?"

Abacate became nervous as we were about to leave. Later we found out why: he had wanted to offer us lunch but was without enough food to do so. Seu Raimundo said he had assured Abacate that we weren't hungry. We made only two more stops that day, hearing still more stories of lives devastated by Tucuruí.

The day was drawing to a close by the time we headed toward home, puttering slowly through the narrow channels. Close on either side of us, spiky and luxuriant, the myriad greens of the flood plain forest were reflected in a broad, shimmering stripe on the surface of the stream. Penny and I remarked how difficult it was to find words to describe what we were seeing, when suddenly a pair of black and white toucans, graceful and swift in spite of their topheavy, torpedo-shaped beaks, veered across our path and up into a thicket of palm. It seemed incredible that such a landscape should be the backdrop to so much suffering.

At the house that evening, everything was quiet. The girls had played a practical joke on Penny, something she said they did to her frequently. This time, they hid her kitten and told her it had wandered away. In spite of the dark, we took our baths in the river, gingerly descending the ladder, fireflies trying to send us coded messages from midstream, and me continually dropping things, first my razor, then my soap, then Dona Denair's soap. Sitting around the kitchen table later with Penny, Marilia, Seu Raimundo and Dona Denair told me about an idea the islanders had come up with, a plan to start a small chicken-raising co-operative on Paruru. With the participation of the union and the local church, they had come up with a concrete project and were hoping to get some money from the Canadian embassy's Small Projects Fund. They had carefully written their request and sent it in through the Bishop's Office, but had been informed that they had missed the deadline for grant applications.

"Well, I have a friend who works at the embassy," I said, "and as a matter of fact, he's in charge of the Small Projects grants." Eyebrows rose around the table. I said I would call my friend from Cametá and ask if he could make an exception for their application. Seu Raimundo went around whistling to himself for the rest of that evening, and Penny told me that was the happiest she had seen him since she had arrived.

A couple of days later, Dona Denair, Elizete and I took a boat, this one belonging to a river merchant called Raimundo Xavier, to Cametá. It was a large, roofed boat, with lengths of nylon rope running along the sides, connecting the rudder to an old steering wheel at the bow. By the time it got to the Gonçalves house, the boat was already full of passengers — two old women, a number of mothers with babies, a trio of teenage girls who moved sternward to sit on a small platform, which held a canister of gas and three big baskets of *açaí*. Elizete sat across from me, a pair of white pumps — her "town shoes" — cradled carefully on her lap.

Raimundo Xavier didn't usually make passenger runs, he told me; he spent most of his time heading down toward the Moju River, parallel to the Tocantins but closer to Belém. Along the way, he bought local products such as lumber, rice and cassava from the river dwellers and brought back items he could sell in Cametá, including tobacco, fish and coils of the tough, thin vine people use to tie together the slats to make fish traps.

As we emerged from the islands and crossed the river, the town of Cametá appeared, lining the shore in front of us, a long, vaguely crenellated strip of white beneath the blue sky. The church with its red roof and white plaster facade stood at one end, set off from a street of pastel turn-of-the-century buildings. At the other end, the picture was seedier: the grubby browns and blacks of the market, the unfinished port, then a smudge of shanties along the shore. Walking up the dock stairs, I told Dona Denair that I would meet up with her that night, and walked to the Prelazia, the Bishop's Office, which was not far away.

There I talked to Aida, a young woman in charge of the church's Pastoral Land Commission in Cametá. With the Rural Workers Union, the Catholic church was beginning to draw people's attention to the issue of the dam, or at least more effectively channel the alarm it had caused. Aida had been part of this process since before the dam was finished.

"The church became involved at the end of 1981," she told me as we sat together in a small meeting room, "when four thousand families living in the areas of Tucuruí, Jacundá and Itapiranga were forced to leave their land." Aida was a short, portly woman with an earnest, round face lightly dotted with freckles. She told me how Eletronorte hadn't even offered the peasants new land in exchange. The company paid them only an indemnity, a *mexeria*, she said, meaning a ridiculously small amount.

Finally, after a campaign of denunciations and protest marches, the company was forced to construct new villages, including public buildings. "The church was asking for 250 acres (100 hectares) per family," she said, "but Eletronorte ended up giving them only about 125 acres (50 hectares). They had to re-demarcate the lands of the Parakanan to do this, so the Indians ended up being moved three times in all." Unfortunately, the land the peasants received was characterized by poor soil, "not even good for growing cassava," as Aida put it, which is lousy soil, indeed. Most of the peasants sold out and left.

By 1986, the church began to focus its efforts on the areas downriver from the dam and moved the pastoral office to Cametá. It managed to get Eletronorte representatives to attend several meetings, but nothing came of them. Now, said Aida, the church was looking for new ideas and possible solutions: fish farms, new methods of treating the water, an education campaign. A young agronomist named Guillherme had joined the staff to help look for agricultural alternatives, new crops such as *guarana* and coffee. "We've also tried to inform various institutions about this," Aida said, "to create an image for people outside the area, a bad image of Eletronorte and the whole question of the dam."

After my chat with Aida, I walked to the telephone company and placed a call to the Canadian embassy in Brasília. My friend there was surprised by my query. They were very interested in funding a project in the lower Tocantins, he said. "But there was no deadline on sending in grant applications. I don't know why the Prelazia said so. Tell them to send their project directly to me."

With that good news to take home to the family, I walked to the far side of the town to see the president of the Rural Workers Union. He was a short, stocky man with a large head and large pouches under his eyes. His name was Francisco Contente, but everyone called him Chicão or Big Chico. He was nothing like the Chico I knew in Xapuri. The predicament of the union in Cametá seemed much worse than that of the union in Xapuri; in some senses the odds were stacked higher against them. Chico Mendes and the rubber tappers had something concrete to fight for in Acre; the workers in Cametá had only things to fight *against* — a river full of polluted water and the Tucuruí Dam.

The current union leaders had succeeded in wresting the union away from the conservative leaders in 1985, then had spent a lot of time "cleaning house," as Chicão put it. They had only about 8500 members in an area where they estimated there were more than 77,000 rural workers. They had no staff, no money, no boats to go out and meet with these people. And it was a hard job to convince the workers that they were different from the old union and that only the workers' participation would keep it that way.

One big problem many rural workers faced, Chicão told me, was landlords. Islands were being bought up, or people would show up with documents indicating they had been owners all along, without the river dwellers knowing it. They would then demand one half of everything produced on the land, or worse, divide it up, install another family and still demand half, effectively leaving the worker with no more than a quarter of what he produced. "It's a very grave problem," said Chicão. "These people are living in a system that is practically feudal."

Most of the union's efforts, however, were focused on the consequences of the dam. The problem extended from the area of the dam itself right down to Limoeira, on the Tocantins River delta, more than 270 miles (450 kilometers) away. Cametá was hit hardest, because there were so many islands in the river at that point. The union had attended half a dozen meetings with Eletronorte, Chicão told me, but nothing had come of them. "Now all they say they will do is pass some money on to the state health agency, Cespe, and dig some artesian wells. They say that they are taking steps. But where is the solution for this problem of the water? The whole region is revolted," he said.

While Chicão admitted that the union still had a lot of organizing to do, "to make strong attempts to raise the consciousness of the workers," as he put it, there were greater problems on the horizon. One was a government plan to turn floodplain farming into a mechanized industry in the region, to replace the small holdings of the river dwellers with large estates. The other was the increasing use of charcoal in the pig-iron factories near the huge Carajás iron ore mine, less than 240 miles (400 kilometers) away. Smelters were using up one acre's worth of forest a day, said Chicão, and the devastation was reaching Marabá, which sat at the confluence of the Tocantins and Araguaia rivers. "Soon, it will arrive here, and then there will be a fight," he said.

Then there were the plans of Eletronorte, which had completed studies of at least seven sites in the Amazon for the installation of hydroelectric dams. Chicão said the union would give the company one last chance to treat them seriously, then they would mount a big publicity campaign with demonstrations in Belém and appeals to the media. "We are going to demand what they have already promised us," said Chicão, meaning the wells and the health measures, "and more. And that has to do with the lake itself, because this situation will only get worse in the next ten years."

The rest of the week passed quickly. One morning we went to the community center on Paruru with Dona Denair — we paddled down in a *casco* — to weigh the local children, some of whom were becoming, according to the graph, dangerously undernourished.

Another afternoon, we watched Seu Raimundo make a shrimp trap in the stream. He used several rolls of palm slats and a piece of fibrous vine called *mucuna*, which Dico beat into pliable strings against the log bridge. A group of poles, which took on meaning only as Seu Raimundo worked, stood upright in the brown scummy water. Seu Raimundo got into the stream and skillfully formed a heart-shaped trap around the poles, fixing the screens to them with lengths of vine. Two walls were put up, leading from the center of the heart-shaped trap to each bank. Hours later, when the tide had receded, we came back and found the stream no more than a series of shallow pools. Inside the trap, shrimp were jumping about in a vain effort to free themselves. The catch amounted to half a basket, but Seu Raimundo told me that, in the past, he would usually get two big baskets full and still have to throw some back into the river.

We also spent an evening visiting the local aldermanic candidate with the big house, Orminda Barra. Dona Orminda was sixty-two and talked proudly and incessantly about her children, one in Brooklyn — "And don't you think New York such a marvelous place?" — and the rest in well-appointed apartments in Belém. But she was very concerned about the poor, she told me. We all had to work together. She was being visited that evening by a personage no less distinguished than Gerson Pires himself, the federal congressman for Cametá. He was state president of the Social Democratic Party (which is nothing of the kind) and the man responsible for the defunct dredge in the river. In a natty polo shirt and light-colored trousers, Pires bounded out of a big wooden boat strung with lights and shook our hands. Sitting with a cold drink on Dona Orminda's porch, he said that no, he didn't have any more news from Eletronorte about compensation for the fishermen. He did want to assure everyone, however, that he thought they would soon start digging artesian wells on the islands. This pipedream solution would have been laughable if it wasn't so easily discredited: there was no way the wells could be drilled into the islands without hitting the same polluted water that flowed along its banks.

My last evening on Paruru I spent chatting with Seu Raimundo. He told me how he had set off at the age of fifteen to work on a pepper farm in Tomé Açu, working almost fifteen years for a Japanese planter. His grandparents had been rubber tappers and had gathered various natural oils from trees, such as *andiroba* and *copaíba*, for trade. His father, a carpenter, had left his mother when Seu Raimundo was quite young, and he grew up learning to farm as much as fish, which is what his stepfather did. Eventually, Seu Raimundo, already with a growing family, had become involved in some small-time river trading, before buying a piece of land on Paruru. "When I worked in pepper, I never owned a thing; only when I started to work for myself did things begin to get better for me," he said. "We always fished just to eat, not to sell. I never bought food; I used to give it away to my neighbors.

"We used to live in paradise." He sighed. "And now how can we feel good with a government like this one that has destroyed it all? I think the only way is the way we work now, in groups, discussing politics or whatever. We don't choose anyone in particular, everyone can speak his mind and give his opinion. That's how we arrive at a decision. But when everything is in the hands of the government, of the higher-ups, well . . . That's why we think a party is much better than where the small person has no say."

We were sitting in lawn chairs on the veranda. A trio of brightly painted octagonal paddles leaned against the door. The river was quiet and constant; the sky was a transparent blue with banks of thin clouds floating against the far horizon, their undersides shirred with red; the day's final breathtaking act before twilight pulled it offstage with the crooked cane of night.

He realized that his involvement might be dangerous, Seu Raimundo said. As someone better off than many others, he had been expected to stick with the cozy setup between the union and the political parties in power. But, he said, "We have an agreement among us to stay in the fight whether it's to live or die. We are ready to work, to debate, to defend our brothers even if we are threatened. In fact, I've been threatened twice by gunmen. It's not a problem," he added, "it's God who knows when we die. It's natural. We have to defend ourselves."

The following morning, after church, Seu Raimundo and Dico took me to Cametá in Mestre Jovico's launch, and that night I caught the boat back to Belém.

FIVE

BETWEEN THE RIVER AND THE SEA

Rodrigues Alves entered the Bay of Guajara and approached the city of Belém. It had been a cold and windy trip, the air redolent of diesel fumes and black pepper. The big wooden riverboat was full of passengers, their hammocks looped in two colorful rows, one on either side of the open deck. Bags, suitcases and cardboard boxes were piled everywhere, down the middle, against stairwells, along the white slat railings. Like some natural traveling alarm clock, a rooster suddenly began to crow in the half-dark.

We passed the floating gas station in Belém's harbor, and soon I could make out the wooden tiers of the Salt Port looming through the early morning mist like an ink sketch still unfinished, the gray sky speckled with circling vultures. Behind a clutter of rusty tin roofs and weatherbeaten sheds, rose the sheer white wall of the Salesian school; to the left I saw the twin towers of Our Lady of Carmel Church. The boat docked and emptied quickly. In spite of the early hour, the port was busy with men wheeling out loads of black pepper and cacao, threading their way through the tired passengers on the wooden boardwalk.

I walked to the square in front of Our Lady of Carmel and caught a bus to the home of my friend Elizete Gaspar. The bus took me past Ver-O-Peso market, through the main square and up Governor Malcher Street. I got off a block from the Cathedral of Nazaré. Elizete lived in a modern eight-story building on a street lined, like many in the area, with mango and chestnut trees. The area around the cathedral used to be the upper-class section of Belém, a gracious district of large, elegant houses, ornate with louvered windows, wide verandas, balustrades and balconies running beneath a shady fretwork of hibiscus and palms.

I had met Elizete in the gold-prospecting town of Itaituba, on the far side of Pará state, on the Tapajós River. Elizete had grown up in the Tapajós region and had recently returned to do research for her master's degree. We quickly became close friends, and her apartment in Belém, which she shared with a younger sister who was expecting her first child, became a second home to me in Brazil.

It was still early when I arrived, and over breakfast I told Elizete about the situation I had seen in Cametá. Even though Cametá was so close to the city, few people in Belém were aware of the suffering of the river dwellers on the Tocantins. Within a short while, however, my early start and the sleepless night on the boat began to catch up with me. I had a hundred things to do that day, but I was so tired I was almost sick. "Try some of this," said Elizete, who jumped up and got a small jar of *guarana*, a kind of dried ground berry, out of the cupboard. "I used to use this all the time in university when it was exam time."

She mixed some of the brown powder with honey and water, and I drank it. It was typical of Elizete to have such a remedy. She had lived in the city for years, but in some ways she retained a number of customs of "the interior." The breakfast table, for example, was usually set with powdered milk and tinned butter and hard, dry biscuits, even though there were supermarkets with fresh milk and butter nearby. She and her sister, Beth, also liked to boil up a batch of *pupunha* palm fruits for breakfast when they were in season, another custom of rural Amazonia. The *guarana* worked wonders. Within minutes, I was feeling full of energy. Elizete told me that the *guarana* had come from the Indians, who liked to use it to hunt at night, for it kept them wide awake and very alert. "You can go down and get it fresh at any one of those tourist stores in the square," she said. "They have big sticks of it and and grate it for you right there with a dried *pirarucu* tongue."

Founded in the early seventeenth century, Belém do Pará is the oldest city in the Amazon. It is poised strategically at the mouth of the great river and is an important link between the river and the Atlantic Ocean. Its relations with Portugal and Europe were traditionally much stronger than those with the south of Brazil. All the products of the region — rubber, hides, oils and medicinals — had to pass through its crowded harbors on their way to foreign markets. The early explorers set out from Belém on their voyages of discovery through the maze of Amazonian waterways, and the Jesuits on their "reductions," their grouping of Indian tribes into large colonies protected by the Catholic Church. Belém was also the headquarters for Portuguese raids against foreign invaders — the Dutch, the French, the English and even the Irish, who set up a short-lived colony on the northern bank of the Taurege River.

More than 350 years later, Belém is still a small provincial city of fewer than a million inhabitants. At a time when the tendency to replace the old with the new seems overwhelming in many other Brazilian cities, Belém remains relatively unscathed. A few modern blocks have broken into its skyline, yet the overall feeling of the place is one of tattered nineteenth-century gentility; an historic city imperceptibly moldering in the humid tropical air. Nonetheless, there is the feeling there of being in the center. It is the capital of all the riverside communities scattered throughout Pará, the only modern city for hundreds of miles. And as well as being the transition point between the river and the sea, it is also the link between the untamed north and the rest of Brazil, between wilderness and civilization, between the realities of the present and the dreams of the future.

Belém feels far more like an ocean port than a river port. In Brazil the Amazon is called the Riomar, or "river sea"; to cross from Belém to the northern bank would mean a journey of more than 200 miles (320 kilometers), and the island of Marajó, the largest in the Amazon delta, is the size of Switzerland.

The ports extend along the city, and spiny with masts and cranes and booms, they seem to draw it in. The Coal Port, the Salt Port, the Açaí Port: their names indicate what was and still is unloaded there. With the constant movement of boats of all sizes in the water and the throngs of people on land, the ports form the heart of Belém's existence. Local newspapers print lists of the big foreign liners and tankers at anchor in the modern harbor, and their ports of origin. Double-decked riverboats clog the smaller wooden wharves, waiting for passengers traveling north to the gold-rich territory of Amapá; or west along the Amazon to Santarém, Manaus and stops along the way; or south down the Tocantins and Araguaia to Cametá, Tucuruí and Marabá.

It is also down by the waterfront that you find the Ver-O-Peso market, where a public scales once invited shoppers to indeed "see the weight" of whatever they had purchased. As crowded with vendors as it is with shoppers, it snakes along the waterfront, an elongated conglomeration of tiny stalls and cavernous stone buildings, all of it in a constant buzz of activity. Ver-O-Peso is dominated by a grandiose market building of cast iron and glass, imported from Liverpool during the days of the rubber boom, rather resembling the Gare St. Lazare in Paris. Elaborate with scrollwork and filigree, a winding staircase in the middle leading to nowhere in particular, it is now used to sell meat and poultry. Inside, great slabs of red beef hang from metal hooks, while defeathered fowl are laid out in pale rows on the marble counters.

Nearby, in a simple brick building, is the fish market, its white-tiled stalls filled with the myriad freshwater abundance of the Amazon. The air inside is thick with the cries of fishmongers attesting to the freshness of their wares. And there they lay, mouths agape, on the stone counters, brown-and-yellow-spotted *surubim* like piscine jaguars; glistening piles of *tamatá*, their black carapaces split open like fruit to reveal the dense yellow flesh inside; slices of silvery pale *filhote*; big *tucunare* with black and gold disks on their tails; ugly, catfish-faced *gurijuba*; dozens of small *pescada* slipped onto stakes through their gills; flat, circular *pacu*, like silvery moons; *xareu*, *curimata*, big-mouthed piranha showing rows of sharp teeth like tiny needles; shrimp and chunks of *pirarucu*, the largest fish in the Amazon, which can grow to the size of an ox. The fishmongers wrap purchases in long green *ravenalia* leaves; little boys weaving through the crowds sell brown paper bags lined with plastic to those who prefer something more hygienic. At either end of the building, vendors hold out baskets of bright green limes, lemons, bouquets of tiny round peppers like red and yellow beads in a nest of green onion, everything necessary to do justice to any fish as it travels, inexorably, toward the cooking pot.

Between the two buildings is another market, a crush of tiny stalls offering what should have no price, but in this case does — health and happiness. Hawking miracle cures, medicinal plants and good-luck charms, the *curandeiros* stand around all day chatting, importuning the curious with loud cries of "*Diga freguês!*," which more or less translates as "Tell me, customer."

One morning as I was walking by the *curandeiros* an old man offered to sell me the dried eye of a dolphin, specially cured with herbs and incantations, which would, he assured, help me to find love. I replied that I already had, and he said, "Well, you can put it in your purse and you'll attract all kinds of good luck, in business, finance, you name it."

The old man's stall was crammed with bizarre objects, and as he slipped the dolphin's eye into a plastic bag, he told me what the objects were used for. Aside from the eyes, he was also selling the dolphin's sexual organs, dried; I didn't know if people were to carry those around as well, but the organs supposedly attracted love, or maybe just an exciting night on the town. He also had a few jars of what looked like water and leaves, labelled "dolphin preparation," to be used as a perfume or in the bath. And like some archaic dating service, the old man could also provide the lovesick and lonely with an alternative, a piece of bull's horn to immerse with themselves in the bathwater.

Goat's horn was to be put in the backyard, he said, "to keep away evil." A small dried snake's head, called a *panegosso*, brought the businessman good luck in trade or commerce. The *curandeiro's* narrow shelves were filled with bottles of various palm oils, and old coffee and mayonnaise jars contained the lard of turtles, snakes, manatees and caimans. Other jars had small snakes coiled inside, one pale blue, the parrot snake, used as an antidote to snakebites. Strings of hooves and paws and caimans' tails dangled from one corner; the tiny wood-deer hooves were to be rubbed against the legs of a small child who refused to walk, while the dried monkeys' paws were for asthma. The old man had some long pink flowers for stomach pains, and hard little oranges, *laranja da terra*, that "were good for any ailment there is." The rest of his space was taken up with bundles of perfumed wood, resins and crinkly patchouli roots, known as *cheiro do Pará*, or "Pará fragrance."

The old man told me that he was seventy-six and had run his stall in the market for fifty years. I asked him where he had learned about all these popular cures, many of which were obviously of Indian origin, and he answered, "We are all servants of the Lord. Some people have the gift of singing, or writing, or playing the guitar. This here is my gift." Then he rooted around among his paper bags and jars until he found one of his business cards, a slip of paper with his name and stall number typed on it. Unfortunately, I lost it somewhere on my travels, and only remember his nickname, Gracas a Deus, or "Thank the Lord."

Past the fish market, the shore turns up and opens out into a square known as the Açaí Port. There the small boats come in from the Tocantins and its many islands with large baskets of *açaí* packed in palm leaves. At night, the vendors haul the baskets out and line them up on the sidewalk, ready for the first early-morning customers. When they have finished, they go to sleep on the curb, presumably oblivious to the radio music blaring from the little palm-thatched bars across the square. And equally oblivious to the *açaí* men, customers sit in the light of the street lamps, drinking beer at rickety tin tables and enjoying the gentle bay breeze after a hot, humid day.

Two possible routes take you away from the port and toward Belém's main square, the Praça da Paz. The quick way is to walk along the shore, past the coffee-colored customs building with its green bars, then to turn up Getúlio Vargas Avenue. The slower is a stroll through the crush of narrow cobbled streets of the old town. There you find a hive of shops and several seventeenth-century churches, their flat white facades, low roofs and trim of narrow molding making them look like sheets of paper burned and curling at the edges. Following the old tram tracks on Rua Santo Antonio, you see various relics of the past: the city library, an imposing structure of indeterminate color, where a chandelier hangs in the lobby, and the elegant Magasin Paris, with its bronze filigree and arched windows.

The Praça da Paz is a wide square of park, the city's tectonic showpiece, and, like the flamboyant theater at its far end, a relic of the rubber boom. Painted in graduated shades of magenta, the theater is Belém's version of the famous opera house in Manaus. A trio of arched doors opens beneath a grand porte cochere surmounted by bronze statues. Low marble balustrades run along the roof. Across from the theater the park unfolds its green lawns, interrupted by fountains, trees and little Grecian-style gazebos.

In the shade of the mango trees that tower over the square, life seems to move at a lethargic pace. The several souvenir shops that line the square cater to few tourists, but serve a more useful function as places to change American dollars at the black-market rate. Small children beg for change, and adherents of Krishna, their hands sprouting sticks of incense, beg for attention. Uniformed schoolgirls loiter in the shade of newsstand awnings and leaf through the magazines to see pictures of their favorite soap-opera stars. Reserving a park bench or two for their clients to sit on, women stir boiling pots of *tacacá* soup on wooden carts shaded by sheets of plastic. Surrounded by tools and old shoes, cobblers sit on the sidewalk, waiting for new customers. Beside them wait the pot menders and the shoe-shine men, leaning against the little wooden feet at the base of their thronelike chairs.

When I arrived in Belém, the city was in the throes of preparations for its annual Círio, a religious procession in honor of the city's patron, Our Lady of Nazareth. Every October, a small wooden statue in a cloak of gold-embroidered silk is carried from the cathedral to the port in a litter covered with white and yellow flowers. Thousands of people, having applied for a place in the procession sometimes years in advance, follow the statue, clinging to the stout rope attached to its back, in the expectation of some divine intercession from the Virgin. In the harbor, the boats are decorated with paper flags and streamers, and at night fireworks are set off by the stevedores and sailors.

Visitors come to Belém from all over the country, booking all the available hotel space and airplane seats for the region's biggest festival. With the city expecting crowds of at least a million, workmen were putting up bleachers in the park behind the theater and along Getúlio Vargas Avenue and decking the mango trees with strings of lights. Vendors of food, drink and all kinds of trinkets were setting up their stalls along Avenida Nazaré and in front of the cathedral. The local newspapers reported, however, that the vendors were upset this year because the usual flocks of wild parakeets that traditionally herald brisk sales had not yet appeared in the mango trees. Some were even demanding the return of the money they had paid for their concessions.

The usual somnolence of the Praça da Paz was interrupted, one sultry afternoon in mid-October, by an unusual sight. Three young

Kaiapo warriors, their heads crowned with bright green parrot feathers, their bodies painted with intricate designs of black genipap dye, were strolling casually along the sidewalk, like vivid tourists from another reality in the noisy urban world of the white man. Taxi drivers, shoppers, passersby, all turned their heads to watch as the trio casually made their way past the Grão Hotel do Pará, the tourist shops and fast-food outlets, pausing just a split second in front of the phone company to let a car turn the corner before crossing the street and disappearing into the crowds moving toward the port.

The three young men had come to Belém with a group of five hundred Kaiapo, men, women and children, entire villages in some cases, all brought in on buses to protest in front of the federal justice building. Two of their leaders, Kube-I and Paulo Paiakan, were being put on trial in Belém, along with an American anthropologist, Darrell Posey, for having "criticized Brazilian Indian policy," denigrating the country's image abroad." If convicted, they could receive up to four years in jail.

The absurd charges had been laid after the three men went to the United States, where the Kaiapo, with Dr. Posey translating for them, told American bankers and congressmen about the fatal damage that would be wrought on their people if a hydroelectric project planned for the Lower Xingu River were to be implemented. At a cost of more than $10 billion, the complex would flood 85 percent of their lands. They spoke of the disaster of the Tucuruí Dam, and also of the Balbina Dam north of Manaus, a white elephant of a project that had poisoned water, taken 80 percent of the lands of the fierce Waimiri-Atroari tribe and effectively reduced their number from 3000 to 350 in less than fifteen years.

When the two Kaiapo and Dr. Posey returned to Brazil, the government unearthed a set of laws dating from the years of the military dictatorship governing the activities of foreigners and specifically prohibiting them from becoming involved in internal political issues and questions of national security. And, as if that were not cynical enough, the federal court representative in the state of Pará charged not only Dr. Posey but the Kaiapo as well.

In protest against the trial, the Kaiapo had grouped in front of the classical white court building on Generalíssimo Deodoro Street. On the day of their protest, I walked to the courthouse, passing a small crowd of residents on the sidewalk wondering what was going on. The

Indians formed a tight knot, bristling with metal-tipped spears and arrows, keening their anger and frustration in an eerie chant pierced by sharp cries. The men wore the same halo of green feathers, and their faces were streaked with red and black paint. A few wore wooden plugs in their lower lip, to make themselves look more ferocious to enemies. Slowly they danced back and forth on the pavement, the bright reds, greens and blacks of the Indians contrasting with the long, solid line of dull olive of the military police standing guard against the courthouse wall. A helicopter suddenly flew overhead, and one young man raised his long arrow heavenward as if to shoot it down.

Scheduled to testify that morning, Kube-I, a big, portly man with long black hair, had showed up for his court appearance in war gear, his face painted black as an indication of his anger. For his part, the judge struck back with the legalities of white society, refusing to allow Kube-I to enter the courtroom because he was not wearing a shirt and tie. He justified his action by saying, "The Indian must become acculturated." The lawyer for the three men, José Carlos Castro, countered by charging the judge with racism, something that had just become possible with the passing of the country's new constitution.

The day after my return from the Tocantins, I had plenty to do. I arranged flights, changed money, got a document I needed from the police station and visited a number of people I wanted to talk to. One of them was a local journalist, Lucio Flavio Pinto, whose bookish, mild mannered appearance and thick glasses belied a scathing tongue and a marked desire to hurl darts of criticism at the Brazilian government. He contributed frequently to the Belém newspaper *O Liberal*, had written a book on the development of Carajás, hosted a weekly evening talk show on television and produced a snappy monthly newsletter called *Personal Journal*. In all of these media, he liked to lambaste the narrow-minded policies of the government in the Amazon. And along the way, he had become an essential source of information for anyone interested in the region.

He was also singularly hard to get hold of, so I was lucky to find Lucio Flavio in his eighth-floor office in a building on Campos Sales Street, across from the municipal library with the chandelier. It was a stuffy, cluttered place, by any writer's standards, with two desks loaded with papers and hardly anywhere to sit. An electric fan tried vainly to disperse the warmth of sun whose light streamed through the plate-glass window. In a conversation often interrupted by telephone calls, Lucio Flavio was extremely outspoken about what was happening in the Amazon, which he felt had become almost a colony of the rest of Brazil.

"I think it's a situation common in all of the Amazon," he said, "in that the region is not given the right to decide which road it will take. All decisions are taken outside of the region. And it has been decided that the Amazon must export, must generate trade in American dollars." It was in order to bring in hard currency, he explained, that the region was forced to grow rapidly, with technology and investments from the outside. He pointed to the Tucuruí Dam as a perfect example of the rapid growth. It was the largest public-works project in the history of the region, built with foreign capital to increase export potential with cheap energy. The enormous iron mine in Carajás was another.

"Why this haste to occupy the Amazon?" he asked. "Why the Northern Headwaters project of the army?" (This was a controversial, multi-million dollar project which envisaged the installation of military bases in the farthest reaches of the Amazon.) "I think it's necessary to have courage to think about the Amazon in an intelligent way. And this, the government doesn't want to do. It's just exploitation for the short term, immediate, without thinking.

"The people who actually live here are merely spectators of the projects," said Lucio Flavio, "because they are not designed to utilize, in the best way, the region's natural resources. The people cannot participate, and this has had a great impact. The native of the Amazon has always imagined himself in a place that is extremely backward, unconnected to the rest of Brazil, the frontiers of which he was lord. And suddenly, the situation experiences in two or three years an evolution that would normally take decades. They construct a hydroelectric dam here, one of the largest in the world, and the average Amazonian doesn't even know what electricity is. In Belém, they have suddenly put in an ultramodern aluminum smelter, when we haven't the faintest information or experience of this kind of metallurgy."

Such a process "completely destroys a man's consciousness of space and time," he went on, a process that does not depend on him or what he wants to see happen. "So he remains floating between a past of extractivism and a present of big projects connected to some of the most advanced economies in the world." What was worse, said Lucio

Flavio, the man of the Amazon was not conscious of what was happening to him and his land. His only role was to provide cheap labor.

In some cases, he said, the well-educated professional was used as "the opener of doors. And he thinks that that is just the greatest, to be the intermediary between the entrepreneur and his own region. He forgets that this region is his patrimony. All he can do is negotiate away his patrimony and accept the money."

In terms of the forces destroying the Amazon, however, Lucio Flavio saw little difference between the poor peasant searching for land and the wealthy rancher availing himself of the latest agricultural technology. "In spite of the distant technologies," he said, "both live from destroying the forest, [the settlers] repeating on a smaller scale exactly what the big landowners are doing. In the end, Joao Silva" — John Doe — "as much as Volkswagen have no idea what they are doing in this environment." Lucio Flavio felt that the great migrations had to stop. Otherwise the Amazon would be devastated. "If Amazonia had been allowed to develop at its own pace," he said, "science might have got here before the waves of migration. We'd have learned how and what to develop in the region without destroying it."

I asked him whether he felt that necessary changes were occurring now, as in Acre, where people were organizing for their rights and to save the forest. He was not as optimistic as I was, although he conceded that the situation was slightly better than during the military dictatorship. "Over time, the social struggle has been a constant waste," he said, "with the killing of popular leaders. It didn't spread because all experiments were violently cut off. Today, I think, it manifests itself more because there is less repression, more possibility of denouncing the injustices." I had to agree with him: ten years ago, Lucio Flavio would probably not have been allowed to print his *Personal Journal*. And just eight years ago Chico Mendes had been put on trial in Manaus merely for helping to organize a public demonstration after the death of Wilson Pinheiro.

Lucio Flavio's office, by coincidence, wasn't far away from that of José Carlos Castro, the lawyer defending Darrell Posey and the two Kaiapo Indians. I decided to drop in on him. Castro has a great reputation in the north as a champion of justice for the little man, defending the accused in some of the most potentially explosive cases brought by the military government in conflicts over land. In the 1970s, he defended two French priests accused of fomenting a peasant ambush that killed a ranch manager; he also defended a third priest, François Jentel, charged with similar activities. Castro has a reputation for being straightforward to the point of rudeness, but I liked him. He was round and rather short, with wavy gray hair and a big mustache. He explained the Kaiapo case to me, describing how the charges had been asked for by a colonel on Brazil's National Security Council.

I commented on how absurd it seemed to charge two Indians under a law pertaining only to foreigners. He agreed and told me that he had already gone to the federal appeal court in Brasília to have the case thrown out. He also told me that he felt this case was one of the most important he had ever taken on. "And also one of the most important in the region of the Amazon," he continued, "from the point of view of the shock between two civilizations, that of the judge and the attorney general on one side, and that of the Indians on the other, or put another way, that of our society, white society, and that of the Other. All in all," he said, "I think that the justice system has revealed itself to be completely unprepared for this case. It has reduced all the culture, values and ethics of the Indian to banalities. The judiciary in Brazil has no familiarity with the sciences, history or anthropology. They think that law is a science above all the others. It is extremely ethnocentric."

Castro told me that he would very much like to bring the case to the attention of the United Nations Human Rights Committee. (A few months after speaking with him, I learned that the federal appeals court had thrown out the case against Posey and the Kaiapo.)

The last person I visited that day was Father Geronimo Trecanni, the head of the Catholic Church's Pastoral Land Commission for the eastern half of Pará. He was a tall, balding Italian who had lived in Brazil for fifteen years. His office, on a wide, quiet street a mile or two from the city center, seemed reserved and austere, with its bare wood-paneled walls. On one wall was hung a very large map of the part of Pará that was in his jurisdiction, on another a simple poster that seemed to sum up what the Pastoral Land Commission was all about. Under a headline reading "Agrarian Reform: Why?" it spelled out in large letters a simple series of facts. "Landowners occupy 417 million hectares in Brazil, 294 million hectares of that is unused or fallow. Multinationals owned 35 million hectares in Brazil. Between 1970 and 1980, 24 million people have migrated from their homes to other states. There exist nearly 11 million unemployed in the cities and

30 million peasants without land. Almost nine million rural workers receive less than a minimum salary [about $50] per month."

News of conflicts over land ownership was fairly regular fare in the Brazilian media. Thousands of peasants were waiting for land, and thousands invaded enormous farms all over the country, only to be dislodged by the most violent means. Frequently the army was called in to help in these expulsions. Yet many Brazilians actively supported land reform. Broad-based committees had been lobbying the government for years to distribute land more fairly, believing that much of the poverty and common crime rampant in Brazil would be curtailed when the poor had some property to call their own, and the means of a livelihood. What's more, small producers grew most of the food in Brazil, while large landowners produced mainly for export. In a country where millions were starving or undernourished, there seemed to be no rational explanation for not enacting land reform.

When President Sarney took office in 1985, he promised a major agrarian reform. Yet after four years and five ministers, of the 108 million acres (43 million hectares) originally promised to the landless, only 11 million (4.2 million) were redistributed. The reasons were as obvious as the arguments in favor of land reform. Most deputies and senators were large landowners. And many powerful businessmen also owned vast acreages. Land was a symbol of prestige that had not dimmed during the centuries between conquest and modern capitalism. No one in power in Brazil had been serious about taking the lands of the wealthy and giving them to the poor, and certainly not Sarney, a major landowner himself.

Thus the conflicts over land had only been exported to the Amazon. There, the violence and repression were the fruits of the inevitable clash between waves of small peasant farmers who claimed what they believed to be *terras da União*, or "ownerless land," and the equally powerful force of moneyed businessmen, attracted by fiscal incentives, easy payoffs to registrars for land rights, and a corrupt police. The result, according to a report issued by the Catholic Church, was hundreds of injuries and assassinations of peasants, peasant leaders and Church and lay people attempting to help the poor secure land over the years. In 1987, 109 people died in agrarian conflicts in Brazil, twenty-four of them in the state of Pará. One peasant who lived in the Parrot's Beak area, probably the most bloody region in the Amazon, said in the report, "The nation ends where the fence of the landowner begins."

Through its Pastoral Land Commission, the Catholic Church was playing a major role in denouncing this barbarity, and for its trouble had earned constant criticism and persecution from the government and the Democratic Ruralist Union (UDR). The UDR had proved itself so much more influential than the Church in government and parliamentary affairs that the country's new constitution, ratified in 1988, was devoid of any law encouraging a more just distribution of land.

Amnesty International also published a damning report on the land situation in rural Brazil, documenting numerous cases in which the judiciary and police acted illegally in support of large landowners, against the peasants. So Father Geronimo drew a picture for me that was, in many respects, common knowledge in Brazil, but with more detail.

He described a case, for example, close to Belém, where sixty-four families had settled on land they believed to be ownerless. Several years later, a landowner showed up and said the land belonged to him. He succeeded in expelling all the families and winning his case in court. But research by the commission staff unearthed a document showing that the perimeters of his property were incorrectly described. The sixty-four families had not been working his land after all. "It was a mistake first of all of the police," said Geronimo, "acting only on the say-so of this landowner, and secondly of the courts for not researching the deed correctly." Another example: On the Canaan Ranch near Marabá, forty-five families were expelled by a dentist from the city of Goiânia who had a court order to expel only one family. The remaining forty-four went back, the dentist sold the land, and the families were expelled again by the new owner with the same court order. By the time the case was ironed out in the courts, the families' houses had been burned down and their crops harvested and sold.

Geronimo also gave me details of some of the more horrific killings in the past, such as one that occurred on the Princesa Ranch near Marabá. In 1986, five men were found floating in the Itacaiunas River. "All of them had been shot and their bodies had been tied together and dumped in the river. All the men were rural workers, accused by the ranch owner of invading his land," he said, "but in fact, they had all received occupants' rights from the state." In the Parrot's Beak, five peasants were killed on the Vale do Juari Ranch, near Colmeia, in Goiás. There was a shoot-out with gunmen, the peasants were expelled three times by the military police, houses were burned down, and those considered the leaders were tortured. Even the local priest and nuns in Colmeia were threatened by the rancher's hired gunmen.

At the moment, according to Geronimo, there were 353 areas of conflict or potential conflict in the state. "And there are two main types of conflict," he continued. "There are those involving occupants who have been on their land for many years, in some cases they were even born there, and those involving settlers who have occupied unused areas, where they have been living for anywhere from two to fifteen years before expulsion attempts were carried out."

The area of the Upper Araguaia River in the south of Pará, part of the Parrot's Beak, had long been one of the most notorious for violence. But, said Father Geronimo, "A new front seems to be opening up now to the west, in the area of São Felix do Xingu. Peasants have been moving into São Felix looking for fresh land, and there have also been reports of slave labor coming to us from there, indicating that big ranchers are arriving also." The slave labor, he explained, occurred when ranchers were in the initial phase of clearing the forest from their land. They would hire contractors, called *gatos* — cats — to go to poverty-stricken towns in the northeast and hire young men to travel to the Amazon on the promise of good pay and free transport. Once the men were on the ranch, of course, the story was quite a different one. Often they were not paid at all, and anyone who complained was either violently beaten or killed. "Lumbermen have also been heading for that area," he said, "and setting up sawmills. Often the peasants can make a little money by selling wood to them. But I think there are going to be a lot of problems there quite soon."

I asked him whether, over the years of struggle and denouncing what was going on in these farming frontiers, the attitudes of Brazil's decision-makers were changing. "Unfortunately," he said, "the attitudes are not changing, only the tactics. The creation of the UDR, for example, is an attempt to put a rational, political face on the violence and inherent injustice. And, in many ways, they have succeeded, as you can see by the outcome of the agrarian reform question in the new constitution."

After years of support work, the Church is as much the target of physical attacks and death threats, he told me, as the rural leaders. "We are constantly labeled Communists," he said with a faint smile. "But when they accuse us of wanting to change society, and I look at the kind of society we have here in these regions, in fact, all over Brazil, I have to admit, I really don't care what they call us. After what I have seen in ten years, I can say, yes, we do want to change the system."

The night before I left for the south of Pará, I spent the evening talking with Elizete about her job at SUDAM, the Superintendency for the Development of the Amazon. She had worked there for five years, and was now away on leave to complete her master's degree. The things she had to say about this government organ were shocking, but not all that surprising. She told me how, for each project that came in, she and a team of co-workers — lawyers, agronomists, veterinarians — would study the application, checking out all aspects of its viability. Her job, she told me, had been to survey the company's assets, and to analyze costs, the market and so on. "But none of this has any influence at all," she said. "What mattered was the applicant's political connections. He would come already recommended by someone. We were just filling out the forms."

If someone who did not have the right political connections applied, however good his project sounded, he was put off.

Elizete said that 1982, an election year, was the "most scandalous. They had a whole chunk of money," she said, "so they were giving it out all over the place, fifty thousand cruzados for one, one hundred thousand for another. A lot of projects were devised just to get the money, and none of them that I know of was actually carried out."

Contrary to what SUDAM's publicity department had told me some months earlier, environmental studies were never undertaken. "They say they won't give money for a ranching project that will destroy virgin forest, but that is just a lie," Elizete said. Not only that but sometimes the land on which companies said they were setting up projects was permanently flooded, or on top of a mountain. "I don't know how many times," said Elizete, "I've heard the technician saying, after coming back from a trip, 'But the place doesn't exist. The geographical location, the parallels the company has given us simply don't exist.' " But there was nothing the staff could say about such obvious fraud. "You never questioned the decisions of the section chief," she said. "All he would say was, 'But the superintendent has ordered it.' It was as if he were a god."

Most of the time, the staff did not take the cases of fraud to their boss. Bribes were common, according to Elizete, everything from trips to the south to new cars. "It was very open among people there," she said. "I mean, if SUDAM ever looked into it . . . A civil servant in Brazil doesn't earn that much. So how come he has an apartment on the beach and takes vacations abroad? But SUDAM will never look into these things because everyone is accepting bribes, the superintendent, his assistants, everyone."

In spite of all the money — $880 million U.S. between 1966 and 1978 just for cattle projects, for example — Elizete thought that none of the hundreds of projects financed by SUDAM ever made any real profit, or proved viable for the region. Most of the time, she said, the grants were only a means of securing ownership of the land. She described it as "an enormous farce, a whole chain of deceit. The land registry office gives a certificate to some guy. The registrar will do anything for money, lots of money. The guy goes in and says, 'I'll give you so much if you put all this land here in my name.' It is just to speculate with land. And that's where the SUDAM official comes in, and he receives his money. All of this has also done a lot to aggravate the problem of land conflicts, especially in the south of Pará."

If its application is accepted by SUDAM, a company receives 40, 50 or 75 percent of its start-up costs in cash; the amount is staggered over the years and adjusted for inflation. "As soon as you entered your project into SUDAM," said Elizete, "you had a profit."

The next morning, I caught a plane destined for the city of Conceição do Araguaia. Below me, I could see the graphic results of SUDAM's generosity to the ranchers: acres and acres of scrubland as far as the eye could see. Our first stop was Marabá, a miserable town on the Tocantins River, miserable not only because it is near the gold-producing hellhole of Serra Pelada, its riches now all but exhausted, but also because it is a major ranching frontier. At that moment, Marabá's jail contained the notorious gunman Sebastião de Terezona, charged with carrying out sixteen assassinations under order, and suspected of several more. And at the end of 1987, police from Marabá had charged on a large group of peacefully protesting miners from Serra Pelada on the modern bridge spanning the Tocantins River, killing an estimated one hundred men and women. I wasn't exactly looking forward to going to Conceição, but I was happy that I would not be visiting Marabá.

Our second stop was Carajás, where a government-ordered reserve of thick green forest enveloped the red gash of the biggest iron-ore pit in the world. Then we zigzagged toward the city of Araguaína, in what used to be the north of Goiás but had just become the state of Tocantins. We flew over ranches with thick, cleared strips around forest, then irregular patches of forest and cleared land like pieces of a puzzle. We crossed a river mottled with silt, an interlocking series of islands shaped like human muscles, then cleared land as far as the eye could see. Almost three hours after taking off, we landed in Conceição.

SIX

THE STRUGGLE FOR LAND

I
T WAS ALMOST DUSK BY THE time we arrived at the shack, and in the dying sunlight the hilly landscape in front of us seemed almost medieval, a palette of blacks, browns and gold. The forest soil had been burned black, leaving rafters of charred boughs amid clumps of new foliage. A brackish pond sat like a smoked mirror beside the path leading up to a tiny cabin of *paxiuba* slats thatched with palm leaves. Carrying the small, bellows-shaped planting machine with which he had been working all day, Antenor Moreira, a tattered, wide-brimmed hat on his head, was coming over a hill. His brother, Domingo, with the same swarthy skin and bushy black beard, followed.

I had walked into this forest clearing from the nearby town of Xinguara accompanied by two women, Maria da Rocha Moreira, and a friend of hers named Marileide. The Pastoral Land Commission in Conceição had suggested I come here to visit a typical family of peasants in an area that was still feeling the mark of violence, even though it had been expropriated by the Ministry of Agriculture.

I had taken a rickety old bus early that morning and headed north up a paved road to Xinguara. There, I had met Maria da Rocha, who had agreed to take me out to her family's small farm. Then the three of us had walked to the shoulder of the highway, to wait for a lift. We had not waited long before someone had stopped his truck and invited us to jump in the back. After a few miles, we had gotten out and taken a logging trail that cut into the forest, but it hadn't lasted long, either. At some point no outsider would have been able to identify, Maria had led us onto an overgrown forest track that took us up and down hills, through ravines and eventually to Maria's land. It was incredibly hot, and tiny fleas buzzed around us constantly. Although the forest had been logged about fifteen years earlier for its valuable woods, it was still close and dense, especially with bushy new growth.

In spite of the walk that had seemed so arduous, Maria da Rocha set to the making of our evening meal with an energy that seemed boundless. She had short, curly hair and eyes like flat black buttons, a small, dark woman of the northeast, where she had been born thirty-one years before. You might even have described her as frail, except that she was anything but. She had, many a time already, hauled in heavy loads of supplies for the farm along the path we had just taken, sacks of seeds, tools, pots and pans.

By then, I had strung up my hammock and collapsed into its welcoming folds, feeling quite guilty about not helping her. Even Marileide, a stocky young mother of three girls, with a snub nose and a booming voice, found herself unable to do much more than chat and smoke a cigarette from the other hammock. But, with what I was to learn was customary hospitality, Maria told us not to worry, that she would have dinner ready in a moment, that we were not to move. I didn't argue. And indeed, as the sky turned dark and the fire burned brightly on a corner of the packed dirt floor, she cooked a pot of beef and rice and opened a paper bag of toasted cassava meal on the built-in bunk that served as both a bed and a table.

We ate our meal in the tiny one-room shack, joined by chickens and a pair of puppies that came in to share the roof when it began to rain. The chickens, however, were not allowed to stay, thanks to a silent but vigilant Domingo beside the doorway. The meal finished, and coffee prepared by Antenor, we talked about what had long been the consuming interest of these people, the politics of land.

Maria and Antenor Moreira were veterans of the fight for land, and references to their struggle punctuated the spirited conversation.

Maria and Marileide talked almost constantly, with Antenor frequently adding a "Yep, that's right, all right" from his seat on the corner table.

One day in 1979, when Antenor was working with three other peasants on a patch of land he had just cleared, they were kidnapped by a group of armed men working for the manager of Tupã Ranch. The ranch's owner lived over a thousand miles away, in São Paulo, but he owned 125,000 acres (50 000 hectares) in the Amazon. The Moreiras were one of about four hundred families who had invaded Tupã Ranch, and taken over a tract of land that was still uncleared. They had all received several threats and demands to leave the area, but with nowhere else to go, no one had obeyed. Crops were set alight, and Maria told me that there were several cases of entire families being massacred. "Various times we would pass by and see just a house and a plot, there was no family," she said.

The four peasants were taken to the ranch house, where they were locked up, beaten and even sexually abused. The lit ends of cigarettes were put in their mouths, and one was forced to gnaw on an old, filthy bone retrieved from the garbage. In a somewhat unusual turn of events, Antenor was not much harmed apart from a severe beating. As Maria described it to me, "The *pistoleiros* kept pushing the men around, insulting them and asking them how they dared to steal this land. And Antenor was honest with them and said, 'Well, I have nowhere else to go, and the owner has so much. I have a family to take care of, so what am I supposed to do?' They seemed to respect him for that," she said. "The other three, there was one old man, just kept their heads down. They were afraid and didn't say anything. The *pistoleiros* offered to let Antenor go, but he said he wouldn't leave without his comrades."

At about nine that night, the men were released. Maria described how Antenor had come home covered with rotten papaya because the gunmen had smashed one onto his head. She had exclaimed at the sight of him, asking him what on earth had happened, and all he could do was laugh. "You know what it's like," she said. "it's your nerves, and the relief of finally being out of that situation."

Antenor had not kept quiet about the episode. He had heard that the Church had begun a special Pastoral Land Commission and was looking for information about the abuses of big landowners from anyone who would come forward. Antenor persuaded the other three men to go to the local church with him and tell their story. And in an attempt to publicize the event, the Pastoral Land Commission sent Antenor and the other three to speak about it publicly, in the city of Goiânia, capital of Goiás, and in Brasília. The papers got hold of the story and printed it. But most significantly, the nastiness of the ranch manager's action induced thousands of peasants in Conceição do Araguaia to take to the streets in the largest protest of its kind in the region's history. The war, however, had just begun. It was to last more than three years.

In 1980, the ranch hired a private militia of some two hundred men from all over the country to enter Tupã Ranch and force the peasants to leave at gunpoint. The gunmen grouped all the peasants together on the road, to make sure that no one tried to sneak back into the ranch. Maria, however, noticed that three men were missing, including Antenor. Angered by what they assumed to be the deaths of the three missing men, the group went into Conceição and protested loudly in front of the office of the government-run Tocantins-Araguaia Executive Land Group, GETAT. The women shook their fists and shouted at the land officials, "everyone," said Maria, "denouncing the action, charging them with the lives of the three missing men. The only thing we didn't do was pin the director, this Dr. Maurício, up against the wall." It turned out that all three men were safe — the gunmen had not been able to find everyone working in the scattered meadows in the forest. But from that experience, Maria added, the peasants had developed a system that eventually worked, the men sneaking onto Tupã Ranch to work and the women keeping up the pressure at GETAT.

Maria went to Brasília and importuned various ministers and government officials to give them land. As usual, promises were made to calm the people down. And finally, a portion of the area was expropriated. The story didn't end all that happily, however, because GETAT decided that only 106 of the 400 families were genuine peasants and that each landholder would receive just 125 acres (50 hectares). The Moreiras lost half their land and, unhappy about the outcome of so much struggle, decided to move to Xinguara, to a ranch called Marajoara, where they had been now for four years.

The experience kept Antenor and Maria solidly in the movement. "You know, Augusta," she said, "before all this, I was neutral. All I did was look after the house and the children. But Antenor, he began to get involved and he motivated me to begin to participate, too." Maria found herself going out in the evenings more and more to talk to women in her neighborhood, just as Antenor would try to organize the men.

She and Marileide had become friends during this period of agitation. Maria became active in Catholic base community health programs and union organizing in the countryside; Marileide had been doing the same in the town of Xinguara. Now, after eight years, Marileide was involved in party politics as well, running as a Workers' Party candidate for councillor in the municipal elections, which were to take place in a couple of weeks. The two women had all kinds of stories about how they had gone to meetings and goaded the more conservative elements in both union and Church to act. They would stand up and ask questions that made leaders uncomfortable; they spoke their minds on issues they felt were not being well handled. They kept interrupting each other as they told these stories, and laughing at the memories.

Marileide told me about a recent public meeting, called by the Workers' Party, where the mayoral candidate, a church worker and relative newcomer to the area named Walterlei, had stood up and told people that the party was not interested in their votes. What they really wanted to do was raise the consciousness of the workers. "Okay, fine," said Marileide in frustration, "but this is an election. Doesn't it raise the workers' confidence to have someone representing them and their interests in the municipal chambers?"

Another time, she said, one of the priests in Xinguara and the leadership of the party told her that the workers were not capable of fighting battles themselves and making their own decisions, that the party intellectuals would do this for them. "And what do you think of that, Augusta?" she fumed. "I think it's wrong. It's undemocratic. Of course, we must make the decisions ourselves, right?" She spoke with all the dissatisfaction of a working class woman with an understanding of how politics affects people far more viscerally than many of those in the party leadership.

When the talk ran out, the women started to sing. They sang every verse of the "Internationale," the anthem of the Workers' Party, and radical marching songs from the Araguaia Guerrilla war of the early 1970s. (This was a conflict launched by a small group of combatants based in the region of the Araguaia River against the military regime.) We made a tiny but enthusiastic rally in the middle of the jungle. Finally, tired out, we fell asleep, even as the cold and damp were seeping into our shelter, which seemed more insubstantial as the night went on.

The next morning, I got up and had a glass of hot coffee. While Maria made breakfast — a reprise of last night's dinner — I crouched on the pile of wood near the fire to warm up. I asked her about the opposition movement in their local Rural Workers Union, a conservative union that was happy to deal with the mainstream political parties in the area.

They were a sizable group, Maria told me, who were trying to bring the union into the left-wing union federation, the CUT. At the moment, the leadership was made up of members of the Communist Party of Brazil, and included among its directors a land dealer who had been threatening to force Antenor off his land in Marajoara. With the membership growing increasingly aware that the union was not concerned with furthering the interests of the workers, the opposition had almost won the last elections — the area around Xinguara was pretty well solidly CUT, said Maria — but an area farther away had voted for the old leadership. She was confident, however, that with the next union elections, their faction would have a majority.

Marileide got up and had a bath in the pool, while I stood outside talking to the affable Antenor. Originally from the state of Maranhão, he told me, he had 125 acres (50 hectares) there, and his brother had about 60 (25 hectares). Domingo, who had neither wife nor family, told me that he had worked in Serra Pelada for a number of years to earn the money to buy his land, but he didn't talk too much about himself. The brothers were growing corn, rice, beans and cassava, rotating their crops regularly to preserve the nutrients in the soil as much as possible. Because it was planting time, Antenor's crops were still young, spread out here and there among stumps and bracken in small patches. Antenor had also planted a number of fruit trees around the cabin, which were already coming up. We three women said goodbye and brought partway along our path by the taciturn Domingo, set off to visit other families in Marajoara.

It was difficult going, as it was to be almost all day. The land of Marajoara was the hilliest Amazonian terrain I had seen, with rounded hummocks mounted at times by enormous rocks and boulders. It had belonged to a rancher called Manoel de Sá. The papers in

Rio had recently carried stories about allegations of slave labor and maltreatment of workers by de Sá, who still owned a sizable chunk of land in the vicinity. Police had investigated the charges and, in the ranch manager's office, found some grisly evidence: two mayonnaise jars containing human ears. And only weeks ago, another mysterious incident had occurred, which had yet to be cleared up. The peasants had found the badly burned corpse of an unidentified man in the charred remains of a shack. The prevalent theory was that, yet again, a ranch worker had fallen afoul of his employer.

We wound our way among the slopes and rises and through tracts of forest thick with hanging vines and low growth underfoot, encountering small clearings here and there, some planted, some still matted with the weeds and grasses that shot up after burning. Marileide and Maria kept up quite a pace until, after a couple of hours, we stopped at the house of an old man named Nazareno. His place was not so much a house as a roof of palm over a structure of rough poles, with an old table and a few rough wooden stools scattered around. Seu Nazareno and a few neighbors stood at the far end, filling sacks with rice. A pile of unwinnowed rice, resembling dry sheaves of barley, had been gathered in a corner.

All the walking and climbing had left me tired and extremely thirsty. Seu Nazareno had planted some papaya trees around his home, one of which was already tall and thick with the bulging green fruit, like rows of breasts around the narrow green trunk. We found a long stick and knocked one down: it was the best midmorning refreshment I could have asked for. Marileide rolled a cigarette from a slip of notebook paper and a pinch of the old man's tobacco and talked to him about her campaign for councillor. Seu Nazareno, a grizzled old man wearing a battered denim cap, was honest about his feelings. "I'm for sure going to vote for you for councillor, Marileide," he said, "but I don't like that guy for mayor, that What's-his-name."

"Walterlei," she said. "No, I know, no one likes him. But you don't have to name candidates from the same party for mayor and alderman."

"Yeah, well, I was wondering about that," said Nazareno.

I left my pack there and we walked on. After about an hour, we arrived at the house of a dark, slim, fairly tall man named Abilo, where we were invited to stay for lunch. Abilo's house was sturdier than many of the others I'd seen, walled in with *paxiúba* slats, divided into two rooms and better furnished. Abilo and his wife, Rita, had seven children and were expecting an eighth. The older ones, said Rita, a perenially calm, smiling woman with neatly coiffed hair, spent the days in Xinguara attending school. Ten-year-old Conceição was fiddling with a transistor radio, trying to listen to the latest hits. A toddler was sleeping in a large bed in the kitchen, protected by a tent of mosquito netting.

We talked about a recent killing that had occurred not far from Abilo's house. A farmer called Tonico, not a big landholder but considerably wealthier with his 500 or so acres (about 200 hectares) than any of the peasants on Marajoara, had been threatening one of the settlers, a man named Pedro. He wanted Pedro's 90 acres (36 hectares) of land — not much to raise a family on — which happened to verge on his property. Tonico had offered to buy, then turned to threats, until finally one day Pedro came across Tonico working in one of his plots with a hired hand. Whether in fear, rage, or frustration no one knew; Pedro cut the man's throat with a sickle. The hired hand said he had neither seen nor heard anything, only turned to find his boss dead. Since that day, Pedro had been hiding in the forest, as much afraid of the union leaders, who he was convinced would sell him out, as of the police. Abilo had gotten together a working party to help Pedro's wife with the planting, he told us. And after lunch, he offered to take us to Pedro's home.

We set out toward Pedro's plot, but never made it. Pedro's closest neighbor, a soft-spoken black man in his fifties, dissuaded us from going. The arrival of strangers would only alarm the family, he said, and they would not want to talk about the incident. The best thing was to leave them alone.

We headed back toward Xinguara, stopping at every house along the way to campaign for Marileide. Everyone repeated the observations of old Nazareno: they liked Marileide, but had no use at all for Walterlei.

We dropped in on Baixinho, a short, stocky man of perhaps forty-five, just in from his fields for a break from work. He and his wife, Zelia, a tall mulatta woman, her head wrapped in a length of white cotton, were originally from the state of Bahia, he told me. The house was clean and swept, with one wall plastered neatly with dry clay. While Baixinho made himself comfortable on the floor, leaning against the wall, we sat on precarious stools at a tiny table covered with a printed handkerchief and drank glasses of water, followed by strong black coffee. The couple had two sons in their early teens, both of them too shy to come in. Dona Zelia was very friendly, however, and asked Marileide to show her how to write the numbers that would correspond with her name on the ballot. In Brazil, the illiterate may name their choice by writing in the corresponding number, and it was unusual to find someone who had difficulty even in doing that. As we were leaving, Marileide made me laugh by remarking matter-of-factly, "Well, I know I have one vote for sure now; Zelia can't write any number but mine."

After several more visits, we found ourselves back at Seu Nazareno's place by midafternoon, and I was forced to carry my pack again. We made a few more stops, often because we had gotten off the right track, but most of our walking was through increasingly difficult and inaccessible segments of dense forest. Tough vines would catch at my pack, I often lost my footing, and roots seemed to stick out everywhere. In a few places, enormous trees had been chopped down, and I wondered how anyone would ever get the lumber out of such a place. There were brooks to cross and fallen logs in our path. I was completely exhausted, and when Maria insisted on taking my pack, I reluctantly agreed.

Finally, we made it to the edge of the forest. From the high ridge where we stood, I could see the town of Xinguara far below, a collection of shacks amid the green. At least, from there, it was all downhill, and the path was relatively clear. The sun was beginning to set, and we walked quickly along a logging trail, making one last stop at a small, well-kept farm, flourishing with fruit and vegetables. It belonged to José Rodrigues, who wasn't at home at the time, although his wife, Waldemira, and his children were. The couple were close friends of Maria da Rocha and Marileide, and later Maria told me that they had bought their land — or back then only the occupant's rights — from José.

Waldemira was a tall, pretty woman with crinkly light-brown hair and blue eyes who insisted we eat something before going farther. We sat beside the house in an open yard dotted with young trees and flowering bushes, with hungry ducks and small pigs that paced resolutely around us, hoping for crumbs.

By the time we left, the sky was growing dark, the air swelling almost visibly with the persistent cries of frogs in the gullies, and, from farther off in the jungle, howler monkeys. We trudged the last bit into town, getting a ride to Maria da Rocha's house in the truck of someone Marileide happened to know.

That night, I took a bath outside in a small rubber basin, hauling the water from the well with only the moonlight to illuminate the scene. Then I climbed into my hammock and fell asleep. Early the next morning, I got up to catch the bus to Conceição. Maria woke up as well and tried to get her daughter Diana, a small lump huddled in a ragged blanket on the floor beside the bed, to wake up and take me to the bus station, to no avail. I said I would find it okay on my own, gave her skinny shoulders a hug and walked up the dawn-quiet street.

In less than half an hour, I was on the road again, heading to Conceição. The trip took me through Rio Maria, the gold-prospecting town of Redenção, with its modern metal bus station, and a number of dusty, godforsaken places of no more than one dirt street and two rows of miserable wooden shacks, all of them plastered with election posters and graffiti. On either side of the road, pastures invaded by brush stretched away toward smoky ridges. Once, we had to slow down for a herd of cattle blocking the road; three cowboys, skinny men in black hats with lassos on their saddle horns, drove them to the side. By noon, I was back in Conceição do Araguaia.

For more than twenty years, Conceição has been a flashpoint in the agrarian conflict in this part of the Amazon. Its name is recognizable even to people in the big cities in the south, and betokens lawlessness. Assassinations, evictions and shoot-outs had become everyday occurrences. It is a sprawling town, surrounded by enormous ranches and built around a small commercial sector dominated by a block of banks and the diocesan cathedral. From time to time, heavy rains would bucket down from the sky, temporarily breaking the hold of a suffocating sun. But usually the town seemed so oppressive that, in spite of the river, just walking down the street could be an ordeal.

With its sandy streets and right-wing politicians who spoke of progress, Conceição remained resolutely rural, a place where there is little to do. On weekends, people would swim in the river, which, during dry season, recedes to leave wide sandy shores for sunbathers. Large signs welcomed tourists to the beaches of Conceição, but, for me, that remained a concept difficult to envision. At the hotel where I stayed, the Tarumã, purportedly the best in town, the desk manager had to take me to four rooms before we found one that did not have something broken. The hotel's hallways were alive at night with the whirring of insects, and the lukewarm pool was littered with garbage. On its wide front porch overlooking the Araguaia River, visiting owners or company executives would often meet in the evenings with their ranch managers, often to discuss the problem of unwanted settlers on their land or to plot the death of anyone who got in the way of their expansion plans. One of the people at the top of their list was a handsome young priest named Ricardo Rezende, who ran the town's office of the Pastoral Land Commission.

During his eleven years in Conceição, various attempts had been made on Ricardo's life, and he had seen many friends and colleagues brutally murdered. I went to visit him at his home, on a quiet, unpaved street, with a big mango tree in the yard.

Ricardo began by showing me his collection of photographs, a grim scrapbook that reminded me of the books of atrocities kept by the Human Rights Commission in San Salvador during the early 1980s. There were photos of Father Josimo Tavares, a priest who had helped settlers gain legal right to the land they occupied, shot on the stairs of the commission office in nearby Imperatriz in May 1986. Adelaide Molinari, a young nun working for the commission near Marabá, lay bathed in blood on the cement floor of the Purara bus station. The three young gunmen accused of killing her that April day in 1986 stood smirking in front of the local pool hall, having just been freed by the police. There were the corpses of peasants who had invaded land. Some were pocked with bullet holes, lying in the sun; some were burned beyond recognition, including, in one brutal case, a young girl of no more than thirteen. Three-year-old Clesio Pereira de Souza lay on a dirt road beside his father, Sebastião, both of them shot in the back a few months previously by gunmen hired by someone who claimed the land that he and a hundred other peasants occupied. When Sebastião's widow went to the police post in Goianesia to register the murder, the police sergeant told her it was impossible; he had no pen or paper. There was a picture of the corpse of Rural Workers Union leader João Canuto, his body punctured by fourteen bullets at close range in front of the Rio Maria cemetery. In another set of photos, Ricardo was shown saying a quick mass over the corpse of a young settler whose family was too afraid to bring the body inside their house for a proper wake. On the last page was a newspaper clipping I had already seen. It told of various "security" firms in the region, such as the ominously named Solution Inc., that would carry out killings, and included a list of prices. Catholic priests were the most expensive.

I asked Ricardo what the response to the violence has been from the local police and judiciary. "Well, the police always work with the big landlords," he said, "and go along on the eviction raids with the ranchers' hired gunmen."

As for the judiciary, he recounted a Kafkaesque tale that had occurred a few years earlier, when a group of peasants had moved onto an unoccupied tract of land that they believed was ownerless. A few years later, they were kicked out by gunmen and military police sent by a claimant to the land named Neif Murad. Their hunting rifles were also confiscated by the police. At the subsequent court case, the commission's lawyer proved that the land was indeed free: records proved that Murad owned only the piece adjoining it. At this point in the court proceedings, Ricardo told me, Murad's lawyer threatened to kill the commission lawyer right in front of the judge's bench. In the face of the threat, the commission demanded that the judge order the local police to accompany the peasants safely to their land. The judge, however, said that he was not competent to do this, a statement with no truth to it, and the commission was forced to appeal to the Secretariat of Public Security in Belém. The secretariat incorrectly claimed that they would have to review the entire case, even though the judge in Conceição had already ruled in the peasants' favor. Months later, the secretariat came to the same conclusion and authorized police to see the peasants back to their land. But the police in Conceição refused to obey the secretariat's orders. In the end, said Ricardo, he had pulled together a large group of neighboring peasants who formed a sort of protective cordon and took the settlers back to the land they should never have been forced off in the first place.

One of the most recent struggles over land, said Ricardo, had occurred at a ranch called Fazenda Bela Vista. About four hundred families had been farming a tract claimed by the ranch's owner, Jurandi Goncalves Siqueira, some for as long as seven years. Suddenly in April 1987 the evictions came. Twelve peasants were put in jail and tortured. When the commission lawyer brought a writ of habeas corpus, the local judge denied it. Crops and houses were burned, but the peasants resisted. Siqueira finally fled the area after three peasants were found murdered, and the land had recently been expropriated.

Meanwhile, horrifying rumors of slave labor on the outlying ranches flew around the town. A few months ago, two young men had related to the police a tale of torture and murder on a ranch of which they knew not even the name. Like many of the workers hired to clear forest and burn it, they had been enticed to the region from some dusty, impoverished town in the northeast with promises of good wages. Upon arriving in the Amazon, however, they had been forced to work twelve to fourteen hours a day. When they were paid nothing at all, they tried to escape. They were picked up, tied to a tree and tortured by the ranch gunmen, who smashed their teeth and poured boiling coffee into their bleeding mouths. Then the workers were left for dead in the forest. Somehow they made it to town, but were unable to say exactly where the ranch was located, and knew only the first names or nicknames of the gunmen. There was nothing anyone could do. It was always extremely difficult to find people who would bring a case against such ranches, said Ricardo. "Usually, they are too broken and scared. But the town is full of rumors of such things, of men being tortured, of entire groups of them, up to forty even, being burned alive inside the bunkhouse at night, so they don't have to be paid."

"Where did that supposedly happen?" I asked. "At Rio Cristalina, the Volkswagen ranch," he replied, "which was recently sold to a Japanese company." In a famous case concerning the ranch, a 350,000-acre (140 000-hectare) spread near Santana do Araguaia, five men denounced the inhumane working conditions to the Ministry of Labor. Both Volkswagen and the government carried out investigations, concluding that the labor contractors, or *gatos*, were at fault. A local judge, however, charged the five men with slandering the German multinational, and ordered them to pay damages. That decision was eventually overturned in appeal.

With the battle moving to the arena of old-time politics, however, things had quieted down. "At election time, the peasants are always given a break, as the local politicians come around and ask for their votes," Ricardo said. He was, in fact, leaving the commission to assume the duties of the parish in Rio Maria. It was a prospect that had greatly gladdened the hearts of Marileide and Maria da Rocha in Xinguara, who felt they would soon have an ally close by. "What we find we really need here now, more than someone like myself, perhaps," said Ricardo, "is an agronomist. This land isn't easy to make a living on. People need a lot of advice. Otherwise, they won't make a go of it. They will sell out, and look for fresh land elsewhere in the region."

Walter had been a truck driver in the neighboring state of Goiás, and on hauls through the lower part of the Pará had been impressed by the lush beauty of the land. He had persuaded his father and five brothers to move with him, and in 1980 they began working for a rancher near Conceição. Eventually, they bought a sixty-three acre (twenty-five hectare) piece from a man who had the singular idea of growing bananas and shipping them to São Paulo. While business was brisk, the owner, "kind of a crazy old guy," as Walter described him, got into debt with the bank and decided to sell out.

One day, during elections for a new president for the union, Walter was asked by one of the candidates, Felipe, to be his driver as he went from village to village campaigning. Walter would sit and listen to Felipe's speeches over and over, and found himself hooked. He became an avid young rural socialist, and only a few months before I met him, had been elected president after Felipe retired.

Walter had a very clear perspective on the situation facing the union. "Since the election campaigns started, things have cooled down, all right," he said. "There are still *pistoleiros* around, but they're not doing anything." In addition, there was a tendency these days on the part of landowners to settle for expropriation, thanks to former Pará governor Jader Barbalho, who had been given the government portfolio of Minister of Agrarian Development and Reform. Barbalho had been offering more than top dollar for land in Pará. Even other parliamentarians had complained that he was enriching old friends in the state with land prices higher than one would pay in the fertile south of Brazil. Walter used the example of Bela Vista. "I saw in the *Official Daily* from Brasília myself," he said, "an announcement about the expropriations. It said that after careful negotiations the government had bought the land for less than that of the current value in the region. But when I worked it out, I found that it came to

The following day, I went to visit Walter Peixoto, the newly elected president of the Rural Workers Union in Conceição. He was thirty-two, a tall fellow, rather shy, with curly reddish hair and a thick beard. I met him in the union building, a large multipurpose barn of a place, almost exactly the same as the union buildings I had seen in Xapuri and Cametá.

it came to about nine hundred new cruzados per *alquiere* [six and a quarter acres, or two and a half hectares], while no one has ever sold land here for more than two hundred. This definitely seems to be some maneuvering on the part of Jader, all right."

In spite of the new mania by politicians and landowners to sell or win votes, said Walter, there were at least ten areas of potential conflict. A typical area was Curral das Pedras, a fraction of a massive estate belonging to the Gomes Reis family of São Paulo. At one time, the Gomes Reis family had owned almost the entire municipality of Conceição do Araguaia, but through various sales and a few expropriations were left with only about 625,000 acres (250 000 hectares). Curral das Pedras was a tract of some 68,000 acres (27 000 hectares) that had been invaded the year before. There the peasants had set up such an effective, almost military style of organization to watch for ranch gunmen and the police, that no one had done much more than threaten to kick them out. A well-known gunman, Luizão, or Big Louis, had tried to buy Walter off, then threatened to go in and kill. An adopted son of the Gomes Reis family, a gunman named Antonio Balbina, had said the same.

We turned to other problems the seven thousand members of the union were facing. The union had been told that the settlers would have to pay the government back for the expropriations after a grace period of five years. "We feel that this is unjust," said Walter. "First of all, the prices are way too high, over double in some cases what the land would normally sell for. How is some guy working on his own and by hand going to pay off such a debt? And second, we feel that the land should have been given to the peasants anyway, where it serves a useful social function. Under the old landlord, that land was not in use. He just lives in his mansion in São Paulo and waits for the prices to go up every day. This way, the land is producing food for the whole region."

But just how good was the land? I asked. Was it worth the struggle and loss of lives for land that might give out after just one generation?

"Look," said Walter, "the weakness of the soil is very great here. It's a subject that comes up at every meeting we have. It varies a lot, but normally you can get about twelve years out of it, in some cases only two. And there are problems with pests, as well. People are worried, because very few are going to have the conditions to stay on the land. The small producer has no financing or possibilities to take out loans. There are hardly any roads, so he's got to put his rice or whatever on the back of a donkey, carry it to the river and bring it in the rest of the way by boat. And the price of rice" — less than $10 U.S., he told me, for a 1300-pound (600-kilo) sack — "was very low at harvest time. It goes up a lot between harvests, but there is no way the guy can keep it and sell it later. He needs the money right away to pay his bills and buy new seed." While it was not difficult to persuade the peasants that planting cacao or fruit trees was a good idea, enabling them to do so was a problem with no visible solution. Such trees took at least three years to mature, and their fruits required effective transport facilities to get them to market.

"The majority of people here are from the northeast," said Walter, "most of them illiterate. And too often, when they have won the struggle for their land, they just think about themselves and not about the guy next door, who doesn't have title yet and will be thrown off. All of these problems make up the great challenge we're facing. But we are also fighting for a new society as well. There is a real lack of people who are conscious of the situation, who realize that just by winning their small battle, the war is not yet over."

Meanwhile, he added, about fifteen or twenty families arrived in town from other states every month. They approached the union to find them land "as if we were the Ministry of Agrarian Reform." Sometimes, he said, the staff at the local ministry office in Conceição sent people to him.

With that, I left. There was a farmer waiting outside who wanted to talk to Walter about having his land expropriated by the ministry. As Walter had said earlier, the news of Jader's good prices had traveled fast.

A few months later, I passed through Conceição again; a certain familiarity with the place made it seem less oppressive. Until suddenly, during a chat with a woman called Ana at the commission office, I learned that Antenor Moreira had been shot and killed only weeks earlier, in December.

I got on the bus to Xinguara and traveled to see Maria, now faced with raising her five children alone. She took me to her house and told me the whole terrible story. Yes, she said, the family had been receiving threats for about four years from a land dealer, Gemiro Siqueira Campos, one of the leaders of the union she and Antenor were trying to reform. "Everyone knew about it," said Maria, "so many people advised us of his plans. But Antenor didn't pay much attention. He gave his life not to have to kill that man."

The whole family had been living in the cabin in Marajoara. It was close to Christmas, and the children were off from school. Maria described how she had roasted some corn for lunch that day, then gone to join Antenor in the field. Then she walked off to get some vegetables for their dinner. At the cabin, the children told her they had heard the dogs barking, "so I thought I better go tell this to Antenor. But suddenly," she said, "I heard a shot. It seemed so loud that it filled the air, and I screamed. There was a horrible screaming, we were all of us, the children and I, almost crazy to hear that shot."

Antenor did not die immediately. The neighbors carried him to the road in a hammock and got him to the hospital in Rio Maria. He was conscious and talking by Christmas Day, but that night, he succumbed to infection. By the next day, he was dead. Now, she told me, she had no choice but to sell the land, and was looking for a cleaning job in the school in town, which would pay her about $50 U.S. a month.

She finished the story and was silent for a minute. Then she looked at me and sighed. "You know, Augusta, I always used to think that somehow, if I worked hard enough, I could change the world. And now, suddenly I'm realizing that it is not so easy." Then she paused before adding, "But I'm not going to give up trying. I know it will be very difficult now without him, raising the children by myself, but I won't give up."

SEVEN

~~~~~~~

THE BISHOP WITH THE WOODEN RING

A FTER MY STAY IN CONCEIÇÃO, I was in the air once again, this time flying south along the Araguaia River to São Felix do Araguaia. The town lay in the northeastern part of the state of Mato Grosso, near the southern border of Pará, just across from the largest inland island in the world, Bananal Island, bounded by the Araguaia and Javaes rivers.

Like Conceição, this part of Mato Grosso had been the scene of land grabbing and violence during the years of migration to the Amazon, and a region heavily favored for grants from SUDAM. Opened up by government road projects, cheek by jowl with the cattle-producing state of Goiás, it was a natural target for those looking for land tracts both big and small.

One typical battle over land rights had occurred near the village of Santa Teresinha, about sixty miles — a hundred kilometres — north of São Felix. The area had been sparsely settled since the early twenties, when migrants from the northeast had arrived there. A church and school had been built there in the thirties. Many more people moved in during the sixties, when hundreds of sharecropping families were pushed off their land in the northeast and the south of Brazil. Then, in 1967, the enormous Codeara ranch claimed the entire area as its own and attempted to expel all the peasants living there. The land the peasants owned was just a tiny fraction of the 450,000 acres (180 000 hectares) the São Paulo–based National Credit Bank owned between Codeara and another ranch, Agropastoril. Nonetheless, the bank set to the dirty work of breaking the peasants' will through a number of tactics that lasted for years. Peasants were routinely threatened and evicted, and many houses were destroyed. At one point, the peasants persuaded 150 ranch laborers to go on strike for a month, but the laborers were quickly replaced.

In his book, *A Church in Amazonia in Conflict with the Latifundia and Social Marginalization*, Dom Pedro Casaldáliga lists scores of examples of maltreatment of laborers. He describes wages of a dollar a day, from which food and transport were subtracted; reports a 70 percent incidence of malaria; says workers were shot when they were too sick to work. There were many other horrifying incidents. He writes about the sight of "some of the laborers, some of them married, with children, weeping on the banks of the Araguaia, in Santa Teresinha, and asking for pity's sake to be given the boat fare so that they could get far away from the companies."

The events in Santa Teresinha reached boiling point when the Codeara ranch, which claimed to own the land the town stood on, refused to let the community, aided by Catholic lay workers and the local priest, François Jentel, construct a health clinic. People from the ranch bulldozed down the building, but it was rebuilt, and this time trenches were dug to defend it. When a group of twenty military police and ranch gunmen came to destroy the building, the thirty-six peasants guarding it shot back. By night, everyone had fled from the scene, but the following day, eighty soldiers arrived in two Brazilian air force aircraft and proceeded to arrest every male in sight, including old men. Jentel was arrested and condemned for subversion at a military trial in the state capital, Cuiabá, before being deported. In the end, only 115 families out of several hundred received title for the land that had all along been theirs. By 1981, the Codeara ranch was admitting that its venture, in spite of $16 U.S. million in tax rebates from SUDAM, was a financial failure. With expenses of more than $3 million U.S. a year and income of less than a third of that, even the poorest peasant was managing his land better than the National Credit Bank.

As I flew over this land that had been ranched and farmed for almost twenty years, the ground below me was a shocking sight, even worse than the endless scrub covering the hills and valleys south of Carajás. The land appeared as a carpet of grayish brown, dotted with small bushy trees, nothing growing between them, not even grass or weeds.

São Felix was similar to Conceição, except that it was more like a frontier town, hot and monotonous. A few Xavante Indians could be seen walking the streets, their faces painted with small fading circles of black. The town's main street stretched along the river, and I ended up staying at the Araguaia Hotel, in a dirty, hot little room, its only window covered with tattered brown paper. It was run by a slatternly woman who liked to sit on the veranda overlooking the river and listen to pop singer Roberto Carlos, cranked up as loud as possible. The place almost made me regret my hostility to the Tarumã Hotel in Conceição. At the Araguaia, I met two wealthy businessmen, and I took consolation from the fact that they had to stay in such a dreadful place, too. One was a young man named Daniel, who owned a ranch nearby, as well as a shoe factory in the south. He purchased tons of hides in Mato Grosso for his factory and had begun, he said, to export to the United States fifteen thousand pairs of loafers a month. He asked me what I was doing in São Felix, and I said I was going to visit its bishop, Dom Pedro Casaldáliga. His countenance changed. "Oh, him," he sniffed and proceeded to malign the man for a good half hour. He finished his discourse by muttering a veiled threat: "But he'll soon shut his mouth, all right."

Before I visited Dom Pedro, I walked a couple of blocks down the street from the Araguaia Hotel to the modern new community center the church had built facing the river. It was made up of various pavilions and offices, including that of the local Pastoral Land Commission. There I spoke to a short, rotund woman, bright-eyed and forthright, named Maria José Moreira de Souza, who came warmly recommended by Ricardo, Ana and the others in Conceição.

Maria José told me that the situation in São Felix was slightly different than that of Conceição, although from 1984 to 1987, it had seemed as though the same relative calm would reign. There was far less migration from the northeast these days, she said, but new waves of people were coming in from the southern Brazilian states of Paraná,

Santa Catarina and Rio Grande do Sul, as well as from the south of neighboring Goiás. They came with some money and certain expectations, attracted by colonizing companies. This was something the big ranches and many businessmen were getting interested in. As their profits from ranching fell, what better solution than to sell off lots to peasants from the south? "The land here is not very good," said Maria José, "and people have many difficulties. In fact, you can really only grow rice and corn here; it's not even good for beans. So people arrive and realize that they have been deceived. Often they don't get the land titles they were promised, and the land isn't as good as they were promised, either. So they occupy other areas, sometimes even of the colonizing company itself. And we are coming back again to the same old cycle: occupation, evictions and violence."

A union leader in Canabrava had been killed a month before I got there, for example, she said. He had encouraged about a hundred families facing eviction to stay, and the ranch owner, believing it would be easier to dislodge them, had him killed. In Vila Rica, a gunman had been killed in a shoot-out with *posseiros*, the ranch owner was wounded, and two peasants were in prison. "The judges here are always on the side of the owner," she said.

I mentioned the appearance of the land as I flew in from Santana, and Maria José said, "You know, when we go out to the countryside, just walking on the ground, you can see the sand underneath. It's pure sand. We can't help but have the impression that, twenty years from now, this will all be a desert."

So is all this worth it? I asked. "It's true that our struggle has to be a global one," she replied, "that we must have an agrarian reform throughout the country. But at the same time, we do know that this land is recoverable. It is possible to live from it, and, for at least those who are already here, to stay on it." They would have to use a lot of calcium and fertilizers, she said, to start plowing with animal traction and, most important, to stop burning. "Now, together with the union, we're working on alternative agriculture," she explained. "But it's hard. Everyone thinks that mechanization is modern and we have to use it. It is the dream of every peasant to own a tractor some day. Imagine trying to convince him that he should use an ox. So we are demanding that the government carry out an ample agrarian reform, that it give land and materials to rural workers so they can make a go of it, not just credits, but animals, seeds and so on, all free. Because, otherwise,

I have to admit that our work here often ends up going against us. After three or four years, his land gives out, the peasant sells and occupies some other place. That's why the ranchers are always accusing us of merely encouraging invasions. But if they are having problems themselves, you can imagine the problems of the peasants.''

A thin, frail man of sixty with a high, square forehead and large brown eyes made even bigger by his thick glasses, Dom Pedro Casaldáliga seems an unlikely sort to inspire hatred. But he has done so for years, wielding a powerful pen that has produced impassioned prose, and hauntingly personal poetry, both guided by his experience and an unwavering sense of principle.

Dom Pedro was born in Cataluña, Spain, the son of an old farming family, and had come to the Amazon as a missionary priest of the Claretain order twenty years before I met him. In 1971 he was named bishop of the newly created diocese of São Felix do Araguaia, an area of 375,000 acres (150 000 hectares). His cathedral was a modest building of white plastered brick, with rows of plain wooden benches inside. A wall at the back displayed a ceremonial feathered headdress of the Xavante tribe and a leather cap typical of the northeastern immigrant farmer. On a side wall hung a photograph of Father Jentel, who had died in France in 1981. A large, colorful mural behind the altar depicted peasants and Indians helping Christ carry the cross from Calvary, and was entitled, Dom Pedro told me, "Easter of the People." There was no gilding, no stained glass, no statues. The place was designed so that its congregation of poor peasants and local workers would feel not just at home but in charge.

Surrounded by trees, a few blocks from the cathedral, Dom Pedro's home was similarly modest, a brick house with an earthen floor and curtains over the doorways. It was full of sunlight that brightened all the colorful posters and postcards on the unplastered walls. We sat in the shade of the back porch to talk, Dom Pedro dressed in a short-sleeved blue shirt, light-colored trousers and rubber sandals. He preferred to be called Pedro, eschewing the traditional religious title Dom. And in place of the traditional heavy gold ring of the Catholic bishop, he wore a thick wooden ring, carved for him by a Xavante Indian.

A few months before I met him, Dom Pedro had been called to task by the Vatican on a number of issues and had had to travel to

Rome. The church hierarchy wanted him to tone down his Liberation Theology, start making an official visit to Rome every five years as he was supposed to (Dom Pedro hadn't been in seventeen years) and above all, stop traveling to Nicaragua. But, without agreeing to much of what they asked, the bishop with the wooden ring had more or less ironed things out with the Pope and his conservative cardinals, and was going to El Salvador instead of Nicaragua. I asked him how it was that he, who came from a conservative Spanish background, had become so radical in his actions. He was arguably one of the most progressive and famous bishops in Latin America.

His voice was gravelly with a slight attack of laryngitis as Dom Pedro described how, in 1968, when he arrived in São Felix, the area was occupied almost exclusively by Indians and peasants on small holdings and was just beginning to attract the greedy attention of the ranchers. "I came here as a missionary," he said, "not to make money, accumulate land or have a beautiful house. So it was a new church that we established here. Perhaps if it had been a traditional, old church, things might have been more difficult. And don't forget we were being influenced greatly by the Latin American Bishops Conference of Medellín." (This was the 1968 meeting that exploded the myth of a conservative, uncaring Church lining up behind the wealthy and the powerful in one of the poorest regions on earth.) But what impelled him most forcefully into the thick of battle, he said, was the utter barbarity of the situation.

"The situation of the peasants, the Indians, the ranch laborers was one that screamed at you," he said. "The big ranchers had arrived and expelled many people, to take away their land and keep it for themselves. It was enough to have just a little Christian faith and social sensitivity to assume this cause. It was obvious that this was a region of slavery, of feudalism, of an inhuman latifundium."

The cruelty of life in the Amazon after the ranchers arrived was brought home quite graphically to Dom Pedro in 1976, in the town of Riberão Bonito. Dom Pedro had traveled there with a priest from São Paulo, Father João Bosco Penedo Burnier. The pair had gone to try to win the freedom of two women who were being tortured by the military police in the town jail. The husband of one of them was a suspect in a fatal shoot-out with the police over land. When the bishop and the priest arrived at the police post, a policeman summarily shot Father João Bosco and killed him. It was, and still is, widely believed that the bullet was meant for Dom Pedro, and that the police had confused the two because the bishop was so much more poorly dressed than the priest. At the seven-day funeral mass for the priest, the local peasants erected a cross in front of the police post bearing a sign that read, "Here Father João Bosco was murdered by a military policeman as he defended freedom." Resentment among the peasants was already running high because of a number of unjust evictions carried out by ranch gunmen and the police; it rose even higher when the police tore down the cross, spitting on it and profaning it. The villagers rioted, and in a body attacked the symbol of their repression, the town jail, with hoes, sticks and anything they could lay their hands on, demolishing it entirely.

A year later, a church was built on the site and named the Sanctuary of the Martyrs. Two years ago, Dom Pedro told me, he organized a pilgrimage to Riberão Bonito and filled the church with photographs of modern martyrs. "There is a photograph of Monsignor Archbishop Romero of El Salvador," he said, "symbolizing the martyrs of Central America. There are photographs of Father João Bosco and Father Josimo Tavares; of Margarida Maria Alves, the sugarcane cutters' leader, killed in the state of Paraiba; of Indians, trade unionists, workers, nuns and brothers and laypeople; in short, various photographs of people who were murdered, symbolizing the martyrs of the people." This Church of the Martyrs was another of the Vatican's bugbears. The Church in Rome suggested that it was not proper to place these photographs in a church because the subjects were not recognized Catholic saints.

During their first months in São Paulo, Dom Pedro told me, he and the other priests would sometimes celebrate mass on the big ranches, including Suia-Missu. The owners of this enormous ranch of 1.4 million acres (560 000 hectares), the Ometto family from São Paulo, had transported by plane the inhabitants of thirty-three Xavante Indian villages on the ranch to an Indian reserve several hundred miles away. In 1972, Suia-Missu was bought by an Italian company, Liquigas, even though the sale of such an area contravened the Brazilian constitution. Liquigas had the idea of mounting a huge beef-growing and packing operation on the ranch, chilling the meat during the flight to Italy. "When we began to discover that the peons lived in horrible conditions," said Dom Pedro, "and we the priests were put up in a hotel with the ranch administrators and pilots, when we said mass with gunmen sitting in the front and the poor laborers timidly standing in the back, we desisted. It made no sense to go out and denounce these people for the killings of peasants and then celebrate mass in their buildings. The place was like enemy territory. It would be like celebrating mass in a salon of the International Monetary Fund . . . or the UDR," he said.

One of the most controversial policies of the "red bishop of São Felix" is his refusal to baptize the children of the rich. "We must give the sacrament of baptism the value that it has," he explained to me. "Baptism is a sacrament that introduces us to the community of those who follow Jesus. When there is no adult consciousness, no personal responsibility, as is the case with a child, it is logical that we must call on the faith of the child's parents or godparents. So if the parents or godparents do not participate in the community, if they exploit and persecute the people, it is logical that they cannot be credible witnesses. They cannot be the legitimate guarantors of the baptism of a child. Either they must change their conduct, or else we wait until the child has grown, and on its own asks to be baptized."

These were the kinds of decisions few if any clergy would make, it being easier to look the other way. But Dom Pedro permitted himself no half measures in his condemnation of injustice. "Just the fact to own so much land when many people have nothing is exploitation," he said. "All accumulation, either personal or entrepreneurial or even collective, such as that of the First World, always exploits. The man who accumulates is he who exploits, he who excludes others. The rich man is always rich at the cost of the poor. Even Pope John Paul himself, whom no one would ever accuse of being a Communist, has repeated various times here in Latin America that the rich are becoming more and more rich at the expense of the poor, who become more and more poor."

For Dom Pedro, it was not enough to dole out charity while the system that required the doling out of such charity remained intact. "Our God is a God of the community," he explained. "There is no room for dichotomy in Christian faith. It must assume the realities of the earth, the compromises of history. It has to bring as far as the ultimate consequences, both social and economic, the authenticity of Christian compromise."

At times, Dom Pedro did sound like a true Marxist, as he is often accused of being, although he disagrees. Nonetheless, he told me that he believed that, for example, "all type of reform is to simply maintain the capitalist structure, the structure of dependence, of empire, of the bourgeoisie and the hierarchy. What we need here," he said, "is the true independence of our people, an end to imperialism, to oligarchies and privileges, and a democracy that is not only political but also economic, social and cultural. And what that means is to transform the current structures." And yes, he said, it was difficult to stick by such principles.

"It is always easier to say yes than to say no," he said. "But the important thing is to affirm your conscience, your faith."

We finished our chat. Dom Pedro had to prepare to say Saturday night mass. I asked him what his goals were now, and he replied that with many more organizations in the area, administrative, political, syndical and so on, after these twenty years, the most important thing "was to stimulate all the more the organization of the people." He recalled how, at the bishops' conference in Medellín, the Church had spoken of "the deaf clamor of the people," and at Puebla, five years later, "the tempestuous clamor of the people." "I hope that in Santo Domingo, at the next conference marking the five-hundredth anniversary of the discovery of America," he said, "we can talk about 'the organized clamor of the people.' "

Meanwhile he would continue in his work as before, riding the dusty rural buses with the peasants from parish to parish, ignoring the death threats he received, because, as he put it, "many people are not just being threatened, they are being killed. If the people carry on their work, in spite of the killings, how can I pay attention when I am just threatened?" I asked him if Monsignor Romero of El Salvador, from whom Dom Pedro had received the last letter the Salvadorean archbishop had written, had been an inspiration to him. "Yes, he and many others," Dom Pedro replied. "Jesus first of all, of course."

As I left his house to walk toward the river, he reminded me that the upcoming week would be a special week of solidarity with the people of El Salvador. Then he went back to the small wooden table where he prepared his only possible answer to the threats and injustice, his sermons and poems and heartrending accounts of life in São Felix.

EIGHT

OLD RAY AND THE GOLDEN CHAPEL

I T WAS STILL EARLY, ABOUT 8:30 in the morning, but the sky was bright, a pale blue airbrushed with luminous cirrus clouds, and the river was the color of milk chocolate, edged in white where it fanned out from the path of the boat. I was aboard the *Fe em Deus* (or "Faith in God," a name that would have pleased the old man at the *curandeiros* market in Belém), heading upriver to Santarém and eventually Manaus. I was surrounded by a tangle of hammocks — stripes, plaids and solids of every color — hung in a pair of uneven rows the entire length of the open deck. Mounds of baggage had been piled between these rows on a low platform of wood slats. Passengers sat on the long benches placed against the railings, chatting with each other or just waiting for the time to pass. Leaning out of their hammocks, below and just a bit to the side of me, two men were playing checkers on a torn-off flap of cardboard, divided in squares drawn with a pen, the pieces made of little circles of cardboard, too.

We had left Belém the previous night. I had flown back there from São Felix to spend a few days before leaving for Manaus. Now, after almost twelve hours of sailing, we were still skirting the Island of Marajó. The Pará River, like the Amazon, was so knotted with islands, fruit of the tons of silt washed down constantly by the current, that it was impossible for me to tell the islands from the shore.

In three days we would arrive in Santarém, and in two more Manaus. It was not the fastest way to travel, but it was certainly the cheapest and, in spite of the somewhat primitive conditions, probably the most comfortable. The *Fe em Deus*, one of three or four boats that left Belém each week, was not a big boat, and it was crowded with at least a hundred passengers. Meals were included in the ticket price, and served on the lower deck. Down a narrow stairwell, odorous with the large sacks of onions packed around it, and past the roaring diesel motor, a pair of long tables was set up, where the passengers ate in shifts. The fare was pretty monotonous. At lunch and dinner, the cook and her assistants would load the tables with huge bowls of stewed beef and various kinds of starches: potatoes, rice, spaghetti and cassava meal. When everyone had eaten, the crew moved the long benches out of the way and bolted the tables to the ceiling, making space for passengers and their hammocks. Past the tables was the galley, and across from it, the few tiny wood cubicles that served as showers and toilets. On the roof of the boat, tables and chairs had been set out, and a snack bar sold beer and soft drinks.

There was nothing much to do but read. The scenery was not exactly exciting in its extravagant but monotonous verdure. We stopped at a few towns in the delta, such as Curralinha, Breves and Antonio Lemos, but not for long. Breves was little more than a collection of sawmills, big airy warehouses standing on stilts over the riverbank, waste lumber piled like giant matchsticks on the shore. Around it, however, the shore was swamped with long thickets of palm trees and silvery-leafed *baoba*, interspersed with enormous cottonwoods and *andirobas*. Lines of *aninga* stood guard in the shallow water, each pointing its single leaf upward like a spear. The wooden houses on stilts, each with its little dock and upright poles, resembled those I'd seen along the shores of the islands in the Tocantins.

Between Breves, on the south part of Marajó island, and Antonio Lemos, on its western shore, we took a narrow strait. The jungle came close on either side. The arching wall of vegetation seemed, as it always did to me, cool and inviting, heavy with dripping vines and flamboyant with bamboo. *Buriti* palms stood out like thick bunches of green feathers, while the occasional *açaí* reared its branches above the fretwork of leaves like an asterisk. Here and there, paths ran beneath the forest cover like burrowings into a great cavern of light and shadow. As we sailed past the few shacks on the riverbank, huddled together in short rows of three or four, people came out in their *cascos* and began to paddle rapidly toward us. The crew flung plastic bags filled with small items of clothing, tied tight like balloons, onto the water. It was a custom, I learned, on this part of the river, and the items found floating in the wake of the boat were much sought after. Antonio Lemos, a town we reached in the afternoon, also had its sawmill, a small white church and one large house with a row of wood shacks spilling up over a crest of sand fringed with long grass. A wooden bridge led over a stream to some more houses, each one connected to the other by a boardwalk on stilts, like a rickety river sidewalk.

As we made our way slowly upriver, I would, from time to time, scan the surface of the water for dolphins. I knew they were in there somewhere, white ones, *tucuxis*, even a few rare pink ones, far more distant and mysterious than those who dance on their tails at marine worlds throughout North America. In Amazonia, the dolphin is truly a marvelous creature, endowed with numerous talents and able to turn himself at will into a handsome young man. Or so I was told, not once but many times. Watching the brown expanse of rolling water, I wanted to see one dolphin, a real one, jumping and diving through the waves like a riverine horse.

Dolphin stories abounded in the Amazon. As television, airplanes and hydroelectric dams increasingly invaded their world, people there still believed that an out-of-wedlock pregnancy was frequently *o filho do boto,* "the dolphin's child." Transformed into a man, the dolphin is, it seems, irresistible, hence the thriving trade in his bits and pieces at the *curandeiros* market in Belém. As the old man there had explained, "Why the dolphin? Well, it's because he's enchanted. If he wants to go to a party, he turns into a man, handsome, unknown. He dances with all the girls and drinks a lot of *cachaça,* a lot. After, when it's dawn, he leaves his clothes and jumps back into the river."

It is said that the handsome stranger at the community dance is recognizable to a certain extent because he never takes off his hat. He cannot let anyone see the air hole on top of his head. When I first heard this detail in Belém, I thought it was so wonderful that I started to say to Elizete, "You know what I just found our? People say the dolphin never takes his hat off at a party because — " And she cut me off, rather bemused, saying, "So no one can see the air hole in his head. I know that. I grew up here."

On Paruru Island, Seu Raimundo had various tales about dolphins. "When we are traveling," he said, "the *tucuxi* dolphin keeps on jumping; it's a sign of a thunderstorm, but he doesn't mess around with anyone. He is the friend of man. If a boat sinks, he helps. But the big dolphin is really bad. When he is turning his belly upward, he is wanting to pull people down. Another dolphin story: My father liked to go out and get some fish after a rain shower. One night, he went out. When he arrived at a certain spot, a huge wave approached and began to tip the canoe. He was worried, didn't know what it was. Then the wave went down. Right after, the animal gave a loud snort. My father got frightened, and the animal gave another snort. And so the animal followed him, my father rowing and the animal accompanying him. My father arrived very frightened and asked for some water, and every night that dolphin went to the same place. We could hear him, right after nightfall, walking around the house. No one saw him, but after some time, it stopped. We believed it was the dolphin because that had never happened until that night."

Abacate had also told me how the dolphins helped the river dweller to catch fish by herding unsuspecting schools into the traps, then patiently waiting for his payoff when the fisherman emptied the trap.

I went to the downtown campus of the Goeldi Museum, in Belém, looking for more information about dolphins from Dr. Napoleão Figueiredo, although it turned out that they were not his specialty. Figueiredo was an eminent ethnologist who had studied religious beliefs in the Amazon. He found and photocopied the relevant pages in the *Dicionário do Folclore Brasileiro*, where I found several accounts of dolphin lore and, particularly, confirmation of the dolphin's penchant for heavy drinking. There was one example of two unknown men who showed up at a party and drank vast amounts of sugarcane brandy. The following day, the river dwellers found two dead dolphins floating in the river. They cut them open and were struck by a very strong reek of liquor.

In 1850, the British naturalist Henry Bates noted, "No other animal in the Amazon is the subject of as many fables as the dolphin."

I never did find out where the belief that the dolphin could turn into a man came from, or how it had spread so generally through such a large region. There were all kinds of theories, some crediting the Indians, others saying it was an Amazonian corruption of European folklore. Europeans, since the time of the ancient Greeks, had always respected the water-bound mammal for its intelligence and beauty, but such respect was a far cry from a belief in actual physical transformations. And why was a dolphin always a rather menacing sexual presence at community gatherings? The more I asked people about this, the more stories I heard, none of them traceable or explicable, except, perhaps, as some psychological outlet for women oppressed in a rural Catholic society and set against a past of Indian legends and the extravagant landscape.

Figuereido also told me about a series of enchanted beings who, in the minds of many people in the Amazon, formed a sort of under-layer of heaven. "They are spiritual entities . . . fixed between two worlds, or as people say here, above the clouds but below the heavens." The result was a mixture of African, native Indian and Christian religious beliefs. "When you have a situation that escapes the reach of the Catholic Church," explained Figuereido, "you go to one of the enchanted ones. Let's say you're having a problem in finding a job, or of love, or just a lack of good luck. You go and ask. He, the enchanted one, then takes your request to the saints."

Scribbling busily on a large sheet of paper, the corpulent, white-haired man began to draw a series of circles and squares, creating a map of the world of these intermediaries. "There is an enormous category of enchanted ones," he explained in his loud voice. "Here, for example, you have the first category, the lords, masters, some more powerful than others. They reflect quite well the social situation in the Amazon, the division of classes here, and include historical figures such as the Marquis of Pombal." An official in the Portuguese government, the Marquis had gained control over Portugal and Brazil around 1750.

"Here, to the side," Figuereido went on, "you have other entities, influenced principally by African cults from Maranhão. These are young, and you also have children. Over here you have the old blacks, the ancestors of former slaves. Here, on this side, you have the indoc-trinators, urban phenomena, greatly influenced by the books of Alain Kardec. They are doctors, nurses, generous people who did kind things during their lives and, as enchanted ones, continue to do so. And here below, you have those who were transformed into snakes, dolphins, fish and birds. This is very much connected to Indian myths. And here you have some recently baptized entities who are still evolving.''

I asked Figuereido how long he had been studying this complicated spiritual world, and he replied, ''Since 1956. And I still don't know a thing!'' He burst into laughter. The Amazon had been through many transformations, he said, and had seen influences from a variety of cultures. ''This was all absorbed here. It's impossible to isolate, to say that this is this and that is that. You have to study it as a block, because these things don't disappear. They are reformulated and reinterpreted.''

Late on the first night of the river trip, the passengers on board the *Fe em Deus* were rudely awakened by what sounded like shell fire, just beyond the curtains of blue tarpaulin between us and the rainy night air. In fact, our ship was just arriving in the harbor of Gurupá and was being greeted by fireworks to celebrate the feast day of the town's patron saint, St. Benedict. It so happened that ''that black saint,'' as one of the crew described him the next day, was also the patron saint of sailors. At least, that was their explanation.

I woke up the next morning to find myself on the Amazon River. A number of passengers had disembarked in Gurupá, so I moved my hammock to the other side of the deck where there was more space. You can only sleep well in a hammock if there is enough room to lie in it slantwise. Next to me, a man lay in his hammock, reading the Bible; on the other side was a man who told me he traveled four times a month to Manaus and bought corn to sell in Belém. I didn't believe him, and speculated that José, as he introduced himself, was probably dealing in a commodity far more lucrative than corn, such as gold.

We were sailing among the dozens of islands, large and small, that formed the Amazon delta. On one side, through a gap in two islands, the river stretched away, flat and gray-blue. On the other side, an island spread a grassy carpet into the water. I watched a man crouched on the bank wash up, sending sprays of water over himself like glass wings. We passed a family of three, paddling in a *casco*. As we motored steadily west and toward the far shore, the landscape seemed to change from thick jungle to rolling grassy mounds, dotted with short trees. A few cattle grazed on the low plain. Then we passed a row of white cottages, clapboard houses with metal roofs and screen doors, which reminded me of the cottages you might see at a northern Ontario lake. José told me we were pulling in to the port of São Raimundo, and the northern look of the cottages suddenly made sense.

Situated at the mouth of the Jari River, São Raimundo was one of two ports used by the Companhia do Jari, a huge agroindustrial complex set up by American billionaire Daniel K. Ludwig. Ludwig had acquired 250,000 acres (100 000 hectares) about sixty miles — a hundred kilometers — to the north, near Monte Dourado, in 1967, and used it to grow rice — 35,000 acres (14 000 hectares) of it on the Jari River floodplain — as well as fast-growing trees for a pulp and paper mill he had had towed across two oceans from Japan. Since 1982, the firm had been in Brazilian hands, but they were losing money as fast as Ludwig had. The cost of energy to run the pulp mill was high, and the crops of rice and trees kept acquiring parasites. Like the failed rubber plantations Henry Ford had set up south of Santarém in Fordlandia and Belterra, the Jari seemed to defy the megalomania of the wealthiest capitalists. The fancy cottages I had seen had been built to American standards for the port's administrative staff.

We passed São Raimundo, and shortly afterward docked at Almerim, a city of paved streets, a few at least, and a line of cream-colored stucco buildings close to the shore. A few passengers disembarked, making their way unconcernedly across the exposed beams of the big dock, which was high up off the water and missing at least half its planking.

Past the town, the shore definitely flattened, then rolled for several miles to the hills in the distance. Buffalo grazed on the grassy plain, and here and there a sluggish stream cut through the sand-colored earth to empty into the river. Aside from the few towns and little wooden dwellings we passed from time to time, the banks of the Amazon seemed remarkably unpopulated. Yet when the river was first discovered, the Spanish chronicler Gaspar de Carvajal saw many villages among the trees and flotillas of canoes moored along the banks. The Indians who lived in those villages were some of the 5 million that historians estimate lived in the Amazon River basin, a number that has been reduced over three centuries to about 250,000.

Soon the channel widened, the shore a distant span of bluffs beneath the blue sky, the odd grassy island moving in between us. The water was littered with stumps and logs and floating pieces of long grass turf, called *canarana*, but there was still no sign of a dolphin.

The following day, a couple of hours after breakfast, we arrived in Santarém, earlier than I expected. The café-au-lait waters of the Amazon were suddenly marbled with the clear azure currents of the Tapajós, a river that ran parallel to the Xingu, and was famous for its clear blue water. Itaituba, where I had met Elizete, was about twenty-four hours away by boat.

Trees and houses covered an expanse of low hills, then we could see tall modern buildings looming above the others. A large island, the Ilha do Meio, appeared to veer off to the right as we approached the harbor. There was a long wall like a cliff below the main street, and scores of small boats were resting on the shingle. The *Fe em Deus* sailed past them, finally pulling in to and mooring at a tall cement dock surmounted by a pair of cranes. The passengers changed their clothes and packed up, rolling hammocks into neat bundles, finding sandals, and other items that had gotten lost. Only the man with the Bible stayed in his hammock, still quietly reading.

Santarém is the third-largest city in the Amazon and looks like most Amazonian cities — the row of trees on one or two main streets, their lower trunks painted white; the modern department stores and banks edging out the old stucco houses of the turn of the century. The city curved, in shades of yellow, pink, white and ocher, around the river. Once again, it was impossible to see the other side of the Amazon, where another fair-sized city, Alenquer, stood.

A long street led along the riverbank, lined in places with warehouses storing jute, pepper, rubber and cacao, and in others with bakeries, clothing shops and a small market. Where the river turned, there was a tree-lined square of restaurants and bars, one tourist shop and a few small hotels.

I didn't stay in the city for long. The day after I arrived, I was on yet another riverboat, this one heading for the Trombetas River, and the town of Oriximiná. We arrived in the morning, and after a long search for telephone tokens, I managed to call a friend of Elizete's, a young lawyer named Ideval. I waited for him at the market, watching the incongruous sight of a huge ocean-going tanker heading upriver toward the bauxite mines of Porto Trombetas.

I had traveled to Oriximiná to meet an old man famous for his tracking skills in the forest. His name was Velho Dico, "Old Ray." He had more or less retired from his profession as a *mateiro*, or woodsman, to take up politics and had twice served as town councillor. I met him in his small sawn-wood house up the hill from the harbor. A row of rough sticks linked with wire marked off his plot of sandy ground from the neighbor's. We went inside and sat down in a plain front room with two old armchairs and a television set on a small table. Old Ray didn't look that old, although he said he was sixty-seven. He was a well-built black man, not very tall, his woolly hair just beginning to turn gray. He had nothing much to do that day, he told me, aside from waiting for the previous day's election results. He had been a member of the Brazilian Democratic Movement Party, he told me, but had become disappointed, convinced that they had betrayed the people. Old Ray had run in the last election as a member of the Christian Democratic Party.

I turned the conversation to his life as a woodsman and asked him how it was possible not only to find his way but particular things, such as a stand of Brazil nut trees or a gold-laden stream, so easily in the forest. And in any forest, whether it be near Cachoeira Porteira, where he was born, or Oriximina, over a hundred miles further south.

"It's easy," he told me. "You know how to get around in a city. You know that such-and-such a street crosses Avenue So-and-so, and that the avenue goes toward the river. And that all the other streets cross it, one after the other. Look, in the forest, every spring goes into a brook, and every brook into a stream, and every stream into a river, like the veins in an arm. For example, if you wanted to leave here and go east, then you leave in the morning with the sun in your face, and to go west, you go with the sun on your back. It's really quite simple.

"The job of a guide," he continued, "is to take the team out, according to the map, only he knows better than the map how to find the minerals. I used to go out with research teams," he said, "head up a river and make a camp. Then three or four men would strike out into the forest with enough food for two weeks or so and a piece of plastic to make a roof at night. And you go with your research equipment. You dig a hole in a brook, get an idea of its configuration, dig there and add some acid to analyze, and already it begins to confess whether it has gold, or tin, or just what. You go along the brook until you find where it starts, then drill there."

Old Ray said he had worked with many geological teams in the past. "I know all the different types of minerals," he said. "I also got a book that describes them."

I asked him how the different companies and government research teams that bought his services knew to contact him, and

Old Ray told me that he had been building up a reputation since the age of twenty-one. "Since that age," he said, "I began to work with people, foreign as well as Brazilian. For some time I worked with an American; I still remember his name, Sargent Smith, and he worked for Chiclets. We'd look for the trees from where you get the gum, and they had a factory in Pendaia. So they all know about me already. Sometimes," he added, "people are jealous of me, but what can I do? It's a gift that I was born with."

Old Ray's parents had been rubber tappers, but by the time he was born, "the market had already closed. That was in 1921. So we had some fields," he said, "and Brazil nuts and palm nuts. When I was older, we cut rosewood to sell." Later, he went to work in the local trading post, making molasses and sugar from the sugarcane his parents grew. Between 1944 and 1948, the family began tapping rubber again, probably as a result of demand created by the war. But the demand subsided again, and Ray moved downriver to Oriximina, where he worked as a carpenter and collected turtle eggs. "After four years of that," he went on, "I went back to Cachoeira Porteira and worked in the post again. And that was where people would find me when they wanted me to show them. I'd find the stands of Brazil nuts for them, and if someone got lost, I'd go out and find the guy." Old Ray told me that he had also hunted jaguars and other large cats, caimans and even *ariranha*, an Amazonian river otter, off and on for years. He recalled the days, for example, when teams of forty or fifty men, in one case two hundred, went out hunting jaguars. "Their skins were very valuable," said Old Ray, "easily worth as much as an ounce of gold. In one trip alone, I'd get eight or ten jaguars, maybe seventy *maracaja* cats and twenty otters. But in 1972, the government brought down a law and stopped everyone from hunting." He told me that the pay wasn't high, but enough to live on, especially before the days of high inflation. "In those days, the poor didn't feel the impact like they do now," he said.

Though he had become used to life in the city, he still missed the life of the forest, and the adventures. "Look, miss," he said, "it so happens that I am accustomed to the jungle. In the city, I always feel longings, I feel bad, a kind of agony. There in the forest, there is health, water. I always feel this longing." He also felt bad about the eventual loss of his skills, as the old woodsmen died and no one cared to take up their profession anymore. "It's all disappearing," he said, "just like the first Indians, the Tupi. Civilization ate up all those Indians. It's the same thing. I feel bad. People don't care about the past, so the past disappears. So much in history disappears, the story of slavery, for example. You ask young people here about slavery and they don't know what you're talking about."

Ideval joined us about halfway through the conversation. He knew the old man quite well, and brought him out on the subject of his dream.

This dream was as much a part of Old Ray's reputation in Oriximiná as were his indubitable skills in the jungle. He had been on a contract in an area called Campos Gerais, an area of small grassy plains and hills. "I had been there before," he recounted. "One night, I was sleeping alone, I didn't see anything, and I had a dream. In this dream, a person showed up, an Indian, and began to speak to me about a chapel made of cut stones with big doors. 'Do you want to go there?' he asked me. 'So let's go, then, but bring Shortie, too. He will also like what there is inside.' And I knew it was gold. So we traveled, and I instructed Shortie to leave markers along the way. We arrived at a stream and I drank some water, and there I saw a stone in the form of a tower with enormous doors."

The Indian told him that the doors were guarded by the spirit of Father Jose Nicolino, a priest who had founded the city of Oriximina in the 1820s. "Everyone thinks he died of malaria," said Old Ray, "but that is not true. He was suffocated, by moving a stone and being killed by escaping gases that had been in there, inside the earth, for millions of years.

"Afterward," the old man continued, "I woke up and asked the aforementioned Shortie to come with me, and we went. But he took along with him his son, a boy of about fifteen. I saw the same trail, the same trees, all marked as in the dream, and finally the stream where the person had showed us the tower. I drank some water again, but my head began to roll and roll, I felt dizzy, and instead of seeing the tower, there was a mountain. When I got back to the city, I still had these headaches and dizzy spells, so I went to the head curer, and he told me that I should have gone just with Shortie, like in the dream. But because he mistrusted me, thought that I might kill him so I wouldn't have to share the gold with him, Shortie had insisted on bringing along his son." Since then, no one had been able to find the Chapel of Gold, guarded by Father Jose Nicolino, although later that day I heard more about it.

We finished our chat with Old Ray and went to Ideval's place for lunch. His mother had prepared a delicious meal of turtle and told me that she knew I was coming that day because there had been a bird, a *vem vem*, in the garden the day before. We watched the results of the elections on television for a while, most of the commentary turning, in rather obvious surprise, around the unexpected win by the Workers' Party in São Paulo.

In the afternoon, Ideval and I went out to look for a man called Odete. We finally found him in the market and took him to a bar for a soft drink. Seu Odete, seventy-seven, was an incredibly tall, thin man, with a physique almost as interesting as his stories of searching for the Chapel of Gold. He had gone looking for it many times, "except that you never got there," he said. Why was he looking for it, I asked him. "Because it's a chapel of gold," he said, "it has gold, except that the priest has to open the doors for you."

Dressed in faded blue jeans and a black, gray and white checked shirt, his waist almost came up to my shoulder. He walked along slightly hunched over like a monkey, his extremely long, skinny arms dangling at his sides. His head, woolly with graying hair, seemed small and round compared to the large body. His ears stuck out like bits of licorice. He didn't remember how he had first heard about the Chapel of Gold. "But it was when I was upriver, hunting alligators," he said. Seu Odete had spent many years hunting alligators, he told us; but had stopped when he was sixty-four. He had also raised cattle for a few years. Now, in spite of his age, he looked after a forest reserve under the direction of the Brazilian Forest Development Institute.

Seu Odete told us about a number of mysterious things that went on at the place where the golden chapel was supposed to be, a place now known as the Hill of Monkeys. He was backed up by two grandchildren, a teenage boy and girl who happened to come along. He told us that people could hear rockets going off on the Hill of Monkeys three times a day, at midday, at six and at eight o'clock precisely, as well as voices praying. These noises could be heard most clearly, he told us, in May. He also spoke of strange stones that looked as though they had been cut very neatly, one with the footprint of a small creature or child. But whenever anyone tried to cut the stones, they always crumbled. What was more, these stones always moved back to their original place when they were taken away. Once someone had removed the stones, built a corral around the cleared space and the next morning found all the stones inside it again.

Seu Odete remembered when Oriximina was just a small place, so small that "when you killed a cow, there was enough meat to go around for the whole place," he said. "There was just this street here and two others going up. You know where the Bank of Brazil is? Well, that was all forest." When I asked him how many children he had, he said, "I'm ashamed to tell you," but finally admitted he had twenty-seven. As we were paying for our drinks, the owner of the bar came up to our table, a jovial man needing a shave, and said jokingly, "Miss, I just have to tell you one thing. It's all lies."

In Santarém the next day, I bought a ticket for Manaus on a boat called the *Rio Guama*. It was early evening when we pulled away from shore, and I could see the line of stores and warehouses, the shops stocked with supplies for gold prospectors, the flashing neon sign of the San Rio clothing store, the line of boats all along the harbor.

At 4 A.M., we docked in Obidos, and I could hear a woman tell her friend, "Oh, it looks like we'll be here for a while. They've got a whole lot of cassava meal to load on." An hour and a half later, the ship's cook poked my foot to wake me up and said, "*Café*."

It was a two-day trip to Manaus. I got to know the captain on this ship, a short, balding man with a mustache, called Pedro Paulo Pereira. Captain Pereira told me that he encountered two main problems while navigating. In summer, when the water was low, he had to be careful not to hit sandbars, which could stall a ship for days. In winter, when the water was high and it rained a great deal, there were big logs and tree trunks, which broke away from the shore and got swept down-river. He showed me the ship's log, and said there were seventy-six passengers on the *Rio Guama*, and nine crew. They were carrying several tons of corn and cassava meal, also oranges, canisters of propane gas for welding, and two cars.

We were officially in the state of Amazonas by then. We stopped first in Parintins, with its floating metal dock. It looked like a fairly large town of old buildings with white railings, a row of square turn-of-the-century facades in pastel, and a gray church with a red cupola on its tower. And closer to Manaus, we pulled up against the floating dock of Itacoatiara, which was connected by a girdered bridge to the shore. I watched two people on a bicycle come down the hill in front of an old four-story building decorated with rows of narrow windows. They rode through the gates and down the bridge, an old man wearing a straw hat perched like a doll on the back, oblivious to all the bumps. The bicycle came to a quick halt on the dock, and the old man jumped off and ran down to the *Rio Guamá*, although he needn't have worried: the crew was still unloading sacks of cassava meal onto the lower deck.

On my last evening on board, I asked Captain Pereira if he had seen any dolphins. "Sheesh, lots," he replied emphatically. "Well, I haven't seen a single one," I said, "and I've been looking since Belém." "You can see them in the evening," said Pereira, "just as dusk is falling. You can see lots of them then."

Following his advice, I stood on the bow as we headed westward through a narrow channel. All around us, the mounded shore was thickly carpeted with green, a darker green wall of trees behind looking like an enchanted forest in the approaching dusk. The gold of the setting sun through the clouds made a stained-glass triptych on the water. A few tiny houses and cattle were visible on the shore as we passed an island, tidy rows of beans quilted into the soft, rich silt. After a few minutes, I saw a splash several feet ahead of us. Pereira, who was at the wheel, gave his bell a gentle ring to alert me. Soon I saw a half dozen more dolphins, emerging as if part of the water itself, then diving quickly. It was as if they swam just near enough to the surface to discreetly show their glistening backs of purple-gray, their dorsal fins slicing cleanly through the river.

NINE

〰〰〰

THE PARIS OF THE TROPICS

WE ARRIVED IN MANAUS EARLY on a Sunday morning, so early that it was not yet dawn. While I tried to get a little more sleep, the other passengers rolled up their hammocks. Mothers gathered their children, and the would-be gold prospectors on the men's half of the boat began to play their transistor radios very loudly.

Our arrival in the city, once touted as the Paris of the Tropics, had little of the exotic about it, and even less of Paris, for that matter. Tall, nondescript buildings and parabolic antennae rose in the distance. A mud land led from the half-finished concrete dock, where we disembarked, past a few parked taxicabs and troops of black buzzards, looking like old judges in stained wigs, to a street of closed-up shops.

There may still be those who, when you say the word "Manaus," close their eyes and think of its famous domed opera house, but a truer image would be, perhaps, the many streams, their banks gray with shacks, that cut through the city, or even its large industrial park. Manaus is a city whose dubious destiny is to always be a boomtown, first rubber, now light industry. The first boom brought the city electric streetcars, the opera, the Rio Negro Palace and a host of similarly sumptuous neoclassical colossi; the *Zona Franca,* or "Free Zone," which refers to the city's tax-free status, has brought it half-completed skyscrapers blackening in the damp, enough household appliances to furnish everyone in the country with a television set, and a population of more than a million.

Because it was a Sunday, there was not much traffic in the streets, and the usual crowds that thronged the city's sidewalks had vanished. Without the four-lane traffic and masses of people to sully the view, it should have been easy to look at Manaus and decide whether or not to like it.

Downtown, the few remaining row buildings of the twenties and thirties, their tall facades dignified with narrow windows and bits of ornate trim, were scattered among hopelessly ugly blocks of concrete and glass. A big yellow cathedral sat on a hill. It dominated a patchwork quilt of grass and trees, intersected by sidewalks and dirty stone walls and littered with all kinds of stands and stalls. Beggars huddled on park benches beneath lengths of plastic sheeting at the bottom of the hill, bubble-roofed bus stops spread in every direction, and beyond them, the docks presented an unvarying face of ribbed metal and concrete buildings.

The elegant mansions of Eduardo Gomes Street had all been torn down and replaced with department stores, fast-food outlets and travel agencies. The once roseate opera house had been painted gray, like all state government buildings. And if you walked far enough along Sete de Setembro Avenue, you crossed three streams emptying into the river, each spreading like a green eruption between hundreds of wooden shacks spotted with heaped-up mounds of garbage.

I walked down Santa Cruz and arrived at the old cast-iron market, which is considered one of the city's main tourist attractions. Rusted and degenerating, the once elaborate structure is as full of stalls outside as inside, the whole place redolent with the odor of rotting produce and car fumes seeping into the steamy air. So many vendors spill onto the sidewalk, where the carbon monoxide can neatly coat their fruits and vegetables before some unfortunate buys them, that the sidewalk becomes impassable. Beside the market, a dock was under construction, prickly with bent and rusted iron rods. Until its completion, only a muddy lane, part of it submerged under filthy water thick with rotting vegetables and dead fish, led to a floating dock. Boatmen rowed you across for the equivalent of a dime, bringing you to a metal platform crowded with stevedores filling or emptying the holds of riverboats bound for Parintins, Obidos and Porto Velho.

Not that all the grandeur of the past was lost. Across from the domed and colonnaded opera, the imposing, elongated Palace of Justice still flaunted its balustrades and plaster eagles; farther down, the headquarters of the once ultraexclusive Ideal Clube, pale green with white trim, sat like a slab of lime Jell-O on the sidewalk.

Balbi Square, better known as Police Square because of the nearby barracks, was ringed with tall, leafy trees and filled with fountains, little bridges and a fancy old band shell. From the newspaper stalls along the sidewalks, you could buy all the major dailies from Rio and São Paulo. And a good thing, too, considering that local papers were thin and pontificatory, and invariably portrayed a dead body on the front page.

The governor's residence on Sete de Setembro, the Rio Negro Palace, resembled some sort of Mediterranean wedding cake, its garden dotted with bronze angels. But its magnificence was turned into a bad, antique joke by its miserable surroundings and by its violent history. It was built by a German rubber baron named Sholz, who was said to have murdered his unfaithful young wife inside its marble halls and to have put out her eyes.

After several visits to the city, I had to admit that Manaus was a place difficult to admire.

The invention of vulcanization and the subsequent demand for raw latex from the Amazon had originally transformed Manaus from a few shacks grouped around an old fort into an elegant city, famed for its orderliness and comfort. Never very big in either population or size until the industrial boom, it became an urban concentration of incredible wealth. The cobblestones for its streets were imported from France; its floating metal dock came from Britain. The rubber barons built themselves palatial homes and outfitted them with the best Europe had to offer — grand pianos, crystal chandeliers, marble bathrooms — and vied with each other to show off their extravagances. According to one story, probably apocryphal, some millionaires even sent their laundry to Europe. Certainly money was no object in a town overflowing with champagne, jeweled ladies and imported culture.

As Brazilian novelist Marcio Souza described it to me while we chatted in his beachfront apartment in Rio, "Manaus was always a very charming town. The dream of the rubber boom was to make it a sort of tropical Paris. Well, I didn't live in a tropical Paris, but a sort of Port au Prince. Well, now it's not even that. It's a combination of Miami and Calcutta."

Seen through his eyes — either in his recollections of what it was like to grow up there, or in his satiric novels — the end of the rubber boom seems to have been as fantastic as the boom itself. "I mean, can you imagine a society that was living in slow motion for fifty years?" asked Marcio. "My father, for example, was a printer, and there were times when he went three, four or five months without pay. Money wasn't circulating in the fifties. They went back to exchange.

"And there was no electricity", said Marcio. "One of the first cities in Latin America to get electricity, to install electric trams and they didn't have it when I was a boy. It all stopped. There wasn't money to fix the generators, which belonged to the British, who just went away and left them. So all during my childhood, I studied at night with a kerosene lantern."

In a novel yet to be published in English, Marcio described the post-boom years in Manaus with typical verve. "In the flooded streets, businessmen ran about like crazy men after the moneylenders. It was the economy of the Stone Age. At the Department of the Interior and Justice, the staff passed the office hours looking after a garden. The Department of Education and Culture specialized in citruses and produced lemons and earth oranges. The Department of Health was developing a noisome production of excellent Leghorn laying hens. The inter-exchange was perfect among the various modalities of domestic production."

Somehow, said Marcio, this strange "un-economy" kept people going. "The rich weren't so rich to be different," he recalled, "and at the same time, people were not so poor they were starving. There wasn't much violence, and when there was a murder, we'd talk about it all year. But at the same time we were connected to the world. There were the big ships in harbor and always direct flights to other countries."

Another strange thing about Manaus, said Marcio, was the lack of connection to the jungle, "because people hate the jungle. They tear it down." He admitted that whenever the acting company he was part of in the sixties and seventies traveled the rivers to other towns, he really missed the city. He was quite paranoid about drowning as well. "I always used to travel with just two bags," he told me. "One held a whole lot of books, and the other a magnificent life jacket, bright yellow, with little lights that lit up in the water. Actually, you should take advantage of the Free Zone when you're in Manaus," he added, "and buy one for yourself. Those boats are dangerous, you know, and you can get good life jackets these days."

But the biggest difference between then and now, said Marcio, was the size of Manaus since the Free Zone was set up. When he was growing up, the city was really just a small town. "My father knew everybody," said Marcio. "Once a cousin arrived from Rio without our address, and he just walked up to one of the cab drivers at the airport, gave him my father's name and was driven right to our door. It was a town of about fifty thousand people. And suddenly, in 1967, in three years, Manaus increased sixfold and they destroyed the city I knew."

The city was still a place where miracles and strange things happened, where the edges of reality tended to blur with the fantastic. As Marcio put it, "There are so many great things happening in the Amazon that I could write an entire encyclopedia, a mad encyclopedia." There is a ghost stalking the corridors of the famous opera house, a young man in eighteenth-century dress, believed to be a traveling actor who caught yellow fever and died. He was seen frequently and had almost become a familiar figure to the theater's old janitor before he retired. It is said that the ghost of the murdered Senhora Sholz frequents the Rio Negro Palace, a ghoulish sight without her eyes, importuning young guards to follow her. And, according to Marcio, there had always been talk of a ghost on the Educandos Bridge — "That is," he joked, "if it hasn't been run over by all the traffic by now."

It is also common in Manaus, indeed throughout the Amazon, to attribute miracles to the dead, especially if they had been unusual persons or had come to some spectacular end. This tendency was most evident when I visited the city's oldest graveyard, St. John the Baptist Cemetery. The cemetery, which covers several city blocks — rather than the horrid market building — should be the chief tourist attraction in Manaus.

Its entrance on Alvaro Maia Boulevard was an ornate roofed gate, resembling a loggia, with several panes of glass broken or missing altogether from the cast-iron roof. Inside, the rows of mausoleums displayed a history of funerary fashion, from the ornate Gothic structures near the gate to the gigantic pair of praying hands in Block Two, which were painted a bright, fleshy pink. Symbols of various religions and cultures poked through the damp foliage and statuary: crosses, Stars of David, crescent moons and stars. Little ceramic photographs were embedded among tiles and carved stonework. The cemetery staff have their work cut out for them: they must constantly scythe and hack away the trees, vines and weeds that invade the fenced-in tombstones and break apart ancient crypts and walls and closet-sized chapels.

I visited the cemetery on a quiet, rainy Saturday. Curious about a number of miracle-working tombs, I began with the most famous, that of a young woman named Etelvina Alenquer, better known as Santa Etelvina. It was an absurd, modernist structure with walls of glass and pale blue stucco. Enclosed in a palisade of metal stakes, the shrine was a low chapel with a sweeping blue roof topped by a cement cross, its panes of glass dirty with soot. Inside, the chapel was littered with junk, torn school notebooks, scraps of paper, bits of clothing, plastic flowers and a few real ones, black and rotting. There was a strong odor of wax as dozens of candles, in spite of the rain, burned and guttered on the blackened pavement, forming dirty, thick pools of molten wax.

The inscription on a big marble slab related that Etelvina was born in the state of Ceará in 1884 and found dead in the Campos Sales section of the city on St. Patrick's Day, 1901. "A perverse hand tore out her life," read the inscription, "the piety of the people of Manaus has put up this monument for her, now amplified by Manaus city hall."

The story goes that Etelvina was attacked by an amorous young soldier, the "perverse hand," who, when she refused to let him have his way with her, stabbed her to death. Now there is even a church named after her; hundreds of people attest to her response to their requests for help, and she is referred to as Saint Etelvina, although she is not officially recognized as such by the Church.

Then there was the grave of Delmo Pereira, "the student martyr." This was a small, waist-high rectangle of cement planted with yellow flowers. Delmo was a young man who was killed in 1951 by a group of irate taxi drivers. It seems that Delmo, rejected by his father and stepmother, got in with a bad bunch who hijacked a taxi one night and killed the driver. Only Delmo was found out, and the other boys, all from influential families, got away. When Delmo was being taken to prison, the taxi drivers of Manaus surrounded the police wagon, took him out and killed him. According to the wife of the president of the Amazonian Academy of Letters, who described the event for me, they beat him up and then ran over him several times with their cars. "In the end," she said, "he was all in pieces. His coffin was no bigger than this, look." And she held her hands about two feet apart.

Eventually Delmo, like Etelvina, began to work miracles and acquired quite a following. I asked the cemetery staff about it. One old man told me that Delmo had been providing miraculous intercessions at least since he began working there, in 1961. He also told me that there was another tomb where people prayed for miracles, that of a little girl "who fell out of a plane." In fact, the child had died in a plane crash in the sixties, but her tomb was also littered with photographs and tokens of gratitude.

The other famous tomb in St. John the Baptist is that of the Rabbi Moyal. It was a nondescript stone slab littered with pebbles, bits of broken brick and fading plastic flowers. The inscription on the tombstone related, in both Portuguese and Hebrew, how Rabbi N. Moyal died in Amazonas of Spanish flu in 1912. Encrusting the wall around the tomb, dozens of succinct little plaques expressed anonymous gratitude to the *ribbi* for his celestial aid. Local newspapers also carried occasional messages of thanks in their classified sections, more proof of the easy coexistence of the supernatural with Manaus' seedy multinational progress.

Later, I got more information about the rabbi's tomb from Inacio Obadia, at the city's synagogue. Inacio, a bearded young man with glasses, was the religious director of Manaus' small Sephardic community. He told me that Rabbi Moyal had arrived in the Amazon in 1909 and had traveled up and down the rivers, asking for donations from Jewish families for a theological school in Jerusalem. Many years later, he said, when word of the miracles began to circulate, "the Jews here were taken by surprise. It wasn't them who discovered that he could work miracles. Suddenly people began to ask for things and these people were answered. If they were not, it wasn't noticed."

The custom of leaving bits of brick and pebbles on the tombstone is a Moroccan Jewish custom, he added. "When we visit the tomb of a relative or a friend, we leave a stone to say we have been there. And when people saw the Jews put a pebble on the tomb, they'd go and put one on, too."

Like much of the Amazon's varied immigrant population — the Syrians and Lebanese, the Japanese, Spanish and the Portuguese — the Moroccan Jews arrived in the Amazon in the early to mid-nineteenth century, when it was an unknown and mysterious place, but one that seemed to offer great possibilities. According to Inacio, Morocco was going through upheavals and economic hardships then. Well-educated young men had few opportunities. A few struck out, along with Iberian settlers and adventurers, and soon letters came back from Brazil enticing more of them to leave. "They heard that it was an El Dorado over here," said Inacio, "an explosion of money, but most of the time, of course, it wasn't true. My grandmother, for example, used to tell us what a shock she had when she first arrived. She came via Europe on a steamship and went to live in a wooden *palafitte* on the river."

Many Jewish families settled in tiny communities along the various rivers, from Belém all the way to Guajará-Mirim on the Bolivian border, trading goods with local Europeans or Indians in return for the so-called wilderness drugs, products such as quinine, cinnamon, clove, ipecac root and so on. When the rubber boom started, they began to trade for rubber. Eventually, however, they left these isolated spots and moved to the cities. "The community here now is the fruit of all the communities of Amazonia," said Inacio, "from the time when each small place had a Jewish community."

It was difficult, he admitted, almost 150 years later, for the Sephardic Jews to retain their culture. The communities in Manaus and Belém were very small, no more than a hundred families each; many had moved to the south, to cities such as Rio and São Paulo. Even the language they spoke, *rakitiia*, was almost lost. "Without schools," said Inacio, who was trying to establish one, "there is no transmission of our cultural legacy. When our grandparents came from Morocco, they carried a huge cultural baggage, a very strong religion. But there was a break, a rupture, in passing this on to their children. With each new generation, there is a weakening."

The day I arrived in Manaus on the *Rio Guama*, the final votes were being counted from the previous week's municipal elections. The loser, a corrupt ex-governor, immortalized as a dolphin in one of Marcio Souza's particularly scathing novels, *The Resistible Rise of the Tucuxi Dolphin*, attracted as much attention in the news media as the winner. Gilberto Mestrinho, the dolphin, went on television that night expected to announce his retirement from politics. But in a classic switch, he declared that he was going to run for governor again in federal elections the following year. "It is the party people are disenchanted with," he summarized, "not me."

When Mestrinho was first elected governor of Amazonas in 1959, a ballot box went missing while being transported by river to Manaus. Its loss may have helped Mestrinho to win. When questioned about it, he said that a dolphin must have leaped up and carried the box to the river's depths. Ever since then, he was nicknamed "the dolphin," the Tucuxi dolphin.

It was because of Mestrinho — who governed from 1959 to 1964, and then again from 1982 to 1986 — that Marcio left Manaus and hied off to Rio. After *The Tucuxi Dolphin* was published, even his parents received threats, and Marcio took them seriously.

The book was a big hit in Manaus, however. Marcio told me that people used to stop him on the street, saying, "Hey, you missed the story about the time the dolphin . . . ." and gave him enough stories to fill another book or two.

The night after I arrived, I went out for a beer with a friend of Marcio's, a schoolteacher of perhaps forty. Ediney Azancoth was a short man, talkative and friendly, with a marvelous sense of humor. He was of Moroccan Jewish descent, but his family had converted to Catholicism a generation or two back. Ediney had never left Manaus, but he was known throughout Brazil, probably the world, because every Souza novel has a character in it called Ediney Azancoth. ("It's a kind of a joke," Marcio had said, with a Cheshire cat smile.)

The real Ediney and I went for a beer to a bar called the Nazaré in St. Sebastian Square, a popular watering hole for young people and artists. It was a funny, lethargic place, a whiff of the past, full of red tin tables and chairs that spilled out its tall, narrow doors onto the sidewalk. Behind the old wooden bar stood an ancient icebox, its defunct motor taken out and deposited on top. Large ceiling fans whirled lazily overhead, while customers slapped down dominoes with a loud clack. The establishment was run by a family, three generations of men working the bar and the tables, all resembling one another.

Ediney's friendship with Marcio stemmed from the days when the two participated in an innovative theater group. They traveled along the Amazon to small towns to perform the plays they wrote themselves.

Opening nights often took place in the opera in Manaus. It was obvious from the way he talked about those years that Ediney missed them. He told me how the group had started in 1968, looking for ways to take popular culture and Indian legends and look at them in a political way. Their first two plays, both based on Indian legends, were very popular. The first, *The Passion of Ajuricaba*, was written by Marcio, and *Dessana, Dessana*, an Indian opera, resulted from a collaboration between Marcio and the poet Aldisio Figueiras. Then came two more productions, *Latex Follies* and *There's a Piranha in the Piranca*, and these raised the ire of the local bourgeoisie.

"Those two plays made a lot of people uncomfortable," said Ediney. "I remember during performances of *Latex Follies*, you could hear seats clacking in the audience when people got angry and left. And one local journalist said the play was insulting to our region's forebears."

The second play had originally been entitled *Zona Franca, Mon Amour*, but they were forced to change the title by military censors. It annoyed a lot of people who were doing very well out of the Free Zone policy. Both plays were harbingers of what was to come. In 1982, the group put on a play called *The Resistible Rise of the Tucuxi Dolphin*, just when Mestrinho was beginning his comeback in Manaus. "Marcio and I started to talk about Mestrinho, and Marcio asked me about some of the stories that used to go around the city in the fifties," said Ediney. "So he began to write the play. He'd come into the theater once he'd written a few pages and read them out to us. But Mestrinho put pressure on the media not to publish ads or give the play any attention. They closed the theater we used to use, and we had to perform in a school, after ten o'clock at night. Even so, it was a success. We had sold-out shows for three weeks."

Nonetheless, the performance spelled the end of their group. The foundation that funded them cut off support, in spite of letters from respected film and theater people all over Brazil. Local intellectuals did not support the group, however, and several members left in disgust. Eventually, Marcio felt he had to leave as well.

Now Ediney worked for the Department of Education. "Sometimes, a few of us talk about getting together again," he told me, "but we still don't have any theater space, and I don't really believe it's ever going to happen."

But as we chatted over our brown liter bottles of beer, people kept coming up to Ediney and slapping him on the back. "I bet you must be celebrating," they would say. "The dolphin finally lost an election."

I probably came closest to the soul of modern Manaus the next day, in the duty-free shopping area, where I went looking for a cheap camera and tape recorder to replace those that had been stolen in Belém. The Free Zone was pretty much confined to a section of the old town, squeezed between the harbor and cathedral, one shop after another packed into the narrow streets. The shops were busy with shoppers from all over the country who were buying televisions, electric fans and stereos for as much as 40 percent less than they cost in the rest of Brazil. The selection of goods was quite amazing. I kept thinking that I would never see so many things for sale in any city within a five-hundred-mile radius, maybe not even in São Paulo.

The area was full of people six days a week. Tourists staying at the posh Hotel Tropical came to shop or arrange jungle excursions at the many travel agencies. Perched at small desks in whatever shade they could find, unofficial scribes sold illegal lottery tickets and their services in filling out government forms. Snack booths advertised every kind of fruit juice imaginable. The sidewalks were full of ambulatory vendors, young men with twenty watches around their arms. During my search for the cheapest tape recorder and camera possible, I was offered everything from condoms to Chanel No. 5.

As often happens in Manaus, a rainstorm broke out while I was looking around, a sudden massive downpour. The sky turned dark and opened up, and the streets filled rapidly with rushing streams of water, as if the Amazon River itself had invaded the city. The streams grew to reach the top of a car's tires, then abated and suddenly stopped. The air quickly resumed that thick feeling of heat and humidity, like a piece of velvet against the cheek.

When the rain let up, I dropped in at the Amazonas Commercial Association and spoke to its president, Jorge Loureiro. A bespectacled, almost cherubic-looking man in his late forties, the owner of a paint and office supplies business, Loureiro believed that the Free Zone was the only thing that could have saved Manaus and its moldering palaces from oblivion. "After the rubber boom," he said, "the city began to empty out. People left, and Amazonas was abandoned, an area without any economic activity whatsoever. The Free Zone is the result of a political decision on the part of the government to keep Amazonas for Brazil." The statement was an ironic one, since the Free Zone was overrun by companies such as Honda, Mitsubishi, Philips, Sharp and a host of other multinationals.

The military government decided to make Manaus into a Free Zone in 1967, Loureiro told me. Companies that took advantage of the unusual location were to be exempt from customs duties and four federal taxes, including income tax. Subsidized land was made available in the industrial park, where the roads were paved, and telex and telephone lines installed. Now there were more than four hundred factories there, employing an estimated seventy thousand workers who fabricated among other items electrical appliances, computer components, watches and cameras. In most cases, the parts were shipped in, put together and shipped out again, doing, according to an article in the *Jornal do Brasil*, $5 billion worth of business a year. Meanwhile, the annual tax-rebate bill for the Brazilian government was estimated at a whopping $1.2 billion U.S, this in a country where children still died of diarrhea.

While the establishment of the Free Zone saved the hides of the old rubber aristocracy and gave rise to a whole new class of managers and entrepreneurs, the Free Zone has not been without its critics. They have pointed out that the Free Zone did not make enough use of local resources, did nothing to develop the region and had attracted too many people to the city for whom there was not enough housing and services. One such critic was the president of the Federal University of Amazonas. I spoke to him in his office in an unattractive modern building on Getúlio Vargas Avenue.

Roberto Viera was an economist and urban planner with a degree from Oxford. With the city's industry locked into making products that were relatively small, light and of high value, he said, the Free Zone did more for the businessmen of São Paulo, who could avoid taxes just by setting up an office in the city, than for the people of Manaus. "The government's investment in industry here has not been accompanied by a corresponding investment in the city," said Viera, "in hospitals, schools, transport and housing. Here at the university, for example, we are still using antiquated lab equipment and are short of teachers, while the Industrial Zone is like an enclave of modernity in a backward city."

A far more trenchant critic of the Free Zone was another professor at the university, Marlene Pardo, who had carried out an exhaustive study of working conditions in the zone. The mother of three grown children, she looked quite youthful with her plump face and long reddish hair tied back in a ponytail, but tired after her day's work. I met her at her apartment in one of the new middle-class housing compounds that have sprung up in the city.

According to Marlene, 70 percent or more of the labor used in the Free Zone was female. "The average age of the women working there is between twenty and twenty-three, and they can start as young as fourteen. A female worker of thirty in Manaus is already old; it's very wearisome work, extremely routine, a work day that is both extensive and intensive. It is like England was, perhaps, a hundred years ago."

One of the worst aspects of this routine for the Free Zone workers, Marlene discovered, was the way it destroyed their old way of life. Whether in the forest or on the riverbank, their old lives were based on seasons, controlled by their needs and will. "People leave there and come here," Marlene said, "and have to change their habits, their time, their whole culture. They must pass the whole day, either standing or sitting, in one place in a line. The change is psychologically violent, also because it is imposed so rapidly."

Migrants to the city were all too often pushed off their land and out of the forest, said Marlene. Her studies had shown that the filthy, overcrowded Manaus of today, with its twenty-seven slums, was the direct result of a policy of bringing people in from the countryside, to exploit their labor in industry. Indeed, this was the end Brazil's rulers had in mind for the rubber tappers, such as those I had met in Acre. And it was clear that it was just such a destiny against which they were fighting, much as they were fighting the destruction of the rain forest.

Although so much of their work force was composed of women, and although the law stipulated that factories employing more than thirty workers had to provide day care, "less than 5 percent of the factories in Manaus actually do so," said Marlene. "Those that do only provide what the people here call 'oven day care,' that is, dozens of children in a small space, badly looked after and improperly fed. The unions have denounced these places to the Ministry of Labor, but none have been closed down."

Most businesses actively discourage women from having children. "Women," she said, "must prove that they are not pregnant to get a job, and sometimes that they have no children. The companies think that the women will miss work too much if they have children at home. They want young, strong, single women. Birth-control pills are handed out in the work place, and abortions are also encouraged. It really is an incredible situation, but women are often the heads of their households here, and they will submit themselves to almost anything to keep their jobs and feed their children. Employers know that women will submit to far worse conditions than men, that's one reason they like them."

Labor contractors were frequently used by the companies, she added. "There are at least twelve such agencies in Manaus, employing fifteen thousand workers. Their jobs are temporary and the salaries below average because the agency takes a cut." The average salary in the Free Zone, she estimated, was one and a half times the official minimum salary, or about $75 U.S. a month.

According to the *Jornal do Brasil*, salaries in Manaus were 200 percent lower than in São Paulo. Workers have often been forced to work overtime without pay (Brazil only brought in a law forcing companies to pay overtime in 1988); accidents were frequent and health risks high. "In the watch factories, for example," said Marlene, "workers spend eight hours a day filing glass, absorbing a lot of glass dust into their lungs. Fumes from paint and solvents are common on the factory floor, and the temperature barbarously high."

In spite of such conditions, it was extremely difficult for the workers to organize into unions, Marlene told me. "Employers keep lists of those who attend meetings, and anyone who participates will never find another job in the Free Zone. Already in Manaus, for every employed person, there are two unemployed."

Marlene felt that the Free Zone policy was formulated for no other reason than to attend to the needs of big business and multinationals who sought to remain competitive by keeping their labor costs low. For her, the idea of calling such a system "development" was absurd. Echoing Lucio Flavio Pinto in Belém, she said, "The government's policies for the Amazon have never tried to create conditions that would root economic development in the products of the Amazon, things like wood, fruit, cacao, fish and jute. Why is there no food processing here," she asked, "or fruit juice and concentrates, or furniture making? Why is most of the food in Manaus imported? The capital invested here does not justify the level of jobs created, nor does it generate conditions of autonomy. It is an artificial model. It generates a lot of profit, but no economic autonomy or social benefits for the people."

It was a far cry from the hellish world described by Marlene to the luxurious home of Jorge Loureiro's sixty-five-year-old-mother, Dona Chloe, whom Marcio Souza had suggested I visit. Dona Chloe had just written a cookbook, which had somehow grown into an autobiography, a passage through lost times.

She lived in a four-story mansion of cream-colored stucco with tall windows and elaborate white trim, standing across from the opera. It was built in 1912, the year after Brazil reached its all-time record for rubber production of almost 45,000 tons (over 40 310 tonnes).

I was admitted through ornate brass and iron double doors and led up a flight of tiled steps into a lounge furnished with antiques. Four mirrored cabinets of jacaranda wood stood against the walls. One held the Baccarat crystal Dona Chloe was given as a wedding present. Another glowed with blue glass from Venice. The parquet flooring was covered with Turkish rugs, and much of the furniture was of exotic wood, woven with caning or upholstered in brocade. We moved to the marble-topped dining-room table, tiny porcelain cups of coffee were preferred, and we talked about Dona Chloe's life.

She had grown up in the town of Sena Madureira, in Acre, where her father, originally from Recife, was a lawyer who eventually became the town magistrate. "He was an extraordinary man, a writer and a poet," she said of him. "It was a pity that my father had to go to Acre. It is a region that has always been forgotten in Brazil." Nonetheless, her father had made a good living working as a lawyer for various large firms in Acre. "He earned a lot of money, but he never saved anything," she said. "We lived with a great deal of comfort."

Dona Chloe's recollections were of a refined Amazonia. She remembered parties, the orchestra tuning up, a turn with her father on the dance floor, the custom of asking the electric company to leave the lights on for a couple of hours longer than usual. She described in great detail the trip she took, at the age of six, to Manaus, "which to me seemed to smell of *tucumare* fish and *cupuaçu*," a delicious, rather acrid fruit. She also remembered the Syrian merchant who came to visit every evening; falling asleep in an armchair; and being frightened of the papier-mâché masks hung on the streets of Sena Madureira for carnival. And throughout it all, she remembered the dishes her mother and the family cook, João, used to prepare: cassava cake, genipap liqueur, stuffed suckling pigs, *pirarucu* in coconut milk, and sweets made with all kinds of regional fruits — green mangoes, cashew, jack-fruit, *jambo* and *cupuaçu*.

In 1933, the family moved to Manaus so the children could go to school; her father stayed in Sena Madureira. The family lived in a large house across the street from the house Dona Chloe lived in now, and she studied piano, typing and "recitation."

"When the ship moored in the port of Manaus," she said, "I was enchanted with all the movement and the beauty of the houses. Electric streetcars, automobiles, lovely ice-cream shops, houses of fashion, hat shops, jewelers, all kinds of unusual things for me." On the street, fishmongers sold fish and quartered turtles from wooden tables. On Sunday afternoons, the family would go to General Osorio Square, sit in the shade in wicker chairs and listen to waltzes played by a military band. "I miss those times so much," she said, "they really were good times."

I asked Dona Chloe how life had changed since the implantation of the Free Zone. "Our life has changed in the following way," she said. "We always used to have good servants. And now these people have been transformed into industrial workers. So it started there; the drama is exactly that. A lot of social problems." Everyone, she said, missed the small city where everyone knew each other. High society had changed completely. "They are new people, completely different," she said. "But from time to time, we invite people, friends, you know, people from the traditional families. From outside, no. We normally just see people from the traditional families living here in Manaus."

After our chat, Dona Chloe showed me around the house, an undoubtedly splendid place, evocative of the rubber boom. There was a pink sitting room in the front with a tiered ceiling painted with flowers, velvet- and brocade-upholstered furniture, and two large oil paintings. Beside it was the music room, a blue room with a white piano and two armchairs of white brocade. We walked to the stairway, a steep, banistered affair, which Dona Chloe eschewed in favor of a small, efficient elevator. Up we went to the top floor with its four bedrooms, each connecting to the other through narrow white doors, and each with a heavily carved wooden bed placed squarely in the center of the room. A wide balcony led off the main bedroom, where the pale gold Byzantine dome of the opera suddenly reared into view. The house also had a rather remarkable bathroom, or rather a bathroom with a remarkable shower. It was a metal semicircular cage, with three large ceramic knobs, and the bather was sprayed from all around. It was made in Scotland, Dona Chloe told me, and she always invited guests to have a look at it.

Dona Chloe also wanted me to go with her to visit what she kept referring to as "the club." The following day, her chauffeur driving, we set off. The club, it turned out, was part of an exclusive housing complex her sons were constructing, not far from the city's municipal beach, which the Loureiro family had donated to the municipality, and the luxurious Hotel Tropical, which also sat on land that had once belonged to the family. They were cutting up and selling what remained as a new neighborhood called Jardim das Americas. Only a few homes had been built so far, but the whole area had been planted with grass and landscaped, the streets paved and named after various nations of the Western Hemisphere.

It was a housing project for the very wealthy, to be staffed by security guards and surrounded by a metal fence. There was also a modern private clubhouse — "the club" Dona Chloe had been referring to, a beautifully tiled bar and two swimming pools. Innumerable flights of steps led down through the foliage to the shore, and well-placed little belvederes overlooked the coffee-colored waters of the Rio Negro. Wide expanses of lawn had been planted everywhere, and flowering trees were set out in tidy rows. There was a large boathouse with a long winch-run ramp for the lowering of cruisers into the river. It all reminded me of the opera, another absurd, luxurious and expensive project set in the jungle. But I also felt assailed by all the brightness; the newly planted trees along the curving avenues seemed to shrink in the powerful heat. Their torsos bare and sweating beneath the oppressive sun, workmen toiled in the flower beds and at the few small construction sites. I couldn't help but wonder how much they earned. But it was a problem getting a cook for the club, Dona Chloe told me. The one they had could make only two common regional dishes, "and people are getting bored. It really is difficult to find good people," she said again. "You no sooner train them and then . . ."

TEN

~~~~~~~

WITH THE YANOMAMI

I ARRIVED IN BOA VISTA AFTER a bus ride of about nineteen hours. The bus had been crowded with men in brightly colored fake-velvet hats and gold nuggets on chains — the sure sign of a prospector — and women and crying children. A woman across the aisle from me, who had boarded the bus on the outskirts of Manaus, carried only a glass and a towel, as if just going to the bathroom rather than another state. She had played *lambada* dance music all night on her companion's tape recorder.

Boa Vista is the capital of Roraima, newly transformed from a territory into a state. Passing through miserable little settlements that clung to the recently paved highway like rotten fruit, the place was the most remote and backward I had yet seen. Because of its remoteness, however — it forms a peak on the very top of Brazil and juts into Venezuela and the Guianas — Roraima and parts of northern Amazonas are home to the last large primitive tribe in the Western Hemisphere, the Yanomami.

Other tribes in Roraima, such as the Wapixana and the Macuxi, dealt with traders and missionaries in the past, but the Yanomami had always avoided the white man. Only recently had they taken to using metal; the use even of shotguns for hunting was extremely rare. There were some nine thousand Yanomami in Brazil and Venezuela, wandering in small groups through the dense equatorial forest that sustained them. They moved every five years or so, building large palm thatch houses, called *malocas*, and tilling small gardens in their temporary settlements.

In 1975, the Brazilian government carried out extensive radar research in the area and discovered deposits of gold, cassiterite and uranium, all of it on Yanomami land. But further geological studies indicated that mining these metals would not be cost effective in such a remote area. Once again, their geography had kept the Yanomami safe, but only for another ten years. No one had anticipated the arrival of miners of a different type, hordes of them, poor, dispossessed, or merely adventurous, who needed little infrastructure to penetrate the forest and its rivers. Scattered through the jungle, they dredged for gold, which had gone up in value, and provided an effective hedge against Brazil's ever-worsening inflation.

By 1987, the state was inundated with gold prospectors. Small planes by the score made frequent trips between Boa Vista and places that had never been on a map before — Paapiu, Wai-wai, Uaiacas, Cutaiba — carrying motorized pumps, food supplies and men. Boa Vista, the sleepy capital of a state whose economy was based on ranching on the savannah-like *campo* which distinguished the Amazon basin there, vibrated with activity. Its boardinghouses and cheap hotels filled up with the thousands of men who arrived, day after day, by bus or plane, looking for a way into the jungle.

Gold-buying houses, with their scales and the chimney stoves for burning off excess mercury and other impurities from the nuggets brought in by the prospectors, lined many of the old streets. Men, young and old, lounged in front of the wide doorways, waiting for a customer to come in from the bush, wanting to convert his weeks of hard work into a night, or two, or three, on the town, with hotels, steak dinners, lots of liquor and *lambada* with tacky women with dyed blonde hair and rubbery tight nylon dresses, in the discotheques.

There was just one problem. The Yanomami did not want white men digging for gold on their lands. And the country's constitution allows them to not to have to like it. Two old constitutions and the latest one specify that all lands used by the Indians for hunting, fishing and agriculture, both currently and potentially, as well as lands important to tribal legend and history, are for the Indians' use alone. No one is allowed onto them without the permission of the National Indian Foundation, or FUNAI. Yet in Brazil, even the fairest laws have a way of going severely astray.

In 1755, the Marquis of Pombal declared that Indians "are to be masters of their estates, just as they are in the wilds. These lands may not be removed from them, and they are not to be molested on them." Yet the result was as much slavery and massacre as before. And, two hundred years later, less than a third of Indian lands are demarcated, while the FUNAI shamelessly works against the Indians' interests.

Lately, the Brazilian government, trying to find some way to steal Indian lands, devised a plan of designating indigenous villages rather than territories. Thus, only the area around the actual village was to be exclusively for indigenous use. The larger surrounding territory, thousands of acres of it, was to be designated as forest reserves, national parks or biological reserves, all of which can be invaded at any time by miners, loggers — or anyone. In the case of the Yanomami, the government planned to demarcate nineteen indigenous areas, stripping away so much of the land to which they were constitutionally entitled that some Yanomami villages were left out. The government also completely ignored the fact that each tribe moved from area to area over the years. So, instead of the 20-million-acre (8.2-million-hectare) block of park that was to be kept for them alone, they were left with a chopped-up carcass of a territory, 71 percent of it open to invasion, theft and unscrupulous whites. The FUNAI, which had for a long time been fitted firmly into the pocket of the nation's military, completely acquiesced in the plan.

I had spoken about all this, while still in Manaus, with Felisberto Damasceno, a young lawyer who worked for the Catholic Indigenous Mission, or CIMI. Felisberto had described the legal battle he was leading in Brazilian courts, because the government decree instituting the system of indigenous villages had less power than the article in the constitution granting Indians the larger block of land. The new plan, however, said Damasceno, was only part of a long-range plan by the government, acting on behalf of the military, to secure Indian lands for capitalist exploitation. "The military considers itself an elite," he said, "those who best know how to develop the Amazon, utilize the mineral resources it contains. Big enterprises join them in this policy, or way of thinking."

The philosophy of the CIMI, on the other hand, was radically and humanely different. Over the centuries, missionaries had destroyed Indian culture by bringing disparate groups into one village, catechizing children and discouraging customs of which they disapproved. In the 1970s, however, the vision changed, and became radically progressive. In Boa Vista, one of the main exponents of the new vision was a lay missionary named Carlo Zacquini.

I met Carlo in the offices of the CCPY, the Committee for the Creation of a Yanomami Park, near the Branco River. I found him to be a rather gaunt, intense, but deeply kind man, who had come from his native Italy to Roraima twenty-four years ago. We chatted on a number of occasions in a comfortable, well-lit lounge in the gray and blue stone house used by the CCPY. Its rooms were silent and empty because the FUNAI had terminated their activities in providing medical and other services to the Yanomami.

When he arrived in Boa Vista, Carlo told me, the FUNAI didn't even have an office there; only a few missionaries worked with the Indian population. Boa Vista was a town of three thousand people then, and Indians were held in such low esteem that when they came to town, they would lie and say they were of mixed blood. Carlo had begun teaching in a technical school. After two and a half years, the Italian fathers with whom he lived asked him to accompany a priest to the Catholic mission on the Catrimani River, which had been set up a couple of years previously. Soon Carlo was looking after the place by himself.

"Ninety percent of my time was taken up just trying to survive," Carlo recounted. "I had to learn to hunt, and to plant a garden. I had never been prepared for anything like this before. I used to go hunting every day with the Indians who had settled near the mission. They mostly used arrows, and I always had to ask them if the animal was edible, because I had to conserve my ammunition. They liked to try to shoot at anything just for fun," he chuckled.

"I also at that time started to learn the language," he said, "asking the names of things, which I compiled into a sort of dictionary." Later, Carlo began to research the Yanomami myths of creation, which are many and diverse and which reflect the many different tribes or peoples who are all lumped together under the name Yanomami. Later, he was joined by a young researcher and talented photographer from São Paulo, Claudia Andujar.

Carlo's routine changed suddenly and brutally after three years or so, when the Brazilian government announced out of the blue that it was going to build a road through Catrimani.

"It was very sudden," he said, "and when I first heard that they were going to build a road, here where there was no one but Indians, I thought the idea was completely absurd. But it became reality, constructed with a speed that was impressive. At that point we began to dedicate our time to helping the Indians survive. That road was a road of genocide," he said, "just as this invasion of prospectors is also a genocide."

Although Carlo was now barred from going into Indian territory, he had been with the Indians to witness the effects of the road. The epidemics began in 1974, with the arrival of the topographical team, less than thirty men, who surveyed and staked out the route the road was to follow. "The path passed through some villages and some village gardens," said Carlo. "In other cases, the Indians, out of curiosity, walked to the path and went to see these strange men.

"Afterward," he went on, "came hundreds of laborers, brought in by contractors to cut down the forest, all by hand, with axes. A plane would leave the food supplies, and a foreman picked it up and distributed it. It was discounted from the workers' wages, so they would eat as little as possible so that they could leave with some profit. A good number of them," he added, "left still owing money to the construction company in spite of all their labor."

Then began a nightmare of sickness, with only Carlo and Claudia to deal with it. Indians walked for days from villages to tell of sick people, and Carlo would arrive with medicines only to find most of them already dead. *Malocas* were found in which the dead bodies still lay because no one had the strength to carry out the funeral rituals. In four villages, they found everyone dead except for one little girl, "as emaciated," said Carlos, "as a stick of burned wood." And the Indians could no longer grow food or hunt. "There were times when they didn't even have the strength to get up to look for wood and make a fire," said Carlo.

He calculated that in the first year, there were twelve epidemics of flu and smallpox. "And the madness continued," he said. "We didn't know what to do. The whole time we were running here and there. As soon as one recovered from one disease, he caught another, and then someone else got it, too. It was terrible."

Carlo stood and went to a large map hanging on the wall. "In 1976, there was another smallpox epidemic and sixty-eight people died, from what we could count. Some were in *malocas* too far away for us to get to. Even some who had been vaccinated got sick." He pointed to a spot on the map showing the Mucajaí Ridge. "Through some aerial surveys that were done, we knew that there were fifteen villages here along this first stretch of the road," he said. "In a later survey, only four Indians were counted," His finger moved slightly up the paper. "Here ahead were ten villages, according to an aerial survey. In a later map made by FUNAI, those villages are no longer there. Our experience taught us," he added, "that the most isolated groups completely disappeared. Certainly these other isolated groups, up here on the map, have disappeared, exterminated."

Carlo estimated that at least a thousand Yanomami Indians died during the construction of the North Perimeter, a road that has never been used.

"The whole thing was like a delirium," he said. "I never had time to sleep. The whole time I was just going after sick people. It really was a public calamity. And there was no one to help. FUNAI did nothing. Once we advised them of a certain epidemic, and two or three months later, if I recall it right, they sent in a team of nurses and some vaccines on a helicopter. Of course, by then the Indians had already died."

As to the impact on the Yanomami since the invasion of gold seekers, Carlo could not be precise. Certainly, the vast flood of men arriving now was far greater than the number of poor devils who had confined themselves to their inhuman labor along the North Perimeter road. But now the government was playing a different game. The Catholic missionaries had been kicked out of Catrimani in 1988, and the teams of medical personnel Carlo used to organize through the CCPY no longer had government permission to work with the Yanomami. "The news indicates that there are many deaths from malaria now," said Carlo. "Many are brought in and die in the hospital here."

Carlo had gone to the Indian hospital just outside Boa Vista a few months earlier to take bananas and cassava to Indian patients who had phoned and told him they were starving. He had no sooner arrived than he was charged with "invasion of domicile" by the FUNAI, a charge he was still facing.

That last time, however, he had seen sixty-four sick Indians. "I've never seen so many here in the city," he said. "All sick." The FUNAI usually brought in a few by plane, he said, but most were brought in by the prospectors; a few walked to the North Perimeter and tried to hitch a ride.

(I later had a conversation with a man named Terencio, the half-Macuxi, half-Wapixana president of CINTER, the Committee of Indigenous Nations of the State of Roraima. Terencio mentioned rather offhandedly that there were usually about a hundred sick Indians at the hospital, the Casa do Indio, nowadays. This was an extraordinary number.)

I asked Carlo if the FUNAI might at least have reliable figures on incidence of sickness, and he almost exploded.

"FUNAI has only people who are either corrupt or incompetent in this area," he said angrily. "The few people you could trust are moved out. There was a case just recently of the chief of the Indian post in the Sururucus, the only one they've ever had there who spoke Yanomami, as a matter of fact. He has just been moved to Manaus to run their craft shop. He was shocked," Carlo went on. "Everyone knew he was moved because he sent internal memos denouncing the situation there. Demagoguery, cynicism, but it's never reached the cynicism of the ones they have in FUNAI now. It's something else now, because it is cynicism and sadism mixed, because really, to put a man like Romero Juca in as governor after everything that he's done is an act of pure sadism."

The palace of the governor of Roraima sits like a cube of chalk, a sterile white block devoid of everything that is not functional, in Boa Vista's main square, recently rebaptized Garimpeiro Place. Any time he wants, Romero Juca can look out a front window and gaze upon the enduring symbol of his state's newest attempt to enrich itself. The square is almost lunar in its bare extensiveness, crossed by wide streets that no one uses. Its center is dominated by a crudely molded statue, a populist monument to greed: a cement man with a big cement hat stooping in a nonexistent stream with his cement pan.

Along one side of the square stands the city's modern cathedral, a tall wing of white wall curving beneath the bell tower, and beside it the house of the bishop, Dom Aldo Mongiani. A tall, distinguished-looking gentleman, Dom Aldo was in no way a radical, but his hackles had most definitely been raised by the way the whites of his diocese were treating the Indians.

Dom Aldo and I sat in the living room of the silent house and drank tiny cups of coffee. He told me how, even before the scandalous treatment of the Yanomami, other tribes in Roraima, such as the Macuxi, had been forced off their land. Now, he told me, many Macuxi were being jailed for trespassing on land they had used for centuries but which had been taken over by ranchers. There were also stories of young Indians in border areas being forced to join the army, even though they were legally exempt from conscription in Brazil.

Since the issues of village demarcation and gold prospecting had come up, however, the government seemed to have declared an outright war against the Church. In May 1988, Dom Aldo received a telephone call from Ronaldo Costa e Couto, minister in charge of the presidential cabinet, asking him to remove — temporarily — the staff from the Catrimani Mission. A fight had occurred some weeks earlier in the village of Paapiu between the Yanomami and some prospectors. Four whites had been killed, as well as four Indians, their bodies mutilated by the prospectors. Though Paapiu was far from Catrimani, "They asked me to take out the priests so that they could take out the prospectors in the region as well," said Dom Aldo.

Shortly afterward, the bishop realized that he had been deceived by the government. Letters and phone calls were made, but the priests were not allowed to return. The Church had to go to court and receive an injunction allowing them to return while the case was ironed out. The FUNAI later contested that order successfully, but two members of the Church staff stayed in anyway. By then, the bishop was heartily regretting the fact that he had not demanded a written request from the minister.

The situation of the Yanomami was worsening every day, said Dom Aldo, and the blame had to be placed on the Brazilian government. "They know what is happening, they know that the Indian needs help, and yet they do nothing. Brazilian society wants the Indian as he is to disappear from the earth, and to integrate in white society. "The whole history of Latin America," he said, "white history, is that of war against the Indian so that his lands can be occupied. As long as the Indian is humiliated, they are content." In white society, in the cities and towns, "the Indian is always marginalized and miserable," he added. "If he were in his own *maloca*, he would be better off."

As bishop of Roraima, Dom Aldo had learned a great deal, he said, most importantly that his role there was to remain in second place, "with the Indian in first. It is necessary to have a new attitude," he said, "supporting and animating the Indian, and respecting his values."

I told him that I wanted to go to the Catrimani, and to another village about forty miles (seventy kilometers) beyond it, Dimini. The former had now been invaded by prospectors but the latter, thanks mainly to its chief of post, Davi Kopenawa Yanomami, was still free. It was illegal for me to go to either, but I was beginning to feel that there would be few places like Dimini left in Roraima within a few years.

Since I arrived in Boa Vista, I had been trying to think of ways to get into Dimini without spending a fortune. Along with Renan Antunes, a friend who worked for a Brazilian magazine, I had come up with a plan to rent a jeep and drive to Catrimani, then walk the rest of the way down the forest-invaded remains of the North Perimeter into Dimini. We thought about going in with Father Guilherme, from the mission, who was in town with a seriously sick Indian child. We even tried to cadge a free ride off one of the supply planes, but none of them went in that direction. Finally it was too late to put the visit off any longer. Davi was planning to leave the village in just two days.

Thursday morning, Renan and I and a photographer named Tarcisio went to the airport and spent a couple of hours trying to bargain with the pilots, who wanted vast sums to take us to Dimini. Some wouldn't take us without authorization from FUNAI, which, of course, none of us had. We had only an invitation from Davi, which did not cut a whole lot of ice with the pilots. Finally we hired a plane from an air-taxi service that did frequent runs for the FUNAI but that asked no questions.

Nonetheless I was nervous. To a certain extent I was aware of the trouble I could get myself into. At Carlo's, I had met a young Swiss anthropologist, Pierrette Birraux, who with her husband, a filmmaker, had been picked up in a Yanomami village on the Sururucus Ridge and accused of being a spy. The police had at first accused her of "illegal prospecting," claiming to have found soil samples among her possessions. But when they could not show the samples, they said she had been a spy. It had taken six months before Pierrette, backed by Brazilian colleagues, federal congressmen and her embassy, succeeded in having the charges dropped.

Standing on the airfield beside the small monoplane, I had visions of uniformed men suddenly looming in front of us and demanding to see the proper authorization to take this trip. Tarcisio arrived after buying cigarettes, and I rushed everybody into the plane. After a fifteen-minute wait on the runway, we finally took off.

As we flew over the flat plain of central Roraima, I could see the savanna below us, dry and ochre in the summer heat. Lines of *buriti* palm meandered without direction, and pools of water formed like knots in a piece of wood. The farther we flew, the more I could relax. In about an hour, we were flying over the Catrimani River, and we could see two blue-tarp roofed dredges slowly making their way up the river. The landscape changed to jungle, pierced with massive granite outcroppings of steely gray, ridged with green. The clouds began to coagulate in thick masses of mist over the forest, and we were afraid for a minute that it might be raining in Dimini, which would mean we would have to return home. But the clear weather held. We flew over the mission, and in about twenty minutes began to circle over Dimini.

"Don't waste any time," Renan said to the pilot. "We should land right away, in case Davi isn't there and the FUNAI woman makes the Indians roll barrels onto the runway to stop us from landing."

We landed with no problem on the grassy strip, coming to rest in front of a half square of low white plastered buildings. A naked boy of perhaps nine years stood staring at us through squinting eyes as we got out. A few other children came to join him, while some women squatted in the shade of the buildings. Now, how to approach Dona Dica, who would know we had arrived without authorization in spite of Davi's invitation.

In fact, it was no problem. Dona Dica, a heavy-set woman of mixed Wapixana and Macuxi blood, a trio of wooden slivers protruding from her chin, peered at us through large, thick-lensed glasses in a friendly way. Yes, Davi had told her that journalists were coming to visit. Our plane took off, and we waved to the pilot with great relief. We had made it to Dimini.

Dona Dica, the FUNAI nurse, showed us around and told us about herself. She had spent part of her childhood in Guiana and spoke fair English. "I speak five languages," she told us with an air of satisfaction. "Macuxi, Wapixana, Yanomamo, Portuguese and English." She had worked fifteen years for the FUNAI, she said, opening the door to her room and telling us to leave our things there. Then we went to the radio room, where a two-way radio stood on a table. Davi's recently awarded certificate from the United Nations was on a shelf. It reminded me of Chico Mendes and the Global 500 award that sat prominently on a shelf in the union hall. Ornaments made from the brightly colored feathers of macaws were pinned along the wall. In the back, Dona Dica showed us the infirmary, an austere whitewashed room, with an old metal camp bed in one corner. To the right, beside the radio room, was a tiny pharmacy.

Davi wasn't there just then; according to Dona Dica he was out hunting. She introduced us to his brother, but he was too shy to speak to us. We wandered around outside in the lessening heat, where a pair of tame macaws paced on a slab of cement. The children stared at us guardedly. Dona Dica introduced us to three women, their faces bristling with bamboo slivers like the whiskers of a jaguar. Their hips were wrapped with wide fringed belts, woven of wild cotton and dyed red with *urucum*. Long rows of beads hung around their necks and crossed their shoulders and breasts. Into the cotton bands around their upper arms, they had stuffed fragrant green leaves. They also inserted these leaves into large holes in their earlobes. One of the women had painted her face red and drawn black dots along the line of her lips. An older woman turned out to be her mother. And there was a rather melancholy-looking woman with beautiful eyes, although I found all of them beautiful, with their shiny straight hair cut like obsidian helmets, and their little touches of vanity, like the leaves. The three were distant relations from another village, Tootobi, who had come to visit. The Yanomami spend a great deal of time visiting, fortifying intervillage relations, walking for days to other *malocas* to stay for days or even weeks at a time.

Davi arrived after about half an hour. His chest was painted with what looked like a dark red snake, and there was red paint on his face. He wore shorts and a cap made of some kind of long-tailed squirrel, and a green macaw feather in his chin, just below the lower lip. "*Ai, shabori,*" Dona Dica yelled at him through the window of the radio room. Davi smiled shyly and shook our hands, looking down and seeming very diffident. He told Dona Dica that he had a sore thumb and needed some treatment. I followed them into the pharmacy, where they began to argue about the trip Davi wanted to take to the national meeting of Indians at the mouth of the Xingu. "No way you're going," she said. "You've done enough traveling. I'll go to the meeting." "No, you won't," Davi replied evenly, "you have to stay here. You have to do what I tell you." Dona Dica paid no attention. "You can't tell me what to do," she countered. I got the impression that the two of them must carry on like this all the time. Later she told Davi that he would have to be back early the next morning to help make lunch for all the visitors who were coming the next day. "No, you have to do it," he told her. "That's woman's work."

We set off for the *maloca*, a good hour's walk from the landing strip. The strip had been built by the Correa Construction Company, as had the low buildings, which had been for the foremen to sleep in. Years after it was abandoned by the company, FUNAI had taken it over and made it an Indian post. Davi became the chief of the post, and considered it his home. But he was not chief of the people of the village we were walking to, which was called Watoriktheri, "place of the people of the winds." Davi was a shaman, or *shabori*, one well versed in the myths and legends of his people, as well as rituals and cures. In fact, he had not come from hunting at all, as Dona Dica had said, but from working a cure, hence the painting on his torso.

A long row of us headed across a grassy meadow, over a stream and onto the remains of the North Perimeter, men in front and women and children behind, the youngest slung in bark strips suspended from the mother's head. Small trees, brush and stately palms rose on either side of the road. A pair of macaws squawked and flew across a wide stream that ran beside us. One of the men raised his bow and arrow for a moment but then thought the better of it, as if remembering what a job it would be to retrieve his arrow from such a place.

After about an hour, our troop turned into the forest. From the road, we walked another half hour or so, until suddenly a magnificent sight reared up in front of us. It was the *maloca*, an enormous oval house of palm, emerging from the forest like some natural part of it, but at the same time completely unlike it. Far off in the background a lofty mountain of gray stone, its summit fringed with green, gleamed in the waning sun.

We entered the *maloca* and found ourselves in a large circular space of black and yellow, a place full of shadows, but like a painting by Rembrandt, with a single source of light high over the middle, which drew the eye. Through the rough hole the sky was visible, a shade of blue turning gold. We stood on an immense floor, shot with shafts of light here and there. There were two big sugar presses made of rough-hewn wood, and a long, hollowed-out log used for ritual meals. We set up our hammocks in the second ring of poles, near Davi's area of the round house. Renan had not had time to buy a hammock in Boa Vista that morning, and hunted up some loose banana leaves to sleep on. Davi laughed at him and said, "White journalist comes to house of Indian and sleeps like a dog on the ground," then found him a spare hammock woven of native cotton.

Before it got too dark, I walked along the broad, shallow stream behind the *maloca* and took a bath in the cool water. On the gravelly bed, I found a long black bow, perhaps five or six feet, as smooth and shiny as onyx. I wondered why it was there, but then realized that immersion in water probably preserved the polished wood. Past the stream, I also found trees with curious markings carved into the bark.

As night descended, the fires were stoked, and they were soon the only source of light other than the stars and moon visible through the hole in the center of the roof. The women sat quietly in their hammocks near the wall with their children. A few men sat in groups and talked. Davi brought us something to eat, a gourd full of banana porridge. Later, we sat in a circle on the ground, in our midst not a fire but a flashlight belonging to Renan.

Davi's struggle, he told us, was for land, for the demarcation of Yanomami territory. "Land is very important," he said, "because the forest has game, fish, fruit, the river, the stream, everything for the Yanomami to eat and to survive. It has health. The land is our life. Without land, we are all dead, everyone. Even the white."

The Yanomami had always been there, he said, and had never moved away. "The Indian existed here before you came, before your father or your mother existed," he said. "He does not come from another country. The first Yanomami is our creator, Omam. We were born here; Omam raised us and left us here. Then the Yanomami grew great and scattered over this land. Omam created everything, even you." Similarly, he said, the white did not discover Brazil, because it always existed, along with the Indians, its first inhabitants.

There are four main Yanomami groups, speaking different languages, each with its own dialect. The myth of creation perpetuated in this particular group of Yanomami said that the world was made of three superimposed layers. Originally there were only two, but the top one became old and worn, and a large piece of it fell, taking with it two men. One of them was Omam, and he fathered the

Yanomami people when he was fishing in a stream and pulled out a woman. She did not, however, have genitalia, only a tiny hole, "like the anus of a hummingbird." Onam took the teeth of a piranha and cut out genitalia, after which he had many children.

The whites and other races were made from the foam or mist that lay along the river. A large bird pushed the foam to the shore and formed it into men, and the shading of the foam reflected the different colors of the human race.

But, said Davi, Onam did not create the prospectors, because he "did not create things to bring harm to the Yanomami. It is the white who manufactured him, just as he manufactures planes, cars and other things that you use. So that is why the prospectors came here."

Prospectors had tried at least once already to get into Dimini to look for gold. A man named Joe Devil had landed a plane, only to be surrounded by the Indians, tied up and painted, in order to frighten him off. "He didn't want to respect us," Davi explained, "so we tied him up so he couldn't go out looking. We called the FUNAI to come out and get him.

"For us, the Yanomami, gold does not mean anything," Davi went on, "because we don't need it. For us, what is of value is land. The white destroys, but the land stays. It cannot run away. But gold does. Whites pick it out, sell all the gold in the city. The Yanomami does not go around with gold around his neck or in his ear like the whites in the city. What has value for us is land, health, life."

I asked him to tell me more about Onam. "Onam is good for us," he said. "He is our chief. He is not like the prospector. He does not destroy the earth and the forest, he does not ruin the river. He doesn't look for gold. He doesn't bring sickness to kill others. Onam is respect, he loves us very much. He likes the Indian and the forest. Onam is very wise, not like the Brazilian government." The government, he said, was just for the whites, wanting riches only for itself and leaving nothing for the Indian. "It cannot see," said Davi, "because it is blinded by the gleam of gold."

But Onam had been responsible for originally separating Indians and whites, according to Davi. "There were many quarrels between whites and Indians. They robbed the Indians, killed them. Onam took them very far away, leaving only Yanomami. There [the white] lived in cities, he made planes and boats, and so he began to come back here and invaded our lands, dirtying our rivers and killing fish."

Davi said that, before, he had always believed the word of the white man, but with the building of the road, and then the arrival of the first prospectors on the Sururucus Ridge, his opinion had changed. "The road brought only sickness," he said, "sickness we never had here before — flu, tuberculosis, malaria, pneumonia — and after they don't give medicines so the Indian can get better. So the Indian began to die."

Yet many Indians were still taken in by the whites, he said, "because he gives many things, a hammock, a pen, a knife. I tell the others not to accept it."

The FUNAI, he admitted, were no help anymore, but his relationship with them was complicated. On one hand, he had much to criticize in the organization; on the other, it was all the Indians had, officially, to protect them. Yet Davi knew FUNAI was lying when it had promised to demarcate their lands. "They are not demarcated. It is only talk in the city. There folks believe it," he said. "They think FUNAI is good, is treating us well. I think it is only helping the prospectors. I think Governor Romero Juca, that it was he who opened it up for the prospectors to get in. The prospectors paid some money to him, I know. When the FUNAI does something good for the Indian, there the white pays for them not to do this anymore. This is a side of FUNAI. If FUNAI would resolve the problem, take out the prospectors and control the region well, they would be worth something. But Romero Juca has done nothing but promise."

On the other hand, said Davi, "If there was no FUNAI, everyone would be dead, like what happened to the Atroari. I like the people of FUNAI. I was raised by them. So I have reason to complain. I am not lying, I am seeing."

Davi said that many paths ran through the forest and allowed them to visit relatives in other villages, some of them hundreds of miles away. Davi had been many times to Paapiu, Uaricoera and Uaiacas, where he had worked as an interpreter. But with the arrival of the miners, he said, things were very bad there. "Now the relatives are suffering very much. They cannot drink water or eat fish because it is contaminated, the water is polluted. The white throws in a lot of, what do you call it? mercury. So then when the relatives drink the water and eat the fish . . . It is not that he dies rapidly, but he becomes slowly sick, becoming weak, until dying. Everyone dies.

"That is why I am fighting," he added, "because when a relative dies, I feel very — how can I say — very sad. Like what happened before. Before there were many of us, when I was small, and the *maloca* was big, very big, then people began to die. Now it is happening again."

We also asked Davi about his activities as a *page*, or shaman. He had been taught by "a great *page*" to protect his people. When someone was sick, he would call on spirits, "who stay on the mountain or in the forest. No one can recognize them but a *page*," he said with a note of satisfaction. "They are very important because when the *page* is working to save another who is sick, they come. There are many of them, some good and some bad also, some very bad. Each one has a name. All of them together are called *shabori*."

This was the same word with which Dona Dica had greeted Davi, and I later learned it referred to both the spirit and the shaman. The *shabori*, the good ones, did many things. They taught the Yanomami what fruits and animals were good and dispersed sickness. "And when it is very hot," said Davi, "when the sun is stopped in the sky, it is because the sun is sad, it is suffering. People get sick. Then we call Abulani, who makes lightning, and another who makes thunder. Abulani gives a great punch, and yes, he makes lightning, it gives a shock, and then it is the thunder who resolves things and sends rain, rain to fall on us and give us health. It cleans the earth."

As a *page*, Davi used a natural hallucinogen called *icacuana*. An extremely powerful substance that comes from a kind of *virola* tree, only the shaman could use it to, as Davi described, "receive and communicate with the spirits, the *shabori* in other places." After inhaling the powder, the shaman went into a sort of trance and saw many things. "You become intoxicated," said Davi, "sort of . . . different. Then you become another person, not just yourself. This is very important. So this allows you to see many things, in the heavens, below the earth, the forest, the jungles, the sun, the moon, day and night. You see everything and the future of the Yanomami." I asked him what that future was, and he grew almost excited. "The future," he said, "is Omam, who looks after us. Omam won't let them, just like that, burn the sky! He won't let them . . . destroy a lot. Because the sky can burn, it is like plastic. The factory is very strong and there the smoke goes into the sky, the winds carry it, and it arrives in the sky and melts it, like plastic. I know this is beginning. I know it is no good. It's bad, not just for me, but for you, too. Families, sons, not just for the Indians." Where did this smoke come from? I asked. "From the factories," he replied, "in your cities. It is just now that I know this, because our *shabori* travels very far, like a satellite that walks through the sky. Yours do not, they are below the sky. Our *shabori* does not want to be on the ground, he lives in the sky. That is why they are seeing this."

After a while, Renan turned to the village chief, or *tuxaua*, known to us simply as Lourival. I was not sure how he would react; Davi had to translate our questions to him as well as the answers. But he spoke animatedly and loudly, pointing in various directions, sitting on his haunches. When he had finished, after about fifteen minutes, Davi told us what he had said.

"He says that he is the son of a *tuxaua* and that everything is fine here. We are happy. Now, eh?" said Davi. "Afterward, it won't work out because of the whites who will arrive in one year or two. He is thinking ahead." Then he gave us Lourival's condensed history of the Yanomami, how they had been alone, and growing; then came the whites, bringing axes and knives, but also sickness. He spoke of the wars between different tribes of Yanomami, and said he did not want the whites, the prospectors, to come there. "They speak badly of us," Davi translated. "They want to end everything, these people he doesn't want here. He is asking that you do not speak the contrary of what he is saying. He wants there only to be Indians, and that the whites respect us and stay on their side. The earth is large. The *tuxaua* says this. This is the land of the Indian."

When he had finished talking, Davi said, "This is what I have to say to you. I am telling the truth."

Our interview over, we fell asleep in our hammocks, everything quiet except for frequent coughing coming from all around us. The dogs kept guard at both doorways, to bark should anyone with evil intentions approach the *maloca* and blow illness into it through a hollow reed.

The next morning, Renan returned to the airstrip ahead of us. I, wrapped in my sheet against the cold, talked with Davi for a while by the fire. I brought out the dry biscuits I had with me, sharing them with the women. One turned out to be Davi's wife, Fatima, the daughter of the chief, Lourival; the other was one of the women visiting from Tootobi. Her name was Luisa, she told me. It was the only communication possible, smiling and saying our names, which was frustrating.

As I walked toward the back exit, I could see the women along our part of the wall preparing breakfast, roasted bananas and steaming white cakes of cassava. Thanks primarily to Davi's salary, half of which he used to buy things for the village, they had a few modern items to make their life somewhat easier, such as metal pans, matches, knives and fishhooks. Here and there, large baskets stood on the ground, threaded through with a bark strap. A woman would loop the strap around her forehead to carry the basket. Smaller bowl-shaped baskets held fluffy piles of white cotton, which the women spun on simple wooden spindles and then wove by hand to make hammocks or the wide belts they wore around their hips. Piles of green bananas sat on rough lofts built over some living areas, and still more baskets hung from the poles, filled with cooked cassava pancakes, like sheaves of moldy paper.

Tarcisio and I took some pictures, then we all set off together for the airstrip. The village was expecting visitors from far away that day, and I knew that with them would come FUNAI officials wanting us to leave. I chatted with Davi as we walked, and he told me how he had learned to speak Portuguese. He had fallen sick with tuberculosis when he was about twelve, he said, and had had to be sent to a hospital in Manaus. He had remained in there for a year or two, learning Portuguese and eventually getting a job with the FUNAI as a translator. For a while he had worked in the village of Tootobi, then Uaicas, before coming to Dimini as chief of post.

Now, however, Davi's outspoken defense of the Yanomami, and the attention it had earned him, seemed to presage his downfall. He had recently travelled to Brasília to pick up his award from the United Nations, only to be told, upon returning to Boa Vista, that he was being demoted and sent away from Dimini. The prospect made him very angry. "I don't want to leave these people," he said. "And I am not going to let a white man be the chief of post here, because there have already been two, and there were problems. The white [chief] only knows how to order the Indian to work, to make his garden, bring him water, hunt game for him, make his meals." If he should be sent away, said Davi, the prospectors would come in for sure. Already the chief of post in Catrimani had told him to let the planes land in Dimini. "He said they would give us lots of money," he said, "but I didn't fall for it." He felt that, increasingly in the FUNAI, anyone who stood up for the Indians against the prospectors was in trouble. "They don't like Indians," he said of the staff in Boa Vista, "only money. If someone likes Indians, the delegates send him away. And who is in favor of the prospectors is made chief of post." Davi's wholehearted rejection of the gold seekers had also earned him death threats, he told me. "That's what they say in the city," he said. "But I am not afraid to die. Whoever kills me, sickness will kill him. He won't escape."

At the airstrip, we found Renan lying comfortably in a hammock in Dona Dica's room, looking through the post's medical records. We went to the cook house for some coffee, and while there, Renan told me that along with the banana porridge we had eaten the previous night, we had also eaten the ashes of someone called Ovaldo. I thought he was joking at first, but Dona Dica, busily preparing meat and rice, confirmed it. "Tell me, Dona Dica," said Renan, "was Ovaldo a chief?"

"No," she replied, "but he was a good man. He was a good hunter who always provided for his family." Her tone seemed to imply that we should be grateful to have eaten some of such a person's ashes. She told us that when someone dies and is burned in the funeral ritual with all his possessions, some of the ashes are saved and sprinkled onto each meal, almost like holy water, as a kind of benediction.

I just had time to take a bath in the stream and wash out my clothes before the village assembled in the shade of the construction company buildings to wait for the plane. And they, long before the three of us, heard it as well. Eventually, we could hear it as well. A coming in from the east, circling and landing on the grassy airstrip. A fairly big plane, the kind that held about twelve passengers, it rolled and came to a halt in front of the radio room. As everyone watched, a hatch opened, and one by one, its occupants slowly emerged, gingerly stepping on to the ground, a whole parade of white Tilley hats and big shiny sunglasses. Then came a couple of plainclothes policemen, inappropriately garbed in suits, followed by the local FUNAI supervisor, Raimundo Nonato, a middle-aged man with glasses and curly hair, and finally a blond man in Bermuda shorts, a diplomat from the embassy in Brasilia. The important guests from far away, former Canadian prime minister Pierre Trudeau and his friends, had arrived.

Considering how important Davi was in the struggle for Indian rights, and the gravity of the current situation of the Yanomami since the invasion of prospectors, it was odd that no one was much interested in asking about their problems. After walking to Watoriktheri, looking around the *maloca*, shooting a few pictures and asking what this or that was used for, they ate lunch. Davi helped Dica put the food on the table but didn't sit down himself. *Tuxaua* Lourival, his lower lip protruding with a wad of *ipadu* — a kind of tobacco that quells hunger and provides a mild stimulant — under his tongue, stood outside and watched through the open window. It struck me as odd how these men, both leaders of a people for whom the thread between survival and death was perilously thin, assumed such postures of diffidence with whites. We really were from some other incomprehensible planet for them, and just as they hid their real names from us with Christian names, they seemed to hide their strength, too, shrinking into a humble, almost childlike stature, which made no sense when I thought about it.

Lunch over, the Canadians presented the Indians with some presents of beads and a couple of rather splendid jackknives, then boarded their plane. Throughout his visit, Trudeau had seemed rather distant and only mildly interested, but he said he was gratified to see the Indians looking so healthy. "It was an agreeable surprise," he told the local correspondent of the *Estado de São Paulo* newspaper, who doubled as a press secretary for Governor Juca. "Brazil is a nation where people are happy, full of hope for the future, with much ahead of them to do." The article went on to say that Trudeau had admitted that he expected to find the Indians in difficult conditions, but instead he found a group of Indians living in a still semiprimitive state, well treated, and knowing how to get along with the whites who visit them. Trudeau was also quoted as saying that he had not seen any of the destruction of the forest everyone talked about abroad, no burnings and few prospectors.

Davi had hoped to leave with the distinguished visitors that afternoon, to begin the trip to the national meeting of Indians that was taking place a few days hence in Altamira. His hopes were quickly dashed, however, when Raimundo Nonato categorically refused to allow him to leave. Davi had done enough traveling already, he said. He had his job to do as chief of post. And he hadn't applied for permission to leave.

That night, in Boa Vista, I was cajoled into attending an official dinner given in Trudeau's honor by the governor, Romero Juca. At 7:30, three big government jeeps arrived to take us to the Casa Grande restaurant, where the dinner was to take place. Once there, we found that we were early, or perhaps, in true Brazilian fashion, everyone else was late.

We all sat and ordered aperitifs. Letters in bad English from the Commercial Association of Roraima were handed out to everyone, outlining "Investments Opportunities in Roraima." Aside from enthusiastic suggestions on mining, agriculture and even tourism, the letter provided an interesting glimpse of the attitudes of Boa Vista's business community concerning the situation with the Indians. The cause of all the trouble, it seemed, was Dom Aldo.

"Unfortunately since the Catholic Bishop took office ten years ago, coming before from one African country," it read, "he keeps the wrong idea that white people can never get along with amerindians and is always suspicious that is going to happen a shock between them. As this shock has never happen, to prove his theory, he keeps teaching the amerindians to act contrary to white people interest, mainly on the farm ranching areas." The missive went on to praise the promise of acculturation. "Since the ancient time of our ancestors Adam e Eve," it said, "the different ethnics groups it was integrated, mixed with each other, becoming more and more beautiful and better. By the other side, the groups isolated has a tendancy to deteriorate, to become more ugly and week [sic]."

While we waited for the governor and his entourage to arrive, I was asked about my book and started talking about why I had come to Roraima. I described the plight of the Yanomami, now that their lands had been invaded by prospectors, and the cynical response of the Brazilian government. Especially the FUNAI. Trudeau replied to my statements, and I was again surprised at how uncaring, even cold, he was. He pointed out to me that even in Canada, we didn't always know how to approach the issue of Indian rights and the preservation of their culture. I found this annoying. "The Brazilian government and the FUNAI do not have to think about how to approach anything," I retorted. "The country's constitution already says what those rights are. They just have to obey the law, something they're quite obviously not doing."

At about this time, Juca arrived with his young wife, Teresa, tanned and kittenish in a spotted strapless dress and pearls. Behind him were various young men to whom he had given ministries in Roraima's government, along with their wives. I was forced to help the embassy official with the translations, repeating in English all the dissimulations and outright lies for the same crowd I had just been lecturing on the evils of FUNAI.

I had always found Juca to be an exceedingly stupid-looking young man, with a blank look on his face, as if someone had just thrown a spitball at his forehead. With his gold-rimmed glasses and thin mustache, he exuded an air of self-satisfaction, to which, in a sense, he has every right. In spite of at least seventeen charges pending against him in Brazilian courts, his army-sponsored nomination for governor of Roraima, in 1988, went off without a hitch.

Juca began his career in the northeastern state of Pernambuco, as secretary of co-ordination — whatever that was — of Recife City Hall. Later he became state secretary of education, head of the housing department and chief of the Cabinet. From there he went on, in short order, to become president of the Rondon Project Foundation. The ministry of the interior liked his work there and brought him to the FUNAI, where, never having studied anthropology or ethnology, and never having had much to do with Indians at all, he was designated president in 1986.

Newspapers flashed headlines about Juca in 1987, when it was discovered that he had been illegally selling off logging rights on Indian lands. Missionaries and anthropologists have called him the biggest thief of Indian lands in modern times. He has demarcated areas more quickly than anyone by reducing the territories by as much as four-fifths of what they should be. He spearheaded the Brazilian government's, really the Brazilian military's, attempt to have Indians who spoke Portuguese and wore clothing deemed non-Indians; and so no longer entitled to a full demarcation of their lands. And when people complained, he firmly closed the doors to anyone considered sympathetic to the Indian cause — anthropologists, priests and lay members of the Catholic Church, doctors and journalists. When I had asked Felisberto in Manaus what he thought of Juca being made governor of Roraima, he said, "Well, we lawyers have a saying. The criminal always returns to the scene of his crimes."

Juca launched into a spiel about the possibilities of tourism and soya-bean farming in the state, then quickly turned to the subject of gold. He said that Brasília would soon be issuing a decree that would remove the prospectors from the outlying areas until the nineteen areas were demarcated. On Indian lands, he said, the constitution did allow nationalized companies to mine for minerals considered to be of interest for national security reasons, "with the permission of congress and, of course, the Indians themselves. No one is going to force anything on them. What's more, the Indians even have a right to 30 percent of the proceeds, which is very generous. You know," he said, "if I find a gold deposit in my backyard, I don't have the right to 30 percent. It must all go to the government."

Juca declared that the state was producing three tonnes of gold every month (in fact it was less than a third of that, according to the National Department of Mineral Research), most of it coming from Indian lands. "The problem with the Indians," he said, "is that when they meet the white man, they want all the things that white society has to offer. But these things can't be provided just like that. FUNAI is doing its best, but it is underfunded. I remember when I was president that there was a great problem with Indians from other countries, such as the Guianas and Colombia, crossing the borders to partake of FUNAI's services for their Brazilian brothers."

The absurdities went on. Trudeau nodded sagely at times, following most of it since he spoke Spanish, while the embassy official and I translated. It was a relief when we all moved to different tables and had dinner, which was a gastronomic failure, beef in a greasy sauce of tinned asparagus and gravy, white rice, mayonnaise salad. When I asked the waiter for a glass of wine or beer, he said he could give us only soft drinks. Beside me sat a woman with wildly moussed hair and long red fingernails, and farther down were a few young men in casual slacks and dress shirts. A pimply young man named Gigi Martins, who wrote the local society column for *A Critica* came in and kissed all the ladies, looking like a hairdresser from some cheap salon in a shopping mall. The Brazilians were in marked contrast to their Canadian guests, who wore comfortable cotton clothes, but especially Trudeau, in his Bermuda shorts, polo shirt and running shoes. The dreadful evening, and the even worse dinner, eventually crawled to a close. I would much rather have eaten banana porridge and Ovaldo's ashes any day.

ELEVEN

THE CATRIMANI

HE RANCHER STUDIED MY press card intently, then looked up and asked, "So what are you doing here, exactly?"

He was a young man, hefty, ruddy-cheeked and bearded, with glittering eyes and a black baseball cap over his curly brown hair. I lied and told him that I wrote for a mining magazine in Canada. "They are really interested in placer mining in Brazil," I explained, "prospectors, you know, as a sort of a feature piece." He looked at my press card again, then at me, then back to the card. Finally he commented, lower lip jutting, "Hmm, not bad."

He turned his attention to the short, swarthy man sitting at the table beside me, who was asking, "Are the police still here?" The rancher, whose nickname was Paludo, was looking through his papers as well. "No, they've gone," he answered. "It's no problem. The area is liberated. And the police weren't here for that, anyway. They were looking for minors, drug dealers, illegal arms. And foreigners." I began to feel even more uncomfortable.

"Now," said the rancher to the short, dark man, "that will be three hundred new cruzados, a hundred for the truck and two hundred for the dredge you've got on it."

"But I haven't got that kind of money on me," the little man protested. "I'm just bringing the stuff in for someone else."

"Got any checks?" asked Paludo.

"No, but I can give you a promissory note," said the other.

"Promissory note? Now what am I going to do with a promissory note? I already got $1,500 U.S. in promissory notes," said Paludo. "Look, you know this money isn't for me. We're charging everyone who goes through with a truck or boat so we can make a fund, hire a lawyer and organize this thing." He began to draw a rough map. "Look, the miners are working in here on this strip between the two Indian *malocas.* Now the priests are trying to get it all declared Indian territory, but all we have to do is organize into a co-op, hire a lawyer, and for that we need money."

Paludo looked up. "Priests?" I asked. "I didn't think there were any missionaries around here," I lied.

"Missionaries, ha! I like to call them mercenaries," Paludo joked. "No, they're gone. Don't worry, you'll get a good story in there. You gotta camera? Take lots of pictures, eh? Now then, when exactly will you be returning to Boa Vista?" he asked, as he began to write my passport number and other particulars into a notebook. Just before I left, he asked me if I wanted to leave a message for anyone who might come later. "Why would I want to do that?" I asked him.

"Well, it can be very dangerous in there, you know," he replied. "It just might be a good idea to leave a message."

I climbed back onto the truck, immensely relieved that the first obstacle had been overcome. I was hitching a ride into the gold-mining camp on the Catrimani River, and Indian area, and knew that the prospectors could be as suspicious of journalists as the FUNAI was. When Paludo had ordered me off the truck, my heart had sunk. I was convinced that he would send me packing. I wouldn't get to my destination, and would have to find some way back to Boa Vista again.

Paludo's ranch was beside the North Perimeter road. A bridge over a stream had burned down a few years before. Some said the Indians did it, but the truth was that a farmer had destroyed it by mistake when he was clearing jungle to plant grass. Now the trucks heading toward the Catrimani River had to pass over a small corner of

Paludo's land, where the streambed was lower, effectively giving him the right of check on everyone going in and out.

There was no bridge across the stream, but a floating pontoon took cars over, while the huge truck I was on drove right through the water, which came about halfway up its massive tires. Once we had crossed the stream, it was only a few more miles to the National Indian Foundation post, run by a Macuxi Indian called Queiroz. Here we had to stop again, and almost everyone got off. I tried to look inconspicuous among the lumber and coils of orange Canaflex tubing, hoping the Indians wouldn't see me. Once again I did not have official permission from the FUNAI to go into Indian land. We had to wait a long time, but no one took any notice of me. Here the issue wasn't who could or could not go in, but how much money could be extracted from them.

After about fifteen minutes, Queiroz finally took down the thick metal chain that was hung across the roadway. A stout, coppery man in red shorts, he watched us drive off, the chain still in his hand. Beside him stood a dumpy woman in a yellow T-shirt across which was stamped, "Land — the right of all Indians."

With its load of equipment — two enormous metal cylinders for the floating dredge, several rolls of six-inch plastic tubing, lumber, diesel gas, all surmounted by a small skiff — the truck plunged into the thick forest, which threatened to completely obliterate the North Perimeter some day. I and about a dozen others clinging to the precarious load were whipped frequently and painfully by branches.

Suddenly, the truck slowed down, and ahead of us I could see a clearing around a deep gorge. Large timbers and planks indicated that there was a bridge over part of it, but as we drew nearer, I could see a wide gap between the disintegrating bank and the bridge, which was standing in the middle of the river. The massive struts of the bridge were grown over with vines, and new planks had been tied together and thrown down to connect it to the precipice.

But my attention was drawn to the side, where a tattered house of dried palm raised its oval roof to the crowns of the trees. A Yanomami woman stood at the side of the road, one hip jutting, dressed in a torn T-shirt and grimy shorts, and smiling provocatively at the men in the truck. Behind her stood another woman, also smiling, this one in a ragged cotton dress and holding a filthy baby in her arms. It was a sight both tragic and shocking, contrasting graphically with what I had seen in Dimini.

We all jumped down from the truck and made our way across the dangerous bridge. As I walked across, I wondered how on earth the big trucks passed over the narrow double tracks to the main bridge, but they did several times, I learned, every day. Another truck stood on the opposite side of the chasm, and we would continue the rest of the trip on it, once it was loaded.

A group of Yanomami men were doing the work, loading cases of soft drinks and two big sides of beef into the back of it. Most of the hundred or more cases had already been stacked in the pick-up, along with some electric generators and two large refrigerated chests. When all the items were loaded, the owner approached the Indians with his arms full of bags of crackers. "Okay," he said, "now who did some work here? Here you go, and you, here's some *bolacha* for you." He handed the crackers to those closest to him. The Indians extended their hands, saying, "*Bolacha, bolacha,*" but there wasn't enough to go around.

The man jumped into the driver's seat and we set off for the river-side camp. The sky was growing dark. There were about twenty of us now, seated between and on top of the gear; the bottles made an uncomfortable seat. Two Indians had come with us, and some of the young men started having some fun with them. They got a big kick out of saying nonsensical things to the Indians and listening to them repeat the phrases exactly, without understanding. Few, if any, Yanomami here spoke Portuguese. "They're pretty funny," the would-be prospectors agreed, "but, man, you can't trust 'em. No, sir. Just turn your back, and you'll find out. But just listen how he repeats everything."

I was still worrying about Paludo and his veiled threat — if that indeed was what it was. I could imagine him on his radio, calling Boa Vista and trying to find out about me. And someone saying, "Well, I don't know about any mining magazine, but she's been seeing a lot of those priests." I asked Tony, one of the four guys I had waited with since the morning for a ride into camp, about Paludo. "Who is that guy anyways?"

Tony curled his lip derisively. "Him?" he said. "*Ele não e nada. He's nothing.*"

I spent the night sleeping in the cab of a truck, an excellent place in that I was safe, warm and buffered from the sound of the diesel generator running just outside. I had expected to find a camp like those I had seen around Itaituba, with some kind of central authority in a wooden shack, a canteen, anything, but this camp was not as established as the mining sites I had seen in Pará. A few tarpaulins had been thrown over rough wood frames, where dozens of men slept in hammocks. Two or three dredges lay moored along the bank of the Catrimani, providing shelter for dozens more. A few unfortunates had no more than a sheet of plastic propped over hammocks they had tied between two trees in the jungle. There was no source of water other than the river, which was a solid brown color. There was no place to buy food, and there were no latrines. In this place, the cab of a truck was like the Rio Hilton.

The next morning, I woke to find just about everyone up already, resuming their work on the boats that were being constructed to sail up the river and dredge its bed for gold. I met one of the young men who had come in with us on the truck. He told me he had already gotten a job on a team going upriver that day and invited me to his tent for a cup of coffee. I sat on a stump and talked to the men lying on hammocks inside. There were about seven of them, with nothing more to do than wait for the dredges to be finished so they could start working. One, a middle-aged man named José Carlos Mendes, was recovering from a bout of malaria. They were all, a young man named Pedrinho told me, from the state of Rondônia, mostly sons of the peasants who had been attracted to the free land there, only to find a difficult life of subsistence farming and malaria. Prospecting was drawing thousands of them off the land and toward the rivers. Now the Madeira, the Mamore and a host of other streams in Rondônia were full of men dredging for gold and tin. Because it was the rainy season there now, they said, they had come north to Roraima, where it was still dry. None of them had found anything yet, but there were rumors that there were big deposits in the upper reaches of the Catrimani, and in Mucajai Ridge, from which it flowed.

The advantage here, they told me, was that anyone with a dredge could explore the river. In places like Jeremias, Baião de Formiga and Paapiu, said José Carlos, "the areas that have gold are already registered by the owner, so it's impossible to get your own area, only by buying. Here, you have the opportunity to start, to look for some virgin land that hasn't been staked or explored." The dredging, however, was far from cheap: it cost about $10,000 U.S. to build a fully-equipped boat.

José Carlos had spent the past fifteen years working as a *garimpeiro*, most recently as a diver. This is the hardest job of all. The divers are connected to the surface only by an air hose. They work four or five hours at a time underwater, sucking up silt with the pump. It was an understatement to call the work dangerous. "No, you can't see anything down there," he said. "You have to dig pretty deep holes, sometimes as deep as twenty feet, and sometimes they cave in. A lot of divers have died in those holes."

"So why do you do it?" I asked. "Why don't you go to São Paulo and get a job?"

"It's the dream of every *garimpeiro* to improve his life, and that's what I hope to do, too," he replied. "The market for work in Brazil is difficult. If you can manage to find a good job, fine. But if tomorrow you lose your job, then you are really out of luck. To be my own boss is worth any sacrifice I have to make." What's more, he said, he made more money as a *garimpeiro* than in any other job he had done.

The Amazon was full of men like Pedrinho and José Carlos, independent prospectors dredging the riverbed and banks for diamonds, gold and tin. They came to the Amazon from all over Brazil, but mostly from the state of Maranhão, which is relatively close to the routes that lead to the goldfields: Itaituba, Alta Floresta in northern Mato Grosso, São Felix do Xingu, Roraima. Some already had some property; others had only a few acres of land or a house; and some had absolutely nothing. Although many, as José Carlos said, dreamed of striking it rich and living the life of a king, the majority simply worked to earn some money in a currency that went up in value as the cruzado went down.

In Pará, northern Mato Grosso and Rondônia, prospecting was pretty well established. Anyone going to these places can find themselves a job on a crew, for which they receive about 6 or 7 percent of the take, plus meals. The rest of the profit goes to the entrepreneurial minority, the owners of the dredging machines and pumps, the people with enough money to find a lode, build an airstrip and set up a business. The image of each man working for himself is a fallacy.

Along with the men who traveled to these out-of-the-way places in search of gold would come camp followers. For example, a team of men usually had a woman working as cook — and also, if she wanted to, as a prostitute. Groups of prostitutes were also flown into camps for short periods of time. And many camps, even the most primitive, set up makeshift discotheques, where the men could spend their gold dust on beer, liquor and women.

Then there were the pilots who earned the equivalent of hundreds of dollars a week flying in men and supplies. In the more established camps, all kinds of rough wooden shops were set up, too, which sold everything from flashy clothes to the latest style of sunglasses. There existed as many ways to spend money in these primitive frontier places as there were nuggets of gold in the goldfields.

The situation in Roraima was similar. Wealthy entrepreneurs were well entrenched, and most of the estimated forty thousand men in the state were in their employ. A few prospectors did go into the jungle looking for a lode. If they found one, staked it out and secured an investor, they would indeed grow rich. José Carlos told me that he had tried it, had run out of food in three days and had almost starved to death.

After chatting with the men, I had a closer look at the dredges in the river. A young man named Vivaldo showed me how they worked: a motor sucked up the silt and water into a sluice lined with either burlap or a sort of carpet with a long, curly nap, which caught the tiny flecks of gold and silt. The rest of the mud and pebbles was washed into the river. There was a smaller air pump for the diver. I walked farther and watched some men sawing wood to make the frames for new dredges. With hard work, a dredge could be built and ready to go in three days, they said. As I turned and walked up the riverbank to the road, I saw two Yanomami boys, in their early teens, showing off their brightly patterned shorts and sunglasses, which they had gotten from the prospectors. Then, gathering the few things I had brought with me, I set off for the mission.

As I walked out of the camp, I was sure I heard a growl, but dismissed it as a figment of my imagination. After all, I was only a few hundred feet from the camp, which was noisy with electric generators, the shouts of men and the sounds of sawing. True enough, the sides of beef that had been chopped up and were drying on hooks in the sun were tempting to any jaguar, but the presence of so many people, I felt, was bound to keep animals far away.

I arrived at the fork of the road where I had to turn to reach the mission. I passed one of the Indians who had come in with us in the truck. He was carrying a load of sugarcane on his back to sell at the camp. At least, I gathered that from his gestures when he pointed to the segmented green stalks across his shoulder and pulled out a thin wad of bank notes — notes that are increasingly worthless due to Brazil's high rate of inflation — from the waistband of his shorts. I tried to ask him if I was taking the right path to the mission, and he waved me on. The sun was hot, and the jungle seemed to throb to a constant buzz. I thought about the growl again and picked up a stout stick to carry with me. Then I saw an older Indian armed for hunting with knives and arrows and followed along behind him.

I followed the hunter until the forest opened into a very wide clearing, where there were two *malocas* and a garden. This place was called Rotiptheri. Some kids came running up to me, asking for crackers, but I indicated that I didn't have any. To an older boy working in the garden, I gave the rice, candles and tobacco I had brought with me from Boa Vista. He also wanted my bag and my red nylon jacket. I felt bad about not being able to give him the jacket, but it was the only thing I had to keep warm at night.

I left the village and carried on through a flat, grassy area. It wasn't long before I found myself at the mission. Here I found a long building of brown-painted slats, its windows covered with green plastic screening, a small porch in front and another one, with a long, sloping roof, behind. There was a round cement well, and farther back three smaller buildings painted white. All kinds of fruit trees were planted in a large yard in front of an empty chicken run. A sign on the wall of the big building said Missão Catrimani, but the black and white paint was peeling and faded.

The first person I saw was Sister Florencia. I almost laughed when I saw her, because one of the ploys Renan thought I might use to get past the FUNAI people and into Catrimani was to say that I was a cousin or sister of the nurse working there. Sister Florencia was a tall, strongly built black woman of perhaps fifty. She wore a light-colored cotton dress with long sleeves and a matching kerchief around her head. I gave her the letter of introduction Father Guilherme had given me in Boa Vista. She put on her glasses to read it, and smiled. "How did you get in here?" she asked. I told her the whole story, how I had hitched into the camp with some prospectors, spent the night there, then walked the couple of miles to the mission. "Would you like to take a bath?" she asked. There was probably nothing I wanted more. As I doused myself with gourdfuls of water in the bathroom, I felt that I had found paradise.

I changed, then went to the kitchen, where Sister Florencia was cooking some fried bananas, along with milky tea and toasted bread. I was so hungry, I couldn't stop myself from fishing out the banana slices before they were done. A teenage boy named Epi, who was mute and slightly retarded, looked in at us through the screen, tapping on it occasionally to get our attention. Sister Florencia looked after him, although he lived in one of the *malocas*, and he spent much of the day following us around, smiling and trying to communicate.

But poor Sister Florencia. The first thing she asked me was whether Father Guilherme was coming back soon. I told her that he was still waiting for a sign of improvement in the very sick child he had taken into the hospital in Boa Vista. Sister Florencia sighed and told me about the situation at the mission. She was there alone, since the government had allowed only two people to go back into the mission after the expulsion, and Guilherme had had to leave temporarily. The FUNAI representative, Elias, who luckily for me was absent that day, and his assistant, a Macuxi named Chico, who was off fishing, made her life hell. And what was more, she had come back to the mission after a fifteen-month absence to find the work of twenty-five years all but destroyed by the FUNAI.

The list of her complaints was endless. They had broken into the lockers of personal possessions belonging to the missionaries and stolen or destroyed most of the contents. The research papers left by a French anthropologist, Bruce Albert, had been thrown out and scattered by the winds. The chickens and other animals had been eaten, the garden overrun by weeds. A jeep and a truck had been wrecked. Medical equipment was missing or broken, as were the generators and water pump. To make more room for themselves, the FUNAI people had moved things out of a storehouse and piled them into the infirmary. Worst of all, the relationship built carefully over the years with the Yanomami was beginning to fall apart. The FUNAI representatives had, in a sense, opened a floodgate. They had broken the bond of mutual respect that had existed between Indian and white, so that Yanomami children had also begun to break things and steal. The mission had made a point of not hiring the Indians to work for them, and encouraging them not to sell their produce for money. But Chico had made a young Yanomami girl work as a nanny for his wife. Other Indians had to work in his garden. The FUNAI gave them candies, crackers and T-shirts. The mission gave them medical care. The conflicting messages from the white world had left many of the Indians confused and distrustful.

The thing about Sister Florencia was that she was a woman who liked a certain sense of order. She subconsciously expected and needed a kind of respect for the processes that slowly built a structure in which the wheels turned as they should, and the machine, however primitive, functioned. The wanton destruction of a world that had seemed to be working well left her frustrated and unhappy. While at first I had hoped that my presence would not upset her working day too much, I soon realized that she needed someone to talk to, to let off steam.

She told me that she had been so upset about being expelled, about the presence of the police and the prospect of leaving her patients behind, that her blood pressure and nerves had been affected. "It arrived at a point," she said, "where I had made up my mind to just go off into the forest and stay in a *maloca*, so I wouldn't have to go away. But then I thought about my family, all the suffering this would cause them, and decided not to do this."

We began our sad tour of the mission, Sister Florencia walking ahead of me, a large bunch of keys in her hand. I told her that I thought the mission looked very nice, but for her it was a mere shell of what it had once been. We began at the garage and workshop. The broken-down truck was parked there — and a dusty dental machine, also broken. The ground and shelves were littered with bits of wire, nails and tools, but the majority of the tools, said Sister Florencia, had disappeared. After looking at the burned-out generator and broken pump, we visited a storeroom, completely disordered, the few remaining items covered with cement powder from a torn sack.

We walked out of the mission and down to the river. As we stood there and talked, Sister Florencia told me that she had been born in Boa Vista, spent part of her childhood in British Guiana and could speak some English. Her father had died when she was a girl, and her mother had remarried. She had a big family, fourteen brothers and sisters, most of them younger than she was. She had worked in the mission for eight years, looking after about 350 Indians in nine villages. But this was more than just the job to which her religious vocation had brought her — it was her whole world.

After a few minutes, two women and a girl of about fourteen came up behind us. The two women were sisters, and the girl the daughter of one of them. Their appearance was somewhat unusual: their skin was pale and freckled, and their hair, cut in the typical bowl style of the Yanomami women, had a reddish tinge. Sister Florencia said one of them, called Nelza, had lost her husband to a jaguar shortly after she arrived. The women asked about me, wanted to know my name, and as we talked they put their hands in my pockets, along the cuff of my shorts, fascinated by these folds of cloth that seemed to have no purpose.

A motorboat came up the river with a couple of men from the camp in it, and they also stopped to chat. Sister Florencia asked them not to go downriver if they were going to fish. She had arranged to let only the Indians fish downriver from the mission, since their supply of food was decreasing. She also asked them to tell everyone in the camp not to shoot should they see a tapir in the forest wearing a red scarf, because it was a pet she had raised from infancy.

We walked back up to the mission, and Sister Florencia showed me the clinic and the small hospital. The hospital was just a round, palm-thatched pavilion, where the Indians could put up hammocks and build fires as they recovered from illness or awaited the birth of a child. Family members could stay there also, to keep the patient company.

Then we visited the two *malocas* near the mission. Sister Florencia told me that they were fairly new. Before they were expelled from the mission, the priests had encouraged the Indians to build the *malocas* farther away, so they could remain independent. The FUNAI representatives, however, had persuaded the Indians to move. Both *malocas* were smaller than the one of Watoriktheri, and closed at the top. The floor of the first was littered with tin cans, a bottle and some pieces of Styrofoam, more evidence of the FUNAI. A small, pretty woman named Mariazinha was weaving a hammock, her work strung up between two poles. Some men were lying around instead of hunting, and many of their hammocks, I could see, were factory-made, gifts from the FUNAI.

As we walked through the second *maloca*, the sister saw a man lying in a hammock, but he wasn't sick, she said, just lazy. She spoke to him in Yanomami, telling him to go out and work, but he paid no attention to her, and those around him laughed. She pointed out another family and said, "They just lost a son, and have been destroying everything he ever touched . . . They were very sad, but they seem to have stopped now." It was the custom of the Yanomami, she told me, to burn a person's possessions when he died so his soul would find peace. Sister Florencia told me that they would even come to her and ask if there were any photos in the mission's albums. "And they ask us to take out the photographs and tear them up right in front of them."

As we were going out, we found a woman named Raimunda sitting in the doorway examining her swollen toe, which the sister had bandaged for her earlier. "Leave it alone," she admonished the woman in Yanomami. "Come to the clinic this afternoon and I will put another dressing on it for you. But you must not touch it."

She took me to the storehouse where the medicines had been kept. It held a bed and a wooden cupboard full of tinned goods. A few pictures of naked women had been pasted to the wall. This, she told me, was where the new chief of post, Elias, stayed.

Nearby was the wooden house where the sister used to live, now taken over by Chico and his family. "You see, this used to be two rooms," said Sister Florencia as we stood on the porch. "I slept in this room here, and in the other was a nursery for babies." She explained to me that Yanomami women frequently kill their babies right after birth, for a whole number of reasons, some of them not necessarily understood by anthropologists. "It is done outside the *maloca*, in the jungle," Sister Florencia said. "The mother herself eliminates the child. If she is angry with her husband or for any other reason, whether it's a boy or a girl, she kills it. I also know two women who won't accept any baby girls; every one that is born they kill. And if it's a question of infidelity, the husband obliges the woman to kill the baby. Sometimes they say beforehand that they will not keep the child, and then maybe another family member will talk her into it, offering to help raise it." Sister Florencia had offered to take in babies, at least fifteen over the years, and raise them to the age of five or six for the families, at which time they would go to the *maloca* to live. The infants had shared the room opposite hers, where she fed and looked after them. In all cases, she said, the families had been happy to have them once they were bigger.

Finally, she showed me the small wooden chapel, a simple building like all the others, where the priests and nuns, rather surreptitiously, it seems, went to pray. They were careful not to show off their religion, said Sister Florencia, but she added, "We don't pray here anymore." Indeed the chapel was piled high with spare furniture from the rooms the FUNAI personnel had taken. At one point, she said, they had confiscated the altar, but in the end it was returned to the mission.

Our conversation was cut short by the arrival of some visitors, three young men from the *garimpeiro* camp with nothing better to do. The first two, nicknamed Minerinho and Roraima, didn't even know what kind of Indians these were on the Catrimani. The third man showed up with Epi, from whom he had bought a couple of long metal-tipped arrows for a pack of cigarettes and a hundred old cruzados. Epi showed them to the sister, and she examined them with a look of disgust. "What can he do with this now?" she asked the man. "What's it worth, ten new centavos? Maybe he can buy one candy." Then the man went into the *maloca* with Epi, though Sister Florencia asked him not to.

"Every day, the *garimpeiros* ask for fruit, sugarcane, and the Indian brings it to them," she complained. "It is all he has to sustain his family, but he prefers to sell, because the Indian is like that. A person asks for something, and he always gives. Even if that was all he had to eat."

When the three men left, Sister Florencia went to the clinic, where half a dozen women and children were waiting. While she administered eye drops, injections and worm remedies to the children, their mothers sat outside chatting quietly. I asked the sister what the women were talking about, and she told me they were saying, "Now that the *garimpeiros* are here, we are all going to get sick. We are going to die."

Meanwhile, the babies kept up their crying. The most common ailments, the sister told me, were malaria, pneumonia, bronchitis and, lately, gastroenteritis. This last complaint seemed to have come from a change in diet, she thought, either from lack of fish and game, because of the presence of the prospectors, or from the refined foodstuffs brought in by the FUNAI. Or it could be the water. No one knows, she said.

According to Sister Florencia, the Indians had begun to speak frequently about the prospectors, or *cariperi* as they called them, now that so many had arrived on the Catrimani. "They are worried about the water," she said, "and wondering if we are going to dig another well here. They are afraid to drink the river water because a woman died recently who lived right on its banks. And now there is the child sick in Boa Vista with Father Guilherme, who had a lot of intestinal infection attributed to dirty water. They have made an immediate connection because this was already being talked about before."

Raimunda came to have her toe looked after again. She had cut it by accident with a machete while visiting at another village and had had to walk for several hours to get back to the mission, by which time it had become infected. Mariazinha, the woman who had been weaving the hammock, came by with a small child and sat beside me, saying nothing but lightly touching my hair. The women all wanted to know my name, then, with some difficulty, told me their Portuguese names. A chubby-cheeked little girl began to play with my hands, and I found out her father was the lazy man who had been lying in the hammock. Her mother had died a few months ago while the mission staff was gone, said Sister Florencia, and she had never found out what had happened. Now the little girl's father had taken another woman and rejected her and her younger brother. She was being looked after by her aunt and grandmother.

As we sat on the porch of the clinic, the sun began to take on the gentler, more golden tones of the afternoon. Just as the sky was beginning to darken slightly, the men came home from hunting and fishing, a group of them, a few paces apart from each other. They carried fish hung on strings of vine and some small game, perhaps a bird, wrapped in banana leaves. They walked by us without looking up. It was as if we didn't exist. "I wonder if the women kill their baby girls because they know that they will have such a difficult life," I said. "That is what some anthropologists say," Sister Florencia replied. "I don't really know. But it is very true that women have a far lower status than the men."

I asked her about the *maloca* I had passed the day before in front of the broken bridge. Life had disintegrated there in Ajarani, she told me, especially after their chief died. "Their culture is already lost. They no longer do their rituals," she said. "And the proof is that when the old man died, they abandoned his body without any ritual, without tears, and followed the prospectors."

Now, one of his sons was calling himself the chief, even though this was impossible, she said, because he had no wife or family, and thus no respect in the community. The son, who called himself Juribeba, had sold out to the prospectors, by all accounts, and had a bad reputation. Once, he had stolen a woman from another *maloca*, making everyone extremely angry. Together with the woman's husband, the Indians had come looking for her, whereupon Juribeba attacked their chief with a machete, slashing his arm. "But at the very moment that he struck with the knife," said Sister Florencia, "an Indian from the other *maloca* let an arrow fly — *taaa* — and hit him right in the chest. He had to go to Boa Vista to be saved."

Her ministrations finished, Sister Florencia told me she was going to make us some supper. I sat on the porch of the big building for a while and wrote in my notebook. João Luis, the tame tapir, came ambling into the yard, and I got some bananas from Sister Florencia to feed to him. He crunched the unpeeled bananas with relish, and applied his long, wet nose to my arms and legs like a soft sponge, begging for more. When all the bananas were eaten, he wandered off to eat some grass, until fat Chico came home from fishing and tried to ride him like a pony, sending the poor beast off into the forest again. "You see?" asked the sister. "You see what these people are like?"

We ate dinner at the big table in the room next to the kitchen, a large, airy place with a few rocking chairs and big, screened windows. Sister Florencia had made a generous meal, more than we could eat, and Epi stood outside, moaning in the dark, trying to tell us he was hungry, too. As she prepared a plate of food for him, she told me about some medical cases she had dealt with, about the incidence of jaguar attacks, and about a chief from one of the outlying *malocas* who had threatened the FUNAI chief of post should anyone in his village die because of the absence of the missionaries. The sister was angry because the FUNAI had accused her of putting the man up to it.

After dinner, I made up a bed for myself in Father Guilherme's room. Sister Florencia gave me some sheets and showed me a cupboard that used to be hers. She stood before it and mentioned everything that had been inside, showing me where things had stood. "Here I had a small statue of Our Lady, and here, all my personal diaries for the past eight years. And then I had two rosaries in this corner, and a box of scraps of cloth over here." Everything the sister had left behind was gone, even embroidered towels her mother had given her. When she had returned a few months ago, she told me, she had seen one of the FUNAI men drying himself with one and said to him, "Excuse me, but that is mine." He only replied, "It *was* yours."

The next morning I was awoken by what sounded like singing coming from the *malocas*. It was still dark, and the singing went on for some time. When I got up, I asked Sister Florencia if she had heard it, too. She told me that it was a "shamanism" to try to improve the hunting.

Since the coming of the prospectors, good-size game was extremely rare, she said.

As I drank my bowl of milk and coffee in the kitchen, we chatted a little about the situation of the Indians. Later I met the chiefs of the two *malocas*, Mauro and Fernando. They were both firmly against the presence of the prospectors, and were very much afraid for the life of the tribe. "The Indians are confronting a great deal of confusion," said the sister after they left. "They are in a great dilemma. They know what has happened with other groups, such as in Paapiu. The problem for them is to know who is going to stay. Will it be FUNAI or the priests? For the Indian, he who gives him more is the one who has more value. It is a very difficult situation for them."

After breakfast, I told the sister I had to go back to the camp to arrange a ride to the city. She insisted on giving me some food, and dug around in a box until she found some wrapped biscuits and a foil sack of water. Both items were labeled in English and claimed to be especially devised for mountain-climbing expeditions. "Where did you get this?" I asked her. "Oh, it's been donated to us from the United States. Here, at least take these biscuits in case you have to spend another day without eating." Sister Florencia also asked me to take a note for Father Guilherme. He had radioed that morning saying that the Indian child had taken a turn for the worse and Sister Florencia was upset by the news. She wondered what treatment the doctors should be giving, and talked to me about it as if we could discover some solution together.

Late that morning, I walked out of the mission the way I had come. The sun was bright and hot, the sky spotted with wispy white clouds. As I came close to Rotiptheri, I could see a group of little boys walking toward me. And as they passed, I saw that two of them had affixed to their heads small model airplanes carved from white Styrofoam, their tiny silver-paper propellers whirling in the breeze.

At the camp, a canteen of sorts had been set up with the two refrigerated chests plugged in and filled with soft drinks. Cans of food and other items were on display on the rough board counters. I got a ride back to Boa Vista with two young men, Antonio and Juquinha, who had trucked some things in for the owner of two dredges being built on the riverbank. During the trip, which was delayed many times, Juquinha commented, "Why don't those priests teach the Indians to dress properly," to stop eating off the ground and all those other primitive things they do? They say they are helping, but I don't see how they are." At one point, when we stopped to give a group of Indians from Ajarani a ride, the bespectacled young man pointed out a child with worms and said, "You see, the mission should make these people change their habits so they don't get sick all the time." I did not bother to tell him that the Indian children were getting a lot sicker from all the "white" food they were getting from the FUNAI and from the water polluted with mercury by the prospectors.

As we passed through the FUNAI post again, I saw Juquinha hand over a roll of money to the gatekeeper, the corpulent Queiroz. "How much did you give him?" asked Antonio, who was driving. "Oh, just five thousand," said Juquinha. That was about three dollars. "Sometimes I give him ten, sometimes five. You have to give him something, but not too much. Not after you've already paid two hundred dollars just to get your dredge in."

I arrived back in Boa Vista that night and learned that Renan and Tarcisio, the journalist and photographer I had traveled with, had already gone. But as a last gesture of goodwill, Renan had asked Dom Aldo if I could stay at the Catholic residence, a big house by the Rio Branco, to help save me some money. I moved in there the next morning.

The residence was a long, two-story building of white stucco, with a rather ornate roof and veranda on either end. It lay between a long stone wall with big iron gates and the Rio Branco, which flowed south to meet the Rio Negro at the border of Amazonas and Roraima. While I was there, I met two priests from a mission in Guiana, Father Peter, a small, gaunt Briton, and Father Matthew, who was Guianese of East Indian descent. Both reminded me of characters from a Graham Greene novel.

Their mission was close to the Brazilian border, they told me, and they drove to Boa Vista once a year to buy supplies and have their jeep tuned up. We had breakfast together every morning and chatted. I asked them if there were any *garimpeiros* in their neck of the woods, and what they were called in English, hoping there might exist a better translation than "independent prospector." "Yes," said Father Peter, "the people call them pork beaters, because they usually get salted pork to eat, which gets filled with worms. They have to beat the pork to get the worms out." Then one dawn I found the two priests packing up their jeep to return home. The jeep, I noticed, had been christened Kateri Tekawitha, a native Canadian saint. Father Peter told me that she had quite a following among Indians in Guiana, as she was the only Amerindian to be canonized by the Catholic Church. They asked me to send them a copy of my book and wished me good luck, then drove through the big cast-iron gates.

While staying at the residence, I also met Dona Laura, a blonde Italian woman of perhaps fifty-five. She was quite fat and spoke Portuguese with a thick accent, talking incessantly whenever I ran into her. I soon learned that she was a former nun, married to a former brother, who had worked for a time in Roraima. She had been a missionary in Somalia, Kenya and Nigeria and preferred Africa, she said, "because the people there are so devout." She and her husband were staying in a little house behind the residence, and she spent her days unpacking donations from other countries, deeming a great deal of it unsuitable. "Things, I don't know, dry food like for people lost in sea, and shoes, enormous, like this," and she held her hands far apart, "for man, all size forty-eight, *ma!* For in Brazil? *Nessuno* has feet so big."

Almost every morning, I went to the Boa Vista airport, to hang around with the pilots and try to get a ride into Paapiu. But it was raining frequently in the Sururucu highlands, making it impossible for planes to land. While I waited, I heard all kinds of odd rumors. One fellow told me he'd heard the IMF would not lend Brazil any more money until the prospectors were removed from Indian lands. (This had already occurred once. In September 1987, the Brazilian air force rounded up all the prospectors, only to see them return in even greater numbers soon after the operation was over.) Others told me of a mysterious airstrip where no plane was allowed to land, but which supposedly belonged to an American company.

The pilots were sensitive about attempts to stop the invasion of prospectors; they were making good money servicing the work sites. Some made more than $1,000 U.S. in gold a week. It was a risky business because the airstrips were cut as short as possible and were very rough. The pilots always flew with the minimum of gas so they could carry more goods in their small planes, which were always overloaded anyway. They hung around for hours in the airport lobby, waiting for someone to hire them, drinking coffee and gossiping, running to the airfield the minute a job came in.

At the time, the mood in Boa Vista was one of absurd and rather harping paranoia. There were frequent articles and editorials in the local paper reacting to international concern over the fate of the rain forest, calling such concern unwarranted interference in the country's private affairs. "This is not the first, nor will it be the last, attempt to internationalize [the Amazon] under the scientific, economic and political allegations of the global population explosion," said one editorial, "suggesting that we receive the excess population." "The Amazon is Brazil," said another. "Let it not be transformed into an international enclave." And from the city of Belo Horizonte, in Brazil's center, thousands of miles from the Amazon, mayor Pimenta da Veiga denounced the existence of an "articulation" of European and North American governments, as well as international organizations, trying to control the Amazon.

For the businessmen of Boa Vista, the debate about the environment was focused exclusively on their attempts to mine the region's gold. The fact that a law had existed for years prohibiting them from entering Indian territory and removing its resources seemed to have completely passed them by. So the most common rumor flying around was that the government was planning to send in the air force again, to take out any non-Indian found on Indian land.

As the rumors intensified, Romero Juca gave a press conference. He was going to Brasilia, he said, to tell the government that if they did expel the prospectors, they would be committing "a grave social and political error. The time has come," said this former guardian of the nation's Indians, "to rescue the respect and the image of the garimpeiro. He is a professional."

Questioned about the "international interference," Juca said that the ecology lobby was just a front for gold-producing countries who wanted to keep gold prices up and their share of the market dominant. He wanted to register all the men working in the goldfields and call them members of a co-operative so they would have a better position in the eyes of the law. And he added, "No country in the world treats its Indians better than Brazil."

It was a pity Adalberto dos Santos could not have been at the press conference to give the sycophantic young journalists another opinion on the "professionalism" of the prospectors in Roraima and to describe the absurdity of trying to form them into co-operatives. I went to see Adalberto, a mechanic, at his shop on the outskirts of Boa Vista, where he told me about his experiences looking for gold in 1988. He had put together a diary of his four-month experience in the jungle, to give to Dom Aldo as evidence to counteract the impressions created by the owners of the goldfields and the local businessmen who shared in the wealth they produced.

Adalberto was thirty-one years old and had been born in Coimbra, Portugal; he had been in Brazil since his youth. The picture he gave me of the life of some prospectors was one of deprivation, danger and arbitrary violence. He told me, for example, how he and four companions had arrived at the gold pits of a man named Come-Onca, or Jaguar Eater, near the Upper Parima. "He gave us an area to work," said Adalberto, "and we had only just cleaned the brush away when one of the *garimpeiros*, Baiano, arrived and said that the Indians were preparing to attack us. Except that this attack never happened. It was a fantasy, a story," Did he think it was an excuse to attack them-selves?, I asked him. "Exactly," he replied.

"The next day, Baiano and three others took their guns and went to the *maloca*, which wasn't far away. And in the evening, they came back laughing, telling us how they had tied up all the men and raped their women, having fun with them in every corner of the *maloca*. The majority of us were entirely against this, and there was a big argument. Me and my four friends decided to leave as soon as we had finished our pit; anyway, the gold from that pit was weak, only one and a half or so ounces [forty grams], and we didn't want friction with anyone."

Four days later, however, said Adalberto, the Indians attacked with shotguns. He and a few others escaped. Later, they went back to collect their few possessions, and learned that four Indians had been killed and one prospector wounded. They left, a group of twelve, and carried on through the forest.

Their trials were far from over. Adalberto's diary described other shocking events in a terse style that makes them seem all the more dreadful. On October 20, the men arrived at the gold pits of Raimundo Careca. "The boss here is a bearded guy," Adalberto wrote. "They stole some Indian women in the upper Catrimani and raped them." On November 16, he wrote, "after eight days of walking we arrived at the Totoobi River. Paulinho Jacaré has died from a snakebite." And on the twenty-first he wrote, "Today, at 1:00 P.M., we crossed the Dimini River, at Anteater Falls. We found some cadavers of Indians, three women, two boys and a girl of maybe fifteen. We noticed that there was a *maloca* near and ran away. At two in the morning, we were surprised by a numerous group of Indians.

Four of my friends were killed. Another was wounded. He died twenty minutes ago."

On November 30, Adalberto emerged from the jungle at an airstrip called Tapirapeco Ridge, where there was a FUNAI post. Of the twelve who had set out from Raimundo Careca's stake, only three had survived.

I asked Adalberto why they had done it. "It is the dream of every *garimpeiro* to strike it rich," he replied. "Few men can conform to working for just a percentage. Unfortunately, the majority have no other choice; they just don't have the money to buy enough food or any equipment. They keep on working for others, for that ridiculous amount of gold."

TWELVE

REMEMBERING THE MASSACRE

They spent the entire morning waiting, more than a hundred Tikuna Indians, men, women and children, at the house of Flores Salvador. The women roasted cassava and bananas over a fire, while the children played; and the men, looking out over the Solimões River, discussed the imminent arrival of the police. Two of their captains, Leovilio and Pedro, had gone into town to bring back the police, to try to resolve the growing problems with their white neighbors. As time passed and still no one showed up, they tried not to lose patience. Once they saw a boat go by with five whites in it, but no one thought it was anything to worry about. As the midday sun grew hot, they moved into the shade beneath the trees or inside the little sawn-wood house of Seu Flores. One o'clock passed, and still there was no sign. Then finally, at about one-thirty, they could hear people coming in from the Capacete Stream, through the woods and toward the house. Three children came running up and said fearfully, "There are white men coming with guns." Salino, captain of the community of Porto Espiritual, was immediately alarmed. "Everyone get over here!" he shouted. "The whites are going to kill us!"

Two schoolteachers, Alcides and Constantino, along with another man, Natalino, decided to go meet them, to see what they wanted. Constantino described what happened. "There were two of them," he said, "one they call Turtle Belly, and a boy of maybe fourteen, Walmir, the son of Jonas, and they were both of them armed. We told them that we had not come to fight with anybody. That we were waiting for the captains, who were bringing the police from Benjamin to resolve the problem of the cow they had killed. And Turtle Belly said not to come any closer; he didn't care what we wanted, we were all going to die that day. Then the boy, he started back, but suddenly turned around and shot. He hit Natalino, who was standing right beside me, and he fell. He lay on the ground crying out, with his hands covering his groin, and then Turtle Belly fired two more shots into Natalino, which hit him in the abdomen."

The first shots acted as a signal to the rest of the gang. The whites seemed to come in from all sides, firing indiscriminately as the Indians screamed and fled for cover. Some ran into the forest, others into the house of Seu Flores. Many Indians attempted to escape the frenzy of killing by running for their canoes. Several fell and were carried away by the swift current of the Solimões; their bodies were never recovered. Twelve-year-old Cristina Julião saw her father fall into the river and watched as he was shot at by whites even as he was drowning. "Why are you killing me?" he asked as he fell, gripping his chest, into the water. The massacre lasted for half an hour.

"Then I heard Oscar call to the criminals," said Constantino, who, wounded, had shut himself into the house, "to get inside his boat, and they went away. Then everything fell silent."

The Indians stayed locked inside the house for another hour, frozen in fear. Maybe there were still others outside, they thought, who would begin blasting at them again. When finally they emerged, they found that fourteen of them had been killed and twenty-seven wounded, one woman as old as seventy-three, and many children even younger than the nervous boy who had started it all as he was about to run away.

The shocking events of Monday, March 28, 1988, will never leave the minds and memories of the Tikuna Indians of the Upper Solimões. Even though the massacre affected four communities close to the city of Benjamin Constant, the horror of it seeped into the lives of every one of the tribe of twenty thousand, the largest Indian tribe in Brazil. That it could have happened so easily, so swiftly, so senselessly, seemed incredible. Such things were not supposed to happen anymore. News of the killing made headlines throughout Brazil and around the world. That none of those who carried out the massacre has yet received a jail sentence went unnoticed.

Nine months after the massacre, I visited the community of São Leopoldo, where the scars of the massacre were still painfully raw. I flew from Manaus to the small border town of Tabatinga and crossed the river to Benjamin Constant. From there, I took a boat to São Leopoldo, once again entering illegally, as I had not requested permission from the FUNAI.

The village was easy to find; a large sign on the bank said "Porto São Leopoldo. Welcome." As I disembarked from the skiff, I was lucky to find the community's captain, Leovilio Ramos Lopes, right there. His brother, the schoolteacher Constantino, had told him I was coming, and we set off toward the village, a walk of about an hour. The sky was dark with impending rain, and as we walked along, eating mangoes, Leovilio told me that he had dreamed the previous night about two tame cows on the riverbank. I wasn't sure if that referred to me and Suely, a pretty blonde linguist from Brasília, who was going to study the Cocama Indians nearby, but I didn't ask.

Soon the village appeared on a rise in the jungle, a collection of small wooden houses on stilts, spread out over a wide area of hard-packed reddish earth dotted with trees. We went to Constantino's house, which was close to the path and quite modern. Inside, a plastic Christmas tree flashed tiny multicolored lights, an incongruous sight in the middle of the dense jungle in one of the most remote parts of Brazil. Constantino's young wife, Franci, sat on the doorstep with her baby son, Christian. An older son, named Mario Sergio, a child of three, was playing nearby with his cousin Leonice, a pretty girl of five or six.

The front room of Constantino's small wooden house was quite festive, painted turquoise, decorated with bright-colored bunches of plastic grapes, a poster of the Brazilian flag surrounded by flashing lights, Constantino's teaching certificates, framed, and a large picture of Jesus, also framed. The room held little furniture, but was divided by a large shelf, which held schoolbooks, a large dictionary and a television set.

We stood outside to talk, beside an *abiu* tree that had a television aerial tied in its uppermost branches. The mosquitoes were pretty bad, but after a while, Constantino took me for a tour of the village, the children tagging along.

Constantino was a slim young man of twenty-three, with sharp features and a faint mustache. Painfully polite, very tidy about his appearance, he was a devout Christian, yet at the same time a staunch supporter of his race and its culture.

He pointed out the school, up on the ridge near the path I had come in by, a large open building of wooden boards painted pale green. He told me that attendance had dropped quite sharply — by more than a third — since the massacre. We turned and made our way down a path parallel with the river, passing several houses, some brightly painted in shades of turquoise and blue, others simply left to become a mottled combination of brown and weather-beaten gray. They all had corrugated metal roofs and two steps leading to the front door. Some had larger palm-thatched pavilions behind them for cooking. We crossed a fetid little stream, bridged by a raft of *paxiuba*, most of the slats missing; then we climbed higher and higher on the bare clay path. Far below, I could see the river again, gleaming in the afternoon sun. And as we walked, the little group following us grew. There was a chubby young man with a guitar, all dressed in white as if going to a party, who strummed and sang as we walked along, an old woman with a grandchild in her arms, who turned out to be Constantino's Aunt Hortensia, and a gaggle of children, the girls all in long, high-necked dresses like nightgowns. Such dress was a tradition in São Leopoldo, begun by Brother José of the Holy Cross.

Up we went to the highest hill in the village, where a white church with Gothic-style windows presided over the little community. Surrounded by towering palms and a picket fence of white and blue, it was the only building on the hill. In front of it stood a large cross bearing letters and the date 25-9-82, and a tall wooden gate topped by a large sign saying "Triumphal Entry of Jesus into Jerusalem."

Constantino opened the narrow doors and we went inside. It was quite small, with rows of plain benches on either side, one for women and the other for men. A red-painted altarpiece behind a wooden lattice was opened as the small group came in and sat down. For a moment, Aunt Hortensia stood framed against an open window, a black silhouette in front of a fretwork of leaves. The service began as the chapel grew dark. There was singing, prayer and readings from the Gospel of Matthew in Tikuna and Portuguese by Constantino and an older man.

The sect of the Santa Cruz, or Holy Cross, was brought to the Upper Solimões by a mystic from the state of Minas who called himself Brother José of the Cross. His real name was José Fernandes Nogueira, and though he had dreamed in his youth of becoming a priest, circumstances prevented him from entering a seminary. Instead, married and with seven children, he slowly began to take on the identity of a priest or missionary. He claimed to have received a vision, and he organized hundreds of pilgrimages throughout Brazil. He began to travel all over his own country and through South America, preaching, baptizing and saying a mass that was a sort of pre-Vatican II imitation of the real thing.

He arrived in the Upper Solimões from Peru in the early seventies, with a reputation as a saint and miracle worker. His teachings, invariably ascetic in content, quickly caught on, especially among the Indian population. Drinking, smoking, dancing and rituals were forbidden, as was any hint of suggestive clothing. Women had to be kept covered up, preferably in long white gowns. Large crosses were erected in every village, as Brother José had preached that the end was near and only those standing near a cross would be saved.

The service lasted perhaps half an hour. When it was over, we stepped outside into the growing dark. The village's eight-horsepower generator had been turned on, and I could see a string of light bulbs winding through the village like a trail of fireflies. I was worried about getting down the steep hill in the dark — moon and stars were completely obscured by clouds — but Aunt Hortensia took my arm and did not let go until we were on level land again.

At Constantino's house, I put up my hammock in the front room and had dinner in the kitchen in the back. The upper part of the walls were open louvers, through which we could see the fading shapes of the trees. A big bunch of green bananas sat in one corner, a screened cabinet in another. There were also an electric fan and a refrigerator, both useless, since neither worked on the power from the small generator. A neighbor and his three children came over to talk to Constantino, so we all ate together. It was a typical dinner of fish, rice and cassava meal, dampened with fish broth. I fell asleep soon afterward in my hammock, the lights of the Christmas tree twinkling through the coarse cotton cover in which I had wrapped myself against cold, mosquitoes and wandering cockroaches.

The next morning, Constantino and I began our journey through the painful passages of memory in São Leopoldo, talking to the men and women most directly affected by the massacre. We stopped first at a large open pavilion, its roof shaggy with dried palm thatch, where Constantino chatted with a group of old people. The men wore white shirts and trousers, the shirts painted with two green and yellow stripes. An old woman wore a long, full-sleeved dress of white with a green and yellow cord around her waist, the prescribed Santa Cruz dress for Sundays. Inside the pavilion, several wheelbarrows were stacked, one on top of the other, in a corner. There was also a thick pair of wooden rollers, used to squeeze the juice from sugarcane, operated by a pair of large wheels in which people had to run, hamsterlike, to provide power. The equipment, like the village generator, had been purchased with proceeds from the communal lands. Everyone had a plot to work outside São Leopoldo, as well as the community property. Much of their income came from the growing and processing of Cassava into a toasted meal called *farinha*, the Amazonian staple that had graced almost every meal I had eaten outside Rio.

We set off for the house of Jordão Pinto. He was sitting on his front stoop, trimming the hair of his son, Pedrinho, a boy of about twelve, with scissors and a comb. As we moved inside, Seu Jordão told me that his son-in-law, Marcos, had been killed in the massacre on the Capacete Stream. Now his daughter Maria, twenty-one, had come to live in his house with her three small children. We left our sandals outside and entered a large, open room, partially divided by benches and hammocks, the rafters hung with items of clothing. The place was full of people, adults and children. Maria, a slim woman with long, curly hair, sat swinging gently in a hammock, feeding her youngest, who was no more than a year old. We sat and talked about the massacre, but when I tried to ask Maria how she felt, she could not answer me. "She understands your question," said Constantino, "but she cannot speak." Putting her hand against her forehead, she could only look down and cry, mumbling a few words in Tikuna to Constantino. "As soon as she knew her husband had died, she felt very sad," he related to me. "She cried a lot and until now still thinks of him. It has been nine months," he added, "and the FUNAI still have not taken care of applying for some kind of pension for her or the other widows."

A Tikuna leader named Paulo Mendes, a heavy young man wearing aviator sunglasses, was visiting with three men from Porto Novo Lima. He broke in and added, "Not only the community of São Leopoldo but all of the communities are so sad, all of the Tikuna are feeling this. Not the kind of sadness where we want to involve ourselves in revenge. But we are all relatives, we are one big family." His tone indicated that the word "sad" was hardly adequate for what he and the others felt. In a language that was not their own, it was the only way they could describe the residue of the massacre.

I asked whether there had been talk of revenge after the incident. At first, Constantino and Paulo assured me that this had never entered anyone's head, but later they admitted that it had. The leader of all the Tikuna communities, Pedro Inacio Pinheiro, had said that justice must be done or the Tikuna would exact justice themselves. But Pedro Inacio was not an adherent to the Santa Cruz sect, and the restraint showed by the men of the villages affected by the massacre had a lot to do with their Christian beliefs. Constantino said that Pedro's words were really a warning to the country that something had to be done. In the village, Constantino had tried to persuade its more angry members that it was wrong to kill, that they should not act like the whites who had attacked them. "That would be wrong," he said.

We then went to a smaller, darker house close by, that of the family of Ernesto Inacio. The place was noisy with the cries of a small infant, while Seu Ernesto's oldest daughter, one of the children who had followed us to the church the day before, played with her friends. Seu Ernesto seemed beaten and almost lifeless when I asked about the massacre. His voice was very low, almost inaudible, so that I could barely understand him. "I think about it all the time," he muttered in an undertone, "about the son I lost and all the other brothers who were lost." The memory was even more agonizing because he, too, had been there when the shooting broke out. Through all the panic, he had wondered where his son Batista had gotten to, unable to look for him, praying that he might be safe. The boy, his oldest, was only ten years old. Batista's body had never been found, carried away like so many by the Solimões. It was not necessary to ask Seu Ernesto how he felt. His entire person showed that he was a crushed man.

It started to rain heavily, and Constantino and I returned to his house. The sound of the shower on the metal roof was so loud we practically had to shout to make ourselves heard. When the rain stopped, we went outside again and across the road to the house of Constantino's parents, Alice and João.

Their home was far more traditional than their son's, and full of children, including Leonice and her younger brother. It consisted of a big open room like a veranda, with a small bedroom off to one side. Like Seu Jordão's, it was furnished with benches and hammocks, along with a couple of chairs, extending to an open-roofed area for cooking and eating. A fire burned on an upraised platform, which seemed to push right into the foliage behind the house. On looking closer, I saw that the platform held a large shallow box, paved with a slab of dry clay. Long pieces of wood barred it from any inquisitive children, and a wooden spit ran across the smoldering sticks beneath it, balancing a couple of roasting bananas.

Sitting on the floor in the middle of the big room, her long skirts spread around her, Dona Alice was weaving *aruma* fibers stripped from the stem of the palm, rather like fine but tough straw. Grasping a few lengths of the thin fiber between her toes, she braided the strands together, continually weaving new fibers into a thick, strong thread with which to make a diamond-patterned hammock or a sturdy bag. The artistry of the Tikuna has long been recognized in Brazil, where they are famous for all kinds of weaving and painting, from baskets, bags and hammocks to fantastic ritual masks made of wood and bark cloth and colorful bark-cloth drawings, called *turi*. Beside her, Dona Alice had a bag of coiled *aruma*. Some of the fibers were pale yellow, others dyed purple with the leaves of the *pacova* plant.

Later in the day, Aunt Hortensia gave me a bag and three slim armbands she had woven, to thank me, I supposed, for taking some pictures of her, her daughter and her granddaughter. The armbands were simple connecting squares of bright color, finely woven and dyed purple, yellow and pink. They were beautiful, but I realized I had yet to see anyone in São Leopoldo wearing the armbands. I wondered if they had fallen out of favor thanks to Brother José.

It showered several more times that afternoon. In the evening we padded through the thick mud to the house of Nilsa Quirim, whose husband, Valentino, had been so cruelly shot and killed as he struggled in the river. The family's house was on the other side of the fetid stream, toward the hill on which the church stood. It was dark inside. Only two kerosene lamps were burning. Four children sat quietly in the corner, including the eldest, Cristina, a pretty girl in a blue-flowered dress wearing a tiny wooden cross on a long white string. Breast feeding a toddler who squirmed around, sleepy and impatient, her hair disheveled, and her face tired, Nilsa looked far older than her thirty-five years. With Constantino translating, she spoke in a low, little-girl's voice about the loss of her husband.

"She feels very sad thinking about her husband," said Constantino, "who has left her with five children, with no one to give them food. Before, when he was alive, they always worked together. Now she must work alone and can't manage as well. Often, there is not enough food for them. The children cry and always ask her, 'Where is our father? Why did he die?'"

Her only future was her children. Once they were older they would be able to help her. The three oldest were girls, and she hoped that when they were old enough to marry, her sons-in-law would help her also.

She had received the news of her husband's death on the afternoon of the day of the massacre. "That night when she was sleeping," said Constantino, "she saw, she felt a person enter the house, something like a person, the soul of her husband. He came inside, then over here, where this little one here — " he gestured to the youngest boy, "was sleeping, and he woke up. It seems it was his father, his soul, who came to see the child one last time, and then he left, going out the back door, through there. After that, she says, she stopped crying."

We left early the next morning, after Constantino closed up his small house and left his little boy, Mario Sergio, with his parents. With Franci carrying the baby, we set off toward the river. The path was muddy, and I kept my balance by treading on the long grass that grew beside it. Along the way, we passed a huge tree, its branches hung with the sock-shaped nests of the oropendula. Just before we arrived at the riverbank, it began to rain, and we ended up spending most of the morning visiting people.

We waited out the first shower on the veranda of the house of the family I had seen when I had arrived from Benjamin with Suely. They were finishing a breakfast of fish and *mapiti*, a fruit that resembles an overgrown grape. Neither Franci, who was white, nor I could understand the conversation, but the family and Constantino seemed to be telling a lot of jokes, frequently kidding each other and bursting into laughter.

As soon as it cleared, we set off in Constantino's small motor-boat, but did not get far. The sky threatened more rain, and Constantino stopped again. This time we visited other relatives of his, a large extended family dominated, it seemed, by women.

The women insisted on feeding us. Franci and I sat in a lean-to made of woven palm, looked after by a pair of aunts who enjoyed being solicitous. They were stocky, motherly creatures in cotton dresses and aprons, each with a tiny pigmy marmoset, speckled fur as fine as feathers and long ringed tails, attached by a long string pinned to their ample bosoms, like pieces of living jewelry. One of the marmosets had an even tinier baby clinging to its back.

Other people who had been caught in the rain joined us, and the atmosphere was like a party. I could understand enough to know that Constantino, as he had done all weekend in Sao Leopoldo, was telling everyone about his trip to the south with the other Tikuna leaders. There was an old man missing a hand; as he sat, he hooked his old blue cap onto his stump and tucked it into his elbow. Constantino's parents showed up with all the children, and even his brother, Leovilio, was there. Two ancient women, gaunt and slow-moving as tortoises, came out of the cabin to look at us, and Constantino told me that one was an aunt, the other her mother. To me they both looked so old, with their wrinkled faces, wild hair tied down with kerchiefs, that I could not tell which was mother and which daughter. The two aunts with the marmosets also had frizzy hair, and I wondered if there had been some inter-racial marriage.

We were in a big yard, surrounded by trees, with the small cabin at one end and the open kitchen at the other. On one side, parallel to the riverbank, ran a wide garden of cassava, the plants standing apart from each other like small trees, under which the ducks and chickens liked to shelter during the rain showers. Cobs of pale yellow corn, their husks tied together, had been hung to dry over long poles held by upright forked sticks and covered with a bit of metal roofing. Several lengths of cut lumber leaned against a *cupuaçu* tree, while nearby there stood a high makeshift table loaded with baskets and bags of things. Two baby parrots sat in the mess, creeping under an over-turned basin to escape whenever I tried to catch one. A long, flat island, planted with corn and cassava, sat in the river just in front of us. A flock of white herons had perched on the few sturdy little trees poking through the long grass at the far end.

The two aunts cooked over an open fire in the palm shelter, boiling a recently killed chicken in a large pot. A wooden table set with dishes and pans of water stood to one side. Over it, a square palm sieve attached to the eaves contained scouring wool and a package of biscuits. The rain temporarily stopped, and the aunts wasted no time in setting out plates of cassava meal, fish and bananas on a table in the middle of the yard. The fish was an ugly black creature, called *bodo*, which I had first seen in the market in Tabatinga. Spiny bits of fish swam in bowls of broth, and when I told Constantino I couldn't eat them — they were just too ugly — he translated this, and everyone laughed.

Finally we left and began the trip to Benjamin, hoping it would not rain again. Constantino's boat was an open wooden canoe powered by a very inadequate little motor. Before we embarked, the old man with one hand ran over and gave me three emerald-colored limes, then ran to his own boat. I waved and called out thanks, and he flashed me an enormous, toothless smile.

Fortunately, the sun held up for the two-hour journey to Benjamin. We passed the Capacete Stream, where the massacre had taken place, and Seu Flores' green-painted house, high up on the bank, shut up and abandoned. Constantino told me that the municipality had said, with a shameful lack of sensitivity, that they were going to turn it into a schoolhouse, a school where no Tikuna child would ever set foot. We also passed a man in a *casco*, plying a bright blue paddle painted with a white flower. Constantino guardedly informed me that the man was one of the whites who had taken part in the massacre. He would have been out of jail for at least two months, I guessed, because the court case was going so slowly and the law allowed a suspect to be imprisoned for a maximum of six months.

Birds flew among the trees and reeds lining the water's edge. Occasionally we would see a man, just his torso visible fishing in a tiny canoe. The disk-shaped paddles of the Tocantins had here become sharp, diamond-shaped paddles, which cleaved the water like glistening spades. As we passed sawn-wood houses, women beating clothes or cleaning fish by the river's edge, men fishing quietly in the reeds, brown children swimming naked in the shallows, I realized that it was impossible for me to tell the whites and the Tikuna apart. Both lived in small wooden shacks, both wore clothes bought in town, and both believed in the same God. Both ate fish and *farinha* three times a day. Both toasted *farinha* and caught fish to sell in Benjamin. Both were poor. Yet one was human and the other an animal, dangerous, untrustworthy, alien, killable.

It was a question I took up that night, when I dropped in on Jussara Gomes, a tall young woman with gold-rimmed glasses from the south who worked in the Centro Magüta, or Tikuna Center, in Benjamin. Although she had first come to the Upper Solimões twelve years earlier, Jussara had been working in the region for about four years. One project she worked on was the setting up of the Tikuna Museum, a revolutionary idea for a place like Benjamin. The other was equally revolutionary, a new course of education in the Tikuna language, based on the creation legends, which were in danger of being lost. Not surprisingly, both the FUNAI and the local government detested both ideas.

We sat in her living room, a simply furnished space with mats and pillows on the floor, and baskets, masks and vividly colored bark-cloth drawings decorating the white walls. The situation was complicated, said Jussara, but the massacre of March 28 clearly reflected all its facets.

The Tikuna, who formed about 40 percent of the population in the municipality of Benjamin, had always been considered the lowest of the low. "He is nothing," said Jussara, "worse than an animal." Then there were the economically repressive circumstances affecting most of the white population in the area. The system of *patrões*, or bosses, was still prevalent among the rural poor, the river dwellers. They were always, I learned, referred to as the *fregues*, or customers, of certain bosses, to whom they owed their loyalty, their labor and their business. They were families with no title to their land, and they depended on one wealthy man for the things they needed to buy, for jobs tapping rubber or cutting lumber, for the sale of their few products and for permission to live on the land fronting the river. The status of the *fregues* matched that of the Indian, but the boss made sure this fact was never acknowledged. The white was better than the Indian, even if the white had Indian blood in his veins.

The whites who had attacked the unarmed Tikuna at the house of Flores Salvador had all been *fregues* of a man named Oscar Castelo Branco, a wizened old man who sold lumber. Oscar claimed that the land that sat between two tracts demarcated as indigenous areas, São Leopoldo and Porto Espiritual, was his, and had allowed some white families to settle there. He had also logged on Indian lands, and had had seven hundred cedar trunks confiscated from him by the police when the Tikuna complained. Oscar owned a floating trading post, where he bought the produce of the local whites and sold them goods in return. He had moored it to the side of Capacete Stream, which was demarcated for the Indians. They had asked him several times to move it until one night, some Indians untied the post and towed it to the other side of the Capacete. In revenge, or perhaps as a challenge, a cow belonging to the Tikuna had been killed.

These acts intensified the ill feeling between the white river dwellers, poor, dependent, always afraid of losing their land, and the Tikuna, who desperately wanted the lands to which they were entitled by the constitution. As time went on, and the problem was not resolved by the FUNAI or the Institute for Agrarian Reform, Oscar Castelo Branco played his "customers" like a guitar, getting just the resonance he required to increase his profits. At the same time it began to be rumored that the chunk of land between the two reserves was finally going to be demarcated. Oscar's *fregues* were afraid they would have to leave and would receive only a paltry financial indemnity for their wooden shacks. And why? Just because of a bunch of Indians.

These were the circumstances that led to the massacre. In an effort to resolve the problems, the Indians had sent two of their captains to fetch the police and a FUNAI representative. But the police never came. Typically, given the ineptitude of authority in the Amazon, the police had no diesel fuel to travel to the Capacete. While the Indians had waited, the whites had prepared to kill them.

It became obvious when I talked to Jussara during time I spent in the Center that the various powers-that-be in Benjamin kept her on pins and needles. Sentiment in the town was strongly against the Tikuna after the massacre; it was considered to be entirely their own fault.

Benjamin was a town of no more than a dozen or so streets criss-crossing the high, flat ridge on the south bank of the Solimões. The river is really the Amazon, but west of Manaus it has a different name. Some believe the name comes from the Sorimões Indians who once lived along its banks; the French traveler La Condamine translated it as the River of Poisons because of a tribe of Indians who used poison-tipped arrows. I had arrived after a very early flight from Manaus to the frontier town of Tabatinga, where army officers stood in the lobby of the airport terminal and watched everyone who disembarked. A few backpacking tourists arrived when I did, so I did not stand out.

The town of Tabatinga was ugly and hot, with few trees and no attractive architecture. The wharf was the worst part of it. Aside from one modern port-authority building and its floating metal dock, it was given over to a long, rambling, filthy market with very little to sell. I walked through it thinking what an inferno of poverty it was. Produce was arrayed on the muddy street, odd-looking produce, such as the ugly black *bodó* fish and the large purple *mapiti* fruit. Miserable shacks clustered in a tangle below and along a ridge at the far end of the market. The reeds along the bank were fouled with garbage and scum. A long, narrow plank led from the muddy shore over the dirty water to the riverboat that made the crossing to Benjamin.

The trip took about an hour. The flat water was laden with silt and littered with branches and other floating vegetation, like a floor that needed sweeping. Benjamin was marginally more attractive than Tabatinga and it was easy to find the hotels: they were the only two four-story buildings in sight. The town's main street sported a few fenced-in almond trees, and there was a modern octagonal church in its center. Cement-block houses that looked like garages served as restaurants, stores and bars and opened onto the hot, unshaded streets. The heat was of a continuous, ovenlike intensity, the kind that kept your clothes permanently damp. Most people spoke Spanish as a second language, and there were often people in town from Colombia or Peru to trade at the market. I spent two weeks there, and it struck me as a very unfriendly place.

The Centro Magüta was set well back on the main street, a simple, airy building of sawn wood divided into several rooms, cool and shaded by a grove of palm trees. It was used as a resource center as well as a place for visiting Tikuna to stay. While I was there, a group of Tikuna, including Constantino, had just returned from a trip to Brasília, São Paulo and Rio, where they spoke to government leaders and took part in a mock trial of those accused of the massacre. Everything had been videotaped, and visitors were invited to sit and watch it on the television monitor.

One afternoon, I walked over to the house of Benjamin's mayor and interviewed him about the situation in town. Sixty-one-year-old João Correia de Oliveira was a dark-skinned man with glittering green eyes. Picking his teeth after lunch on the front porch of his house, he turned out to be a difficult and far from articulate individual. But what he said to me was indicative of how many people in Benjamin saw the massacre.

The first thing he said when I asked him about it was, "Oh, you've already really turned up the drama in that situation," referring to the press. It all happened because of certain organizations, he said, meaning the people at the Center, and even the church, people who had what he called "dreadful orientation, people who are not of this region, who come from other places."

"So," he went on, "there happened the dramatic situation, where cultured people — and there were already these threats and rumors — were warned and alert that they would have to leave their land. And it wasn't the Indians' land, it was the whites' land. People who had been here for generations and generations, eighty years, and were going to lose their land and not receive other land, or only get an insignificant quantity of money. There was no justice in that sense. And so this situation of a shock formed between the two classes."

He felt profoundly sorry about it, said Correia, and prayed to God "that persons coming to the Indian orient him correctly, proportioning peace and harmony, because war gets you no place.

"So we hope that such a drama never occurs again," he said, "in which people die without deserving to; simply carried away by the influence of others. I know the behavior of the people here," he finished, suggesting that the Tikuna were not normally given to "threats and rumors."

The mayor admitted that a school was indeed functioning on the site of the massacre, and had been since the previous June, less than three months after the event. He had set it up there, he said, because now there was a police post there as well, and thus the school would be "better protected."

The following day, I took the boat back to Tabatinga. I ran into Constantino again; he was there to check into the FUNAI office and sign a form showing that he was back from his trip. I did not know that Indians had to do that sort of thing; it reminded me of the pass laws under apartheid in South Africa. We separated at the dock because there were army personnel there, and I walked a bit beyond the FUNAI office to the local prosecuting ministry. I wanted to talk to the local prosecuting attorney who was bringing the state's case against the twelve men charged with carrying out the massacre. His name was Caio Bessa

Cyrino, a young man who looked very earnest in his thick glasses, dressed most unsuitably in a three-piece suit.

Caio explained that there had been some delays in the process, which was currently in the criminal instruction phase, because the case had been erroneously sent to the federal courts at first, instead of the state court. Then the elections of mid-November had caused another interruption. "So now," he said, "the judge is hearing the accused as well as the witnesses for the defence and the prosecution. Once the cases have been summed up, he must decide whether the case goes to a jury trial." Caio thought the case might be wrapped up in about six weeks.

I told him I had heard he wanted the trial to take place in Manaus instead of Benjamin. "Well," he said, "the law stipulates that the jury trial be held in the locality of the crime. But since we in the public ministry do not feel that there is the right climate for a trial in Benjamin — there are still segments of society who have what I would call a prejudicial posture against Indians in that municipality — we can ask to have the trial moved." He could have it moved only to the nearest municipality, however, which was not Manaus, but Tabatinga. And the people of Tabatinga, he felt, had a different perspective on the case and on the Indian population as a whole. "The indigenous population of Benjamin Constant strongly refuses to be the cheap labor of the entrepreneurs there," he explained, "the logging and fish-buying companies, and that is why different ideas have diffused through the white population there. But Tabatinga is different; its economy is based far more on trade and commerce. There is still a risk, but of less intensity than in Benjamin."

I asked Caio what he thought about the case. I hoped he might be able to explain what had been bothering me since my arrival. Did he not find it incredible at times that he was prosecuting such a bizarre case? Had he gathered any insight as to how the killing in cold blood of unarmed adults and children could have happened?

He looked thoughtful for a moment and admitted that he had asked himself the same thing many times. "It really reflects the situation that you can see all over Brazil," he said. "You know that you can turn on your television any night, and on the six o'clock news watch military policemen beating workers on strike, students, the oppressed and the exploited. That is how I see this situation. These settlers are also oppressed, and at the same time the truth is that they committed this grave crime, one which was practically genocidal. If the level of distribution of land, income and political power were equal in Brazil, if the genuine rights of the Indians were respected all along, we would not have to go around resolving these occupants' rights. Because this problem has been there for a long time. If each and every Brazilian citizen, like these defendants, had the right to a piece of land they could call their own, without owing favors to some entrepreneur, this massacre would never have happened. They would have had their own land to work, on which to live. These men had their own land to work, on which to live. These men had lived as long as fifteen years without having to pay a cent to Oscar Castello Branco. So it's possible that you can find some kind of answer there; it is the only corollary I've been able to find. Because I understand the solidarity they have with Castelo Branco, but what I can't understand is the form, the brutal form, it took. The fact is, these men are as Indian or almost Indian as the Tikuna. They are an army in rags, yet capable of decimation."

Caio had also noticed the difference between reaction to the massacre abroad and in the area. "While in other parts of Brazil, and throughout the world, people are still shocked about the massacre, here I have noticed a certain indifference to it all. I don't know why exactly, but I believe, to a certain extent, that it is due to the way the ideology of the dominating classes manages to pass into the whole population."

While in Tabatinga, I took the opportunity of crossing the border into Colombia for the afternoon to see the city of Leticia. It cost less than a dollar to take a van down the street and into the neighboring city, and I could only tell I had crossed the border because the buildings began to look more prosperous, the signs changed to Spanish, and the beach-ball colors of the Colombian flag could be seen flying over public offices. But as I stepped out of the van in a different country, it felt like far more than the language had changed. Leticia was the state capital of a tiny province that pokes out of the rest of Colombia to insinuate itself between Brazil and Peru. It seemed like a small, tropical show-piece of a town, with cream-colored buildings, wide, shady streets, all of them paved, and a wonderful modern library building, which also housed a museum. It was possible to buy Tikuna artifacts in Leticia; they were made in Brazil but not available anywhere there.

The next day, in Benjamin, I met the head captain of the Tikuna tribe, Pedro Inacio, who had returned from Manaus. He too had been at the mock trial in São Paulo and was now planning to return to his village, Vendaval.

I also planned to go to Vendaval, to see a village that was known to be more traditional than the communities closer to Benjamin, and which had definitively cut any ties with the sect of Santa Cruz. I asked Pedro Inacio what he thought about the sect. "We did not feel that this sect was good for the Tikuna," he explained, "because it forbade us from following our traditions and customs. And these things had been passed down to us from our fathers and forefathers for centuries. So a few people decided to move and are now in a village across the river from us."

Pedro Inacio was a small man with bowl-cut black hair and a face both stubborn and gentle. He was a great defender of the Tikuna culture and was adamant that justice be done after the massacre. It was he who had warned that if justice was not done, the Tikuna would exact their own justice.

Leadership among the Tikuna was based on various things: heredity, to a certain extent, strength of purpose, the ability to deal with the white man, courage. For these latter qualities, Pedro Inacio was a good choice. An articulate, thoughtful man, he showed no deference to the whites in Benjamin or in Brasília. He preferred life in the village to life in the white world, but he did not reject the white world, and he was politically astute. He refused to let drop the demand that Tikuna land be demarcated when the FUNAI and the Brazilian government found the excuse that Tikuna territory was in a national security zone because it was close to the border. If the FUNAI would not demarcate their land, he said, the Tikuna would do it themselves. During the trip to the south, he had told reporters, "If the government does not help us, we will resolve this in another way. There could be much violence, but we are not afraid of death. We will die for the right to our native land and we will be buried there."

In 1986, the Tikuna had formed a council and elected Pedro Inacio as its leader. At the same time, he told me, they had discussed how they could act politically to help the Tikuna secure their rights. "We discussed various political parties in Brazil," he said, "and decided to opt for the Workers' Party. It is the party that represents all the poor and suffering in Brazil, the workers, those people who do not have a voice in this country, who suffer injustices all the time, without anything being done. Now, in the last elections, we succeeded in electing four councillors."

I asked him if their activity in the Workers' Party might be a way of bridging the gap between the Tikuna and the poor whites of the area. It was certainly something they would like, he said, but so far, unfortunately, things had not worked out that way. "It's unfortunate because the poor white, the worker here, even though he is in the same situation as us, he does not know this, he isn't conscious of the problem. They are dependent on the bosses, and so far, they still vote for other parties, the ones the boss tells them to vote for, the parties of the big men. There are very few whites in the Workers' Party here," he added. "The great majority of members are Tikuna."

Pedro Inacio's point of view corresponded to that of Chico Mendes and the rubber tappers of Acre, who had realized that, once their own council was formed, they had to join with the Indians to stem the tide of destruction and insure the rights of the downtrodden and exploited in Amazonia. Chico called the new organization they were setting up with rubber tappers and Indians the Union of People of the Forest, and it represented a major step forward in resolving the problems of each group.

According to Pedro Inacio, the election of four councillors, one in each municipality in the Upper Solimões, had been a great boost to the confidence of the Tikuna. Now, he said, they would travel to Brasilia to meet with other Indian tribes, each of them carrying the documentation that proved what land was theirs according to the constitution. "The FUNAI," he said, "which claims to protect us, refuses to demarcate our territory because they say that it's inside a zone of national security. They want to enclose us in indigenous villages. We have to organize ourselves to fight for our rights, not only the Tikuna but all the indigenous of Brazil."

I hoped to get to know Pedro Inacio better, but he had little time that day. The motor of the Center's boat had broken, and the part, ordered from Peru, had still not arrived. Pedro Inacio told me that he was going to spend a day with his family, all of whom were staying at the house of his daughter in Porto Novo Lima, and so I arranged to get to Vendaval somehow and meet him there in the next few days.

THIRTEEN

THE PEOPLE OF YOI

T HE TRIP TO VENDAVAL WAS long and almost ridiculously arduous.

I went with one of the village's schoolteachers, Reinaldo do Carmo, who had also been to the mock trial. There were eight or nine of us traveling in an aluminum motorboat, and the trip started out fine, until, partway through the afternoon, it began to rain. We quickly covered all the goods, including the enormous cassette tape recorder Reinaldo had bought in Manaus, and ourselves with bits of plastic sheeting, hoping that the rain would soon stop. It didn't. It continued to pour down in bursts and bucketfuls, even as the sky turned black, and we were still miles and miles away from the village. The temperature turned very cold as the water dripped and ran incessantly underneath the sheeting. Our arms slowly grew wet, as well as our feet. I pulled out my hammock to keep myself warm, and soon it, too, was soaked. Our backs began to ache from hunching over and holding up the plastic. Occasionally, I lifted it to look out, and saw nothing but sheets of rain pinging on the clay-colored water and a strip of green shore.

At about eight that night, we stopped to let someone off. It still rained, so we remained under the plastic sheeting. I didn't think I could possibly feel more uncomfortable until I began to notice that I was beginning to itch all over. Motionless at the riverbank, we were a target for hungry mosquitoes and soon everyone was scratching and fidgeting. The owner of the boat took ages to come back, and we must have sat in misery for at least half an hour. Finally he returned and set off again. We would not be able to reach Vendaval that night, Reinaldo informed me, so we were going to stop in the village of Belém do Solimões.

We arrived at the village at about nine-thirty and clambered up the muddy bank through the rain. After waiting for an hour for someone to open the community center, we found ourselves somewhere to sleep. But it was incredibly cold, and everything I had brought with me was wet and clammy. Nonetheless, I strung up my hammock and managed to get some sleep.

I woke up at about 5 A.M., as if from a nightmare. Reinaldo was curled up on the floor on a paper poster of the Brazilian flag. He must have had an awful night, I thought. But at least the rain had stopped. As we left Belém do Solimões in the gray dawn, I could see a fairly large village of wooden houses, complete with a telecommunications pole, indicating that there was a phone or radio there.

We entered a stream and made one more brief stop to let a passenger off at his house. The boat came to rest beside a bunch of huge lily pads, torn with the weight and the force of the rain, in front of a rambling wooden cabin. Reinaldo and a few others got out also and came back with some cold roast fish. It was shared out as we set off again, but when Reinaldo offered me a piece I turned it down; it was too early for me to contemplate such a meal. A few minutes later, he said, "Everyone is worried because you're not eating. You must be hungry." I said not to worry, I had a few crackers that were still dry and would eat those instead.

By the time I arrived in Vendaval, I was cold, wet, hungry and extremely miserable, until the hot sun slowly dried me out, and Reinaldo gave me a cup of coffee. I barely noticed the beautiful sight of the dawn-misted channel of river between an island and the shore, dotted with little wooden *cascos*, each one containing a man holding out a line for fish.

Unlike São Leopoldo, which was inland and surrounded by jungle, Vendaval, which means "windmill," stretched along the river, high up on a flat ridge. It seemed to resemble any Amazonian village with its rows of sawn-wood houses, the stamped earth dotted with all kinds of fruit trees and palms. And while Constantino's Christmas tree had seemed an incongruous sight in São Leopoldo, in Vendaval I saw a small flock of about six woolly sheep that really looked as if they'd rather be somewhere else.

Reinaldo lived in a house not far from the river but facing a few other houses. It had once been the schoolhouse, he told me, but the village built a larger one, and he began to live in the old one after adding a kitchen. He lived with his wife, Yilda, and three children, Enildo, Rosiane and the youngest one who, though almost two years old, did not have a name yet, so was just called the Tikuna word for "man."

The house was small and closed in, like the houses of better-off peasants in the Amazon. The first half of the house was divided in two, with a curtain over the doorway, through which I once saw a spider as big as my palm sitting on the wall next to the mirror. The main living room was where I slept in a hammock of *tucuma*-palm fibers, beside a table and bench. For the first couple of days, I was an object of curiosity among the children, who could fill a doorway faster than anything I had ever seen, just standing and staring. Most of the time, people sat in the kitchen, which had a table with stools, a raised clay stove on a platform and nine big baskets of *farinha*, which Reinaldo had bought for his own use and to resell. There were a few fishing spears stuck onto the rafters, and in a corner, a dusty folded-up baby stroller.

It was not until the next day that I had a good look around. A line of trees ran between the river and the broad track that served as a street. Almost every house in the long row had a number and a cross painted on a small slab of wood. Reinaldo pointed out the schoolhouse and the community center, simple wood buildings like all the others.

We stopped at one house where an older woman with long black hair was skillfully sewing palm thread around a long, pliable strip of palm stem with a wooden needle. She worked slowly, and I enjoyed watching her, although we could not communicate very well. She would point to things like the needle or a bird and say its name, after which I would repeat the word, to the great amusement of the children who came around to watch. The woman sat on a bench outside, beneath a large palm shelter built to cover the family's cassava-roasting pan. A round clay oven had been built up, like a large knob, in the center of the yard, and on top of it was the huge flat-bottomed pan, perhaps four or five feet in diameter. Wooden paddles for stirring rested against it.

Reinaldo and I stopped next at a large house constructed in the traditional style of the Tikuna. When I saw the place, airy and pale gold in the sunlight, I had to wonder why so many Indians were turning to the building of small enclosed sawn-wood shacks. Was it simply because they were "white," as Jussara described it? This traditional home was so much more comfortable, pleasant, full of space and light. In fact the place was not really a house at all, in the Western sense. It was almost completely open to the world outside, with a high palm roof that sloped almost to the ground, and only one slat wall. Most of its area was taken up with the large open space where I found a bench to sit on; a smaller platform, filled with hammocks and clothing, had been built in a corner against the wall. Down from there and extending along the wall were a number of objects, big baskets and square sieves, a pair of diamond-shaped paddles, their tips painted black, a large clay pot, brooms, and a hammock. Half a dozen wooden staffs, beautifully carved with animals, birds and other figures, had been wedged into the rafters beneath the neat creases of the dried palm roof. A drum was hanging from a pole. A bag and some rolls of painted bark cloth lay on a small makeshift loft. Many of these items had been used in a recent Festa da Moça Nova, the coming-of-age ritual of the family's oldest daughter.

Chubby and slant-eyed, the daughter was sprawled on her stomach on the platform with some younger friends, her father and a small boy of perhaps two. She must have been about thirteen years old. A few wisps of black hair peeked out from the kerchief she wore around her head. Most of her hair had been shorn or pulled out during the ritual, and she would have to wear the kerchief until it had grown out again. Two bands of woven palm had been tied just below her knees. She had to wear these until they wore out and broke off. But in a nonchalant juxtaposition of modern and traditional rituals, she had colored her fingernails with a coat of pink nail polish.

The Moca Nova ritual was the most important of the Tikuna life calendar, and involved a great deal of preparation. Reinaldo explained that the house had been built around it. The large open area where I sat had been used to accommodate the guests. In the ritual, the Tikuna girl spends three days inside a little corral or hut of bark cloth painted with all manner of figures and designs. Nowadays, even planes and motorboats mingle with the drawings of forest animals, birds and mythical creatures. After the three days, the girl's hair is plucked out by the women of her nation. (Every Tikuna belongs to a nation, represented by an animal or a bird. Reinaldo, for example, was of the currasow nation, as was the girl at the house. No Tikuna is allowed to marry someone from the same nation.) During and after the hair-pulling ceremony, young men wearing big, brightly adorned masks dance in front of the girl, and also among the guests. There is always a large clay tub of fermented cassava juice, to which the guests liberally help themselves.

Thanks to the proscriptions of Brother José da Cruz, the ritual had been abandoned in some villages. Vendaval was one of the few places where it was still an important event.

I sat for a while and watched the girl's mother weave a basket with lengths of green palm stem, the ground around her covered by little clouds of green filament, which she had peeled off the thin strips. The family's pet monkey kept running among the litter of pots and brooms along the wall, throwing around the coils of green fiber and making a general nuisance of himself.

We wandered around the village a little more, then Reinaldo and I turned and headed for home. On our way, I noticed that a large group of people had gathered in front of one of the houses in the long row along the river. They had collected, I could see as I drew closer, large piles of *carama* palm leaves and long *paxiuba* slats. I stood and watched as they formed into small groups, each with a bunch of leaves, which they began to twist, one by one, onto the slats. It was obvious they were making a new roof. Each leaf-covered slat would be laid across the beams, one on top of the other, to make a thick yet airy roof. Reinaldo commented that such roofs left a house a lot cooler than corrugated metal, but that metal had the advantage of allowing you to place buckets at the eaves to catch clean rainwater.

By the time we got home, lunch was ready. Reinaldo, his brother-in-law and I ate at the table, while Yilda, her sister and the children sat on the floor in a large circle. After lunch, Yilda put the dishes into a big pot and went down to the riverbank to wash them. A couple of boats were moored there, so she sat in one of them, rinsing everything, then scrubbing with soap, then rinsing again in the swift coffee-colored current. She also had a fish to clean, and while she worked, her sister bathed her oldest boy in the shallows.

Behind them, the river scene was lush and peaceful, the sun slowly beginning to wane. Off to the side, a narrow green spit widened into a headland crowned with trees. I watched a man in a *casco* row across the channel's mirrorlike surface, and farther upstream, a bunch of children played on a half-submerged log, their active bodies making busy black silhouettes against the lowering rays. I picked up the pot of clean dishes and indicated that I would carry them up to the house. Yilda could understand what I was saying, but was too shy to speak to me in Portuguese, so we never managed to communicate very much.

The Tikuna have had contact with the white man for more than three hundred years. Some anthropologists believe that the Tikuna originally came from farther inland to occupy the banks of the Solimões when slavery and the presence of rival Portuguese and Spanish colonists had driven the Omagua and Yurimagua tribes to Peru. The Tikuna were frequently forced to gather forest products for the profits of the Portuguese garrison commander in Tabatinga, were sold into slavery and were even sent to fight during the war with Paraguay in the 1860s. During the rubber boom, the Solimões River was an important thoroughfare between Iquitos, in Peru, and the Atlantic Ocean.

But the Tikuna, who call themselves the Magüta, say that they come from the land of Evare, which lies not far from Vendaval, inland from the Solimões. Their ancestors were fished out of the river by Yoi, the first man, and became human once they were on land. Yoi himself experienced an unusual birth, through a series of events that I found interesting because there was no attempt, in these legends, to describe an all powerful, father-like being. "Before the world existed," goes the legend, "Ngutapa already existed." Ngutapa had a wife whom he treated rather badly. Once, when she was annoying him, he tied her to a tree and left her there. The wife persuaded some wasps to sting Ngutapa in revenge, and when they did so, a huge swelling began to grow in his knee. Out of the swelling were born Yoi, a brother and two sisters, all armed with important weapons the Tikuna would use to hunt. Yoi and his brother, Ipi, were constant rivals and could be quite harsh to one another. Once when Ipi saw a trap set in the forest, he got angry. In trying to take it apart, he was caught in the trap and hanged. He died and turned into a wood deer. And Yoi's response was to say, "That will teach you!" (Ipi did come back to life later.)

These tales and many others like them made up the new school-book *Our People*, which was liberally illustrated with colorful naive drawings done by adults and children. The Tikuna had prepared the book with the help of the Center. The production of the book led to the preparation of a second, which was ready to be printed while I was in Benjamin.

Jussara had told me about the educational program she and an anthropologist, João Pacheco de Oliveira, had devised with the Tikuna leaders and teachers. It had begun with a request from the Indians, who spoke to their elders and gathered stories about the creation of man and the world according to the ancient legends. The more they questioned, the more stories they heard, until *Our People* brought the stories together in Portuguese and Tikuna.

Two years before the massacre, the Center had tried to bring whites and Indians closer together through another education project. Concerned about the tensions that the demarcation process would create, the group decided to begin a program of teacher training, combining Tikuna and white river dwellers. "We wanted to discuss the problems of demarcation and also the discrimination with which the Tikuna has always lived," Jussara had told me. "Teachers are very respected by the river dwellers. They are considered to be people who know more than most. So we thought about doing a booklet, and during classes collected stories and legends of the river dwellers. There was a very interesting dynamic between the two groups during classes," she had added. "They tried to balance their differences, and the Indians talked about their customs."

The following year, they carried out another program of teacher training. It, too, had worked well, according to Jussara, and there was a party afterward. But the attempt to bring the two races to a common view of their problems was no match for the power of the bosses. One of Jussara's students, a young man named Wanderlei, was one of the attackers on March 28. "They tell me that he was one of those who shot the most," she had said with a sigh. "He went after people who had fallen into the river, wounded, and kept shooting."

The staff at the FUNAI disliked the teacher-training idea from the beginning. After the massacre, they clamped down at the Center and on the Tikuna teachers. João Pacheco was barred by them from entering Indian territory anywhere in Brazil, and he returned to Rio to teach at the federal university. Jussara was also barred from entering Indian territory and could no longer travel into the villages to organize training courses for new Tikuna teachers. The teachers were also persecuted. In 1988, the FUNAI forbade any Tikuna teachers from participating in training courses upon pain of losing their jobs. "The prohibition really messes us up," Jussara had told me. "The original idea was to give the training courses in the village. The teachers had been complaining to the municipality that the courses are always done in the city. So we don't know what to do, and the teachers really want these courses."

In spite of the FUNAI, the teachers remained enthusiastic. "First of all, we wanted a book put together by the Tikuna," said Reinaldo, who had been taught at a Lutheran mission, "a book that told about the history of our ancestors. But once it was ready, we thought that we could apply it in the schools also. When we were doing the research, we did it so that we would be able to pass this on to our children, because we had often the children don't even know about our own customs. So we had begun to worry about that."

Previously, he said, the educational system had not worked all that well. Teachers were poorly trained and had classes that were too large. Children were taught in Portuguese in the schools and spoke Tikuna at home; they rarely had a chance to consolidate their speaking skills in Portuguese and could not read and write in their own language. As a result, few adults were literate. Some men could speak Portuguese from their experience of trading in the city, and some teenagers could write it. But, according to Reinaldo, the majority could do neither. "So there were three main points we wanted to take care of," he said, "to safeguard our legends, to teach Portuguese using everyday things in the area, and also to teach Tikuna. I think that both languages are important, because generally, we have to learn to master Portuguese to go into the city and deal with the whites."

He felt it was important to save the customs and culture of the tribe, because, as he put it, "We are not like the white, and some people didn't know any more about it. That was why we were afraid of losing it all. Now we are developing something, doing something, realizing that we cannot lose our customs."

Many years ago, he said, the stories and legends of the Tikuna people were not written but passed down orally. "People told them to their children and grandchildren," he said. "When I was small, I listened to an old woman who told me the story of dawn, how it was. She told it to her children and everyone listened. You would hear them many times."

Even for a teacher such as Constantino, who was a very devout member of the Santa Cruz, religion and legends were not in opposition. "Both things are good," he had told me in São Leopoldo. "*Our People* has rescued our past and helped the children learn about it." In Benjamin, Pedro Inacio had said, "School shouldn't only be for learning to read and write, but also to learn things of the Tikuna that are used in every community, remedies of the forest, what kinds of trees serve for fevers, headaches and other things, as well as things like what kinds of monkeys exist in our nature, what kinds of insects. To study in Tikuna and also Portuguese, to one day be able to discuss with the authorities outside the problems of land, to know how to talk with the white. Whites don't respect us because we speak only a little Portuguese. But because we wear shoes, clothing, watches, they say we are not Indians anymore. But we are Indians, because we know from where we came, who is our god, who made the earth, water, the forest, animals and fish. So school is for our children to learn this."

The days in Vendaval were punctuated with visits, an integral part of life in the Amazon. One day after I had done the dishes and gone for a swim in the river, I looked toward the other end of the village and saw a big white boat coming into the channel. It was the river trader, or *marreteiro*, making a call. I watched as it pulled up at the quay, a half-submerged pile of logs tied together at the riverbank. Reinaldo came out with Man in his arms and asked if I wanted to go down and look.

The entire village, it seemed, had assembled on the bank, but only the ubiquitous groups of children had actually ventured onto the boat and were hanging inside the doorways of the storeroom and sitting on the railings. Reinaldo and Man and I crossed the long, precarious plank onto the deck.

The boat resembled those I had traveled on, except that what was usually the crew's quarters had been opened up and turned into a store with a counter. The owner, Mico Mafre, traveled up and down the river with his wife and three kids, selling items for cash, baskets of *farinha*, bananas, even a chicken. He had quite a selection of goods in that small space: soap, deodorant, Lux talcum powder, nail polish, face powder and various elixirs arranged in neat rows. There were boxes of batteries, effervescent stomach tablets and Andrews liver salts; T-shirts, underwear and acrylic shorts lay across the counter in thick piles; plastic sandals and suitcases hung from ropes attached to the wooden-slat ceiling. There were a few foodstuffs — tinned guava paste, beans, packages of crackers. There was even a chamber pot.

Reinaldo asked to see some fishhooks and also the medicines and batteries. There were so many things he wanted to buy that he decided to sell all the baskets of *farinha* he had stocked in the kitchen. When he came back from all his dealing that evening, he had spent everything. But, he told me, he had gotten a good price for the *farinha*. It cost two thousand cruzados to buy locally, he said; he could get double that in Benjamin, but Mico Mafre was offering three thousand, saving Reinaldo the trip into town.

The river trader went to the next village with loads of *farinha* in the hull, several piles of bananas and pineapples on the deck and two imprisoned roosters, one of whom attempted to make a frustrated getaway.

The next day, Frei Arsenio, the local priest, came to visit. He was a tall, graying, slightly disheveled Italian in old baggy trousers, blue running shoes and an election-propaganda T-shirt, which, he joked, he was only wearing now that the elections were over. He chatted with Reinaldo about the elections for a while, but he had come by, he said, because he knew there were a few baptisms to do. He arranged to return in exactly two weeks to do them and say a mass. We chatted for a while, and he told me that he was based in Belém do Solimões and had been in the area for twenty years, attending to nine thousand Tikuna and whites in seventeen communities.

I asked him about the Santa Cruz sect. Brother José had arrived at a time of transition within the Catholic Church, said Frei Arsenio, and of social transition among the Tikuna. There had been a breakdown in the system of bosses, and the Santa Cruz addressed religious and social needs, which the Church at the time did not clearly recognize. "But when things began to improve for the Tikuna," he said, "the sect began to break down, and is beginning to disappear." Brother José had died a few years ago, and no one had appeared to take his place, although a few, quickly brought under the influence of the region's bosses, had tried. Brother José had acted with the blessing of the army and the bosses; but more as a bulwark against the power of the established Church.

After a lunch of squash and fish, I got a ride with Miguel, a man I recognized from the wretched boat trip from Benjamin, who was going downriver to the white village of Santa Rita do Weil. There, I had been told by many people, the boat from Manaus would pass on its twice-weekly trip to Benjamin and would stop to take on passengers. It always came by in the evening, so I knew I had plenty of time.

Miguel let me off at a floating trading post, moored to the bank, with several skiffs tied to it. I walked inside the big warehouse and asked if I could wait there for the boat to Manaus. But a heavy man in shorts informed me that the Manaus boat had already gone by the night before, and the next one wasn't due for another four days.

To say my heart sank or that I was seized by desperation would be an understatement. It was the most horrible situation I could be in. There was nothing in Santa Rita but a few cabins and some cows. I would have nothing to do for four days; I would miss my flight to Manaus and my flight from there to Rio, and possibly even my flight to Canada. I knew there was a telephone somewhere in Santa Rita — I had seen the telecommunications pole — and I set off to look for it. I eventually found it, only to be informed by the friendly townspeople that the phone was locked up because they had not yet finished counting the votes in São Paulo de Olivença, the nearest town, so they didn't know who was mayor yet, and the mayor always gave a crony the job of looking after the phone. Maybe I could try again tomorrow. The whole situation seemed completely unreal.

I met a woman on the riverbank who asked me what I was doing in Santa Rita, and when I explained my predicament, she told me that a fish dealer was traveling to Benjamin the next day. I went to his house, but the fish dealer, and may he rot in hell forever for this, refused to take me along.

Just as it seemed things could not get any worse, the owner of the floating trading post, Reginaldo Müller, told me I could stay there. He also said boats passed by all the time heading for Benjamin. He pulled a bottle of Orange Crush out of the refrigerated chest and set about fixing me a meal with some of the tinned food he was selling. He slung up a new hammock over the pile of salted *pirarucu* fish, and was for the next two days (he was wrong about the boats passing all the time) an exemplary host.

Seu Reginaldo's family lived in Tabatinga, but he seemed to prefer the life of a bachelor in the wilds of Santa Rita. "I live alone here," he said to me, "but I wouldn't live anywhere else. This is air you can breathe." And it was not only the air. There was never anyone around to tell him to tidy up and put on a clean shirt. His friends came over every day to play cards and chew the fat. Reginaldo spent most of the day in his hammock, overseeing the local boys who worked for him repacking baskets of *farinha* with fresh leaves or weighing fish the locals brought in to sell. A man named João, the husband of the woman I had met on the riverbank, worked behind the counter, and the days passed with gossip, jokes and idle conversation.

The first night I slept there, lying over the great pile of salted fish, I could hear the sounds of scurrying and thought to myself, wrapped up from head to toe as usual in my sheet, that there must be some really big cockroaches in there. Then I suddenly heard my glasses fall from where I had placed them, on a stack of boxes of crackers. Not cockroaches. Rats. Their gnawing filled the night, and I prayed they wouldn't decide to go for a stroll on me. It took me a long time to fall asleep again, and when I did, I dreamed I was in Paris, buying books on the quays of the Seine.

I woke at dawn and sat outside with the two dogs. In a little while a man came out and said good morning. He turned out to be Reginaldo's cousin, Zeca. He went in and I heard him say to Reginaldo, "Man, I hardly got a wink of sleep last night. A rat jumped right on me! Crunch, crunch, crunch, I could hear them chewing on things all night long." His cousin, however, didn't seem to be concerned.

Zeca, a strapping man of maybe thirty-five, with sandy hair and a mustache, kept us entertained all day with his stories. He had long led the life of a rake, he admitted, and even though he was now a born-again Christian, "a believer" as the Brazilians call them, he still had a kind of wisecracking way of speaking that made him always sound as though he were joking. The others asked him how he had become born again, and he said, "Well, it all began when the police came and threw me in jail in Tabatinga. Now that is not a pleasant experience, and I know, because I've been in jail fifty-four times, usually but not exclusively for drunkenness." The last time, he said, he and five others were unjustly accused of trying to steal a boat. While he was in jail, a minister had come around to talk to them and read the Bible. "And I said to him, brother, when I get out of here, I'm heading straight for your church."

Zeca would tell us we were all sinners in a way that made everyone laugh. He assured me several times that if I prayed hard, God would send a boat. The rest of the time the conversation ranged over everything from the nature of the devil to snakes and hair oil. Zeca said he didn't like to use it: "It makes my forehead shine."

With me there, the men made comparisons between Brazilian and North Americans. They told me repeatedly that the Brazilian — actually the Amazonian — was inherently lazy. "You could plant a thousand cacao trees on the little island up there and they would come up just beautiful," said Reginaldo, to give one example, "but does anybody do it?" Another time, over dinner, they told me what a disaster it was when people ran out of *farinha*, as they sometimes did at the end of the rainy season. "So why don't you grow more cassava and store the *farinha*?" I asked. "Didn't we tell you the Amazonian was lazy?" both men replied at the same time.

In spite of the joking, I was in the depths of depression, with nothing to do, not even a book to read. Everyone was friendly, but I wanted badly to get back to civilization. Still no boats came by. Reginaldo was going to take his boat to Tabatinga soon, but he had to wait until he had a ton of fish, and the fish were only coming in dribs and drabs. I scanned the horizon downriver for hours with Reginaldo's binoculars, but saw nothing more than a few local motorboats and canoes. On the third day, when I had already been up for about five hours, had gone back to my hammock, and was beginning to cry, Reginaldo came in with a quizzical look on his face and got his binoculars. "It looks like there's a big refrigerated boat coming," he muttered. I jumped out of the hammock and ran onto the boardwalk. Reginaldo gave me the binoculars, but all I could see was a tiny speck. In a few minutes, however, others confirmed that it was indeed a large boat heading upriver. We watched and waited for half an hour, during which time I began to worry that maybe the captain might not let me on board. As the boat approached, I got my stuff together and we went out in the motorboat. Reginaldo hailed the vessel, and it slowed down. By that point, I was incredibly excited and only hoped that I wouldn't suffer another disappointment. As we pulled close enough for me to see the bow, I became convinced

I would not be let down. The boat had an auspicious name, one that seemed to sum up my whole trip. It was called the *Corajoso*, the Courageous.

EPILOGUE

ABOUT TWENTY HOURS AFTER I climbed on board the *Corajoso*, I was back in Tabatinga. The trip had been comfortable, and the owner of the boat, Waldeci Queiroz, a heavy young man traveling with his wife, Francisca, their little boy and a crew of about seven, was as hospitable and friendly as everyone I'd met during my trips through the Amazon. Early in the morning, just before we reached Tabatinga, as the morning sun shone on the Solimões and its brown surface gleamed like molten chrome, I noticed a school of dolphins swimming alongside of us and realized this was my goodbye to Amazonia.

I had only a day in Manaus before catching my plane for the south. Christmas lights were up in the streets already. There were plastic replicas of evergreen trees for sale on the sidewalks in the Free Zone, and the local newspaper carried a headline story announcing that there had been a record number of homicides in Manaus that year.

Back at the small apartment I shared in Rio, four months' worth of copies of the *Jornal do Brasil* stacked in my bedroom, I had to admit that it felt good to be there. I felt bad about just one thing. A conference on the environment, which I knew Chico Mendes had been planning to attend, had taken place a week earlier than I thought. I had missed seeing Chico by about a day.

Shortly afterward, I flew back to Canada. The day before Christmas, I was at a party at a friend's house, when someone showed me a copy of the Toronto *Globe and Mail*. On the second page I read what I never thought would happen: Chico Mendes had been shot, killed by a bullet through the heart.

I flew back to Brazil in mid-January and was in Manaus for the carnival, in February. With Chico Mendes suddenly all the rage now that he was dead, and requests for articles from the oddest places, talk about a Hollywood movie, and well-meaning Chico Mendes Committees springing up all over the map, I still couldn't shake my feelings of incredible sadness and bitterness at Chico's sudden loss.

And travelling back again, quickly this time, through the Amazon, there was more bad news. Penny Magee, the American anthropologist who had been studying the effects of the Tucuruí Dam, was back in Belém; she had finished her research in Paruru. She told me that the Gonçalves family were almost starving. Once, they had eaten nothing but squash for three days in a row, she said; another time they had had to share among them only three tiny *mapara* fish; another time a young caiman was divided among twenty-eight people. Penny and Marília had returned to Belém with the palms of their hands peeling, a sign, a doctor had told them, of malnutrition.

In November 1988, Ricardo Rezende, the young priest from Conceicao do Araguaia, had been severely injured in a car accident in Belém, in circumstances that were never clarified. He was now in Juiz da Fora, in the state of Minas Gerais, where his family lived, waiting for an operation to insert a plastic plate in his head. A Socialist Party of Brazil deputy in the state legislature, João Carlos Batista, who had long fought for peasants' rights, was shot in his apartment building parking garage after repeatedly complaining of threats to his life. Lucio Flavio Pinto, the journalist I had interviewed, had also begun to receive death threats.

In Xinguara, Marileide had received more votes than any other candidate for councillor, but without a *bancada* — enough Workers' Party candidates along with her — she was barred from taking a seat in the town hall. Now, her husband wanted her to quit politics once and for all. Maria da Rocha was suddenly a widow, forced to sell the land for which she and Antenor had fought so hard. The forces for change in the Amazon, it seemed, were suffering incredible setbacks, as the destruction of the forest and the disintegration of its communities continued unabated.

My journey led me inexorably to Acre, where it had all begun. I arrived there on a hot, sunny day almost a year since my first trip to Rio Branco.

There I met Reginaldo Castilo, a former classmate of my friend Elizete Gaspar, in Belém. A professor at the Federal University of Acre, Reginaldo had kept a thick file of newspaper clippings in the last few months. As I pored over the clippings, I began to realize that Chico's death was more than an act of revenge by Darli Alves, as the news media had tirelessly suggested, and it became my self-appointed task to get as nearly as possible to the bottom of this while in Rio Branco.

In July, Chico had gone to Curitiba, the capital of Paraná, to attend a conference on extractive reserves. While there, he was told about a judge's order, dating from 1973, for the imprisonment of Darli Alves and his brother Alvarino on murder charges. Chico asked for a copy of the order and, by the time he returned to Xapuri from a national conference of the CUT trade union federation in Belo Horizonte, the document had arrived. On September 26, he handed it to Mauro Sposito, the chief of the federal police in Rio Branco. But the letter sat in a drawer in the police station until October 13 because, Sposito later claimed, the envelope was open, and the police needed local authorization to act. On October 17, Adair Longhini, the judge in Xapuri, sent a telex to Sposito. He made a point of typing and sending it himself, because a half-brother of the Alveses worked as a registrar in his office. Finally, military police were sent to Fazenda Paraná to pick up the two men. There, however, they found that the two were long gone, and the hired gunmen laughed in their faces.

In a letter addressed to Sposito and made public in the local papers on December 3, Chico wrote: "On that occasion, there was much speculation and doubts about who must have advised the gunmen [of the impending arrest]. And to my surprise and that of all the comrades, we have been informed that it was you who was the author of this advice. The information comes from the gunmen themselves and from the [Alves] sons, who took pride in saying that their fathers had many friends, including the federal police, who kept them up on everything."

In the same letter, Chico said he was afraid that "there exists a plot among the gunmen of Darli Alves, the death squad, and the federal police to bring about a slaughter of the leaders of the rubber tappers' movement."

The following day, however, Sposito countered with a clutch of contradictory accusations and outright lies in an attempt to smear Chico's reputation. First, he claimed that Chico had been a "collaborator" of the federal police since 1980, "giving information on the rural area, having as well furnished data that made it possible to identify clandestine organizations under the cover of political parties." Sposito also charged that Chico and the rubber tappers' movement "were being subsidized by a multinational alien entity." By this he meant the Ford Foundation, incorrectly described as an organization, "subsidized by the Ford Motor Corporation." He provided reporters with a piece of stolen mail, an innocuous letter from the foundation's Peter May in Rio.

On December 6, a sinister article of no more than a paragraph appeared in the daily *O Rio Branco*, a newspaper that belonged to João Branco, the president of the Democratic Ruralist Union, and Narciso Mendes, a deputy with the right-wing Liberal Front Party. This note announced the imminent "explosion of a two-hundred-megaton bomb," "which would have global repercussions." Just below the article was yet another criticism of Chico Mendes. It was as if some kind of signal had been sent.

On the 13th, Chico dropped in on his younger brother, Zuza, a rubber tapper who lived in Seringal Santa Fe. He told Zuza that he didn't think he'd live long. "But, Chico," Zuza said to him, "why don't you get out? Go away for a while until things cool down." But in that calm, reasonable way of his, Chico disagreed. "Look, Zuza," he said, "I've been fighting here for more than twenty years, together with the comrades. I've never run away and I've never sold out. I'm not going to run away now, because my place is here. Don't worry about me. I want you to look after yourself." Then, Zuza told me later, Chico smiled and said that he had dreamed the night before about their mother. She had been smiling and waving to him, Chico said, and when he approached her, she showed him a comfortable bed she had made up for him in a field surrounded by flowers.

Two days later, Chico was in the small city of Sena Madureira, in the northern part of the state, close to the border with Amazonas. Genesio de Natividad, a lawyer working for Acre's Pastoral Land Commission, accompanied him on this trip to organize new union locals.

Describing one meeting to me, Genesio said, "It took place in a sort of community health center, in the courtyard. There were more than five hundred rubber tappers there, men and women, who had never been approached before by the union. So I opened with a short introduction and told them about Chico. Then Chico took the microphone and began talking to them. And from where I was sitting, right there in front, I could see in the audience some people, some old men, men who had spent their entire lives working for the bosses in the forest, and there were tears in their eyes. No one had ever told them before that they had dignity and that they had rights. Chico was very pleased with that first meeting. I know it meant more to him than all the international accolades."

In Xapuri a couple of days later, Chico was happy about the arrival of a new truck that had been donated to the union. He said to his comrades, "Now with this truck, the Toyota, and the two boats, we are going to break past the UDR very slowly, winning more victories for our resistence movement." By then the governor had assigned him a pair of bodyguards, two inexperienced military police in their mid-twenties who had one ancient .38 revolver between them.

Chico wanted to get used to the new truck. On December 22, a Thursday, he drove around Xapuri with Elenira and Sandino and all their friends. With the truck full of children, he stopped frequently to chat with friends and acquaintances. Chico's wife, Ilza, noticed how much time and attention he gave his children that day. "He would stop to kiss them all the time. He was happier to be back from this trip than any other," she said. During his trip around town, Chico stopped at the hospital to pick up some medicines for the union to distribute on the rubber reserves. There, he spoke to Sister Zelia, and told her he did not think he would live to see the new year. "But he said it without fear, without anxiety," she said, "like someone saying see you later."

In the evening, he played several games of dominoes with Gomercindo and the two bodyguards. At around 6:30, Ilza asked them to stop so she could put dinner on the table. Gomercindo stood and said he had to go on his motorcycle to pick something up but would be back in ten minutes or so. Chico grabbed a towel and said he was going to take a shower in the bathhouse outside. He flicked the switch, but the electric bulb in the little cement cubicle had burned out. When he opened the door to the backyard, he said, "Eesh, it's dark out there. Those guys could be ambushing me."

The two young corporals did not budge from the table. Chico got a flashlight and stepped through the door once again. Suddenly a loud series of blasts rang through the seemingly impenetrable darkness. Chico was hit by at least twenty-six pieces of heavy lead, which ripped through his shirt and pierced his shoulder and heart. He fell into the kitchen, then staggered into the narrow corridor in front of the children's room, where he crumpled onto the floor and died. The two soldiers jumped up and ran, actually knocking Ilza aside in their haste to escape. They didn't even bother to use the door, but jumped through the open windows and took off. Ilza ran out, screaming. Gomercindo returned about then and saw the commotion, neighbors coming out and surrounding the house. "The police post is right near there," he told me later, "and the guys were just standing on the sidewalk in front, not doing anything. So I yelled at them, but they didn't do anything. Then someone shouted and said Chico was only wounded, so I jumped onto my bike and rode off to find a car. By the time I got back, they were taking him out of the house — another car had gotten there — but he was already dead."

Chico's body was taken to the hospital. Gilson Pescador stood by him. About an hour after the shooting, the first journalists arrived. They were from *O Rio Branco* and said they had made the journey from the capital to Xapuri in just an hour and a half, which is physically impossible. It was obvious that they had known in advance that Chico Mendes would be killed.

The news went out very early — only fifteen minutes after the shooting — on Radio Diffusora do Acre, a station that belonged to the municipality of Rio Branco and employed a half-brother of Darli Alves.

The state was also on alert. A bus with thirty military police was immediately sent to Xapuri to quell any riotous behaviour by the inhabitants upon hearing the news of Chico's death. The governor wanted Chico to be buried in Rio Branco rather than Xapuri, to avoid any confrontations. Gilson Pescador told me that Flaviano Melo seemed annoyed when he heard of Chico's death: "Now I guess I will have to cancel my Christmas trip to Rio," he sighed.

On December 23, the head of public security named a special police inspector, Delegado Nilson Alves de Oliveira, to investigate the case. Both the head of the federal police, Romeu Tuma, and the acting minister of justice, flew into Rio Branco in the days that followed, to look things over and assure the press that justice would be done.

In an attempt to catch the Alves brothers and three of their gunmen, the federal police began what they called Operation Broom, but which might more appropriately have been called Operation Rake. It accomplished nothing. Darci Alves, the son, turned himself in after a few days, as did his father, Darli, by prior arrangement with his lawyer. Alvarino Alves and the gunmen, the three Pereira brothers, have never been caught. Various local ranchers were questioned by the police, then freed. Another Alves son, Oloci, was picked up after he was spotted driving down the road by a soap-opera actress big in the ecological movement in Brazil.

The investigations and attention were focused almost exclusively on the Alveses and their gunmen. A reenactment of the crime led the police investigator, Delegado Nilson, to believe that Darci was there but that another gunman had pulled the trigger. A piece of paper found in Darci's wallet contained a notation: "Xapuri, December 22, 7 o'clock." That was the exact hour of the murder. The notation was followed by another date — December 26, 1 o'clock," the hour and day Darci turned himself in.

The police took over the Paraná Ranch, and there followed a slew of stories about the weird goings-on of the Alves family. A sister of one of the gunmen and the wife of another told police that Darci and the gunman had come home at about eleven o'clock on Thursday night. Darci had said, with an air of satisfaction, "Now there won't be any more trouble in Xapuri." More tales of murder began to emerge, most of them recounted by a boy named Genesio Barbosa, who at the age of seven was given to Darli by his mother, who had had an affair with the rancher. Genesio, then fourteen or fifteen, claimed to have seen various murders.

In each case, the boy told me, he had been threatened, and warned that if he ever told, the same would happen to him. Genesio also told me and a church lawyer about some of the visitors to the Paraná

Ranch. They included the former mayor of Xapuri, Wanderley Vianna, the former mayor of Rio Branco, Adalberto Aragão, UDR president João Branco, police chief Enock Pessoa and lawyers Rubem Torres and Luiz Azevedo. Azevedo was a partner of PFL deputy João Tezza.

In 1987, two Bolivians were killed at the ranch and buried in the form of a cross. The assassinations of certain men who had annoyed the Alves family had also been ordered by the two brothers. Maria Goretti Pereira, wife of the gunman Amadeus, called the place "a paradise for *pistoleiros*." Slave labor was the rule, and no one was paid in cash for work done there; workers only received credit at the storehouse for food and clothing.

As much as the family's allegedly violent proclivities, their sexual appetites were also fodder for the newspapers during the weeks after the killing of Chico Mendes. Darli, a wizened little man with thick spectacles, had five wives, three of them living on the ranch, and claimed to have thirty children. Alvarino had two wives. Darli's and Alvarino's father, Sebastião, had had three; his third wife the daughter of his second wife.

Darli was often referred to as "a real macho." His wives, although they fought when they were all put together in the main house, said he looked after them, was affectionate and "good in bed."

One of them, twenty-three-year-old Francisca, committed suicide on January 8 while under house arrest on the Alves ranch. When he heard about the death, Darli cried for a moment, then brightened when reporters began to question him on his sexual prowess. "Darli Alves swears he knows how to put out the fire in chicks," ran the headline of one newspaper story devoted exclusively to that extremely macabre part of the conversation. The story quoted Darli as saying: "Macho like me in bed, I have yet to see. My only fault is to like women." In spite of his fifty-four years, he said, "I go to bed with a woman and give four times a night with the greatest normality. What gets a woman is not good looks, money or brains, but to be a macho in bed."

In early March, the tenor of the newspaper stories changed. The coverage of the Chico Mendes case stopped, and articles criticizing the rubber tappers' movement began to appear. The rubber tappers were virulently excoriated in the press for being against the expropriation of two local ranches, an accusation both unfounded and untrue.

In mid-March, the big news in the Rio Branco papers concerned plans to pave a road through the northern part of the state to the Peruvian border. The $300-million U.S. project would allow products from Acre, Rondônia and Mato Grosso to reach lucrative new markets in the Far East. The Japanese consul in Manaus visited the state in early February, feeding the aspirations of Governor Melo. At one point the Japanese government said it would loan Brazil the money to pave the road. But it is said that, at a Group of Seven summit in Tokyo, U.S. president George Bush talked his then counterpart Noboru Takeshita out of it. Melo was convinced that the cause lay primarily with the four American congressmen who had visited Acre on January 16, and who had not believed him when he said the road would not destroy the forest. Articles, editorials and public announcements were made, rejecting "the interference of foreign governments in internal matters . . . under the pretext of the preservation of the Amazon." This also acted to exacerbate the campaign against the rubber tappers.

In fact, the movement's leaders said they were happy with the idea of paving the road, because it would help to raise the price of their products and lower the price of goods they needed to buy. But they wanted to see the road paved only after the land flanking it was designated as reserves. This would protect the rubber tappers and the Indians living there. Again the rubber tappers were accused of being against progress, when in fact, their side of the story was simply never heard.

I called Flaminio Araripe, the journalist who had given me a ride home from Seringal Cachoeira the year before. We met for a beer at the pool of the Pinheiro Palace Hotel, which was deserted then, on a quiet afternoon between rain showers. Flaminio seemed uncomfortable at first, but he explained one of the reasons for the changes in the newspaper.

After the death of Chico Mendes, he told me, the print run of A Gazeta, one of the two dailies published in Acre, had jumped from two thousand copies a day to twelve thousand. Recently, however, his editor-in-chief, Silvio Martinello, was called to a meeting at the office of Governor Melo, whose wife owns a majority of shares in the paper. At the meeting was a very wealthy rancher from Mato Grosso who said he wanted to invest $6 million U.S. in Acre but first wanted the coverage of the Chico Mendes case and the rubber tappers' movement stopped. At the same time, Flaminio told me, the governor was turning his ambitions to a seat in the senate in Brasilia. To be elected, he needed money and support from the state's landowners. He knew the rubber tappers would vote for the Workers' Party anyway, so he had decided to cast his line in richer waters.

A couple of days later, I went to the newspaper office to talk to Martinello. He confirmed newspaper reports I had seen that he had received a death threat from a former mayor of Rio Branco and one-time kingpin in the ruling party, the PMDB. A friend of this politician had warned Martinello to stop publishing allegations concerning his involvement in the plot to kill Chico Mendes, "or he would lose his head." Martinello didn't seem too perturbed by the threat. In any case, the tone of coverage had already changed. "This climate of threats has existed for a long time," he explained calmly. "But there is a risk and it is very real. Osmarino, for example," he said, naming the newly elected president of the Rural Workers Union in Brasiléia, "now he could be killed at any time." Martinello said this with such matter-of-fact conviction, it was as if he already knew of another plot.

Meanwhile, the friends and supporters of Chico Mendes had formed a committee, and they proved to be far better at getting information than the police. They received a number of tip-offs, one concerning the ex-mayor of Rio Branco. He had been seen with Darci Alves three days after Chico's murder, before the young man turned himself in. Two other big ranchers were seen celebrating Chico's death in a bar in Brasiléia almost four hours before Chico was killed. The Chico Mendes Committee also made frequent statements to the press, complaining about the inefficiency of the investigation.

In spite of the police presence, several leaders of the rubber tappers' movement — including Julio Barbosa, the new president of the union in Xapuri; Gilson Pescador; Chico's cousin, Raimundo Barros; Osmarino; and others — were receiving frequent death threats. Then the acting president of the Court of Justice, Judge Eva Evangelista de Araujo Souza, began to receive such threats. On the night of January 3, her daughter received an anonymous telephone call from someone who said, "Tell the *doutora* that I am being well paid to do this task and that she better not get mixed up in this Chico Mendes case." Later, the same person called again and said, "Tell *doutora* Eva not to go to the courts today, because when she's going up the steps, her head could roll like that of Chico Mendes."

Eva Evangelista had been pressing for the appointment of a second judge in the case; she also wanted a permanent public prosecutor in Xapuri. At the time, only one city in the interior of the state had a public prosecutor on site. The other prosecutors stayed in Rio Branco. Half of them, she said, were on holidays.

Early on a Monday morning, I went to the large building that housed the bishop's office, just across a paved driveway from the city's large Roman-style cathedral, to see Genesio, the Pastoral Commission lawyer. During our conversation about the recent events surrounding Chico's death, Genesio went over the anomalies and puzzles many people felt were not being addressed by the police investigations. Why had *O Rio Branco* printed that strange and obviously untrue story about a two-hundred-megaton bomb on December 6? How had their reporters known beforehand that Chico Mendes was going to be killed? The Chico Mendes Committee also wanted to know why the police did not cordon off and investigate the patch of land behind Chico's house where the murderers had waited, until the day after the assassination. A witness had come forward to tell the bishop, Dom Moacyr Grecchi, that he had been at a card game at the Rio Branco Club on December 17 and had overheard the ex-mayor and another businessman say that Chico Mendes would be killed in five days. Why had not the police checked out the allegation? And why had two important police authorities been promoted to new jobs while there were strong suspicions that they had been in collusion with the criminals?

I had felt from the beginning that there was more behind Chico's death than the quest for revenge of a far wealthy old rancher like Darli Alves. Nonetheless, the actions of the authorities, the confidence with which the lives of the rubber tappers were threatened, and many other details such as those Genesio had outlined, seemed to indicate that the network of those involved in the plot was indeed wide and far-reaching. Chico Mendes and the movement he led made many in the ruling class in Acre long to be rid of him. While many foreign journalists and visitors had thought Chico's international standing was a sort of shield, we had all been proved wrong.

The significance of the plan to construct a new road to the Pacific was that the road would considerably widen the field of those who stood to gain from Chico's death and from the death of the workers' movement as well. The road would cause an increase in value of the land surrounding it; many businessmen would gain handsome profits. If some people had thought far enough ahead, they would have realized that a campaign by Chico might have effectively stymied their project.

After I talked to Genesio, I went upstairs to talk to the bishop. Originally from the state of Santa Catarina, Dom Moacyr, fifty-five, was a big man, with straight, thinning hair and thick glasses. With his rapid, articulate speech he gave off an air of efficiency and constant busyness. I asked him about the threats to his life. A phone call had woken him up in the middle of the night, said Dom Moacyr, and the caller "spoke like someone who was very tense and worried; it wasn't a joke. He told me his name, his nickname, which was Goiano, and said he was calling from Rondônia. He said that he had been contracted to kill Chico Mendes and me. 'But I am not a person who kills,' he said two or three times, 'I only rob cars.' And he said, 'I only ask one thing, don't go to Xapuri alone and be very careful.' And then he added, 'Try hard that there should be a little justice because everyone is involved in this.'"

Dom Moacyr said that he hoped the national and international mobilization around the issue of Brazil's rapidly disappearing rain forests would have some effect. "You can't look at the Amazon as separate from the rest of Brazil," he said. "So the best solution for the Amazon is an agrarian reform in the south, center west and northeast of the country. And an end to the fiscal incentives. The money of the people should not be wasted on the private interests of certain people, most of whom are bandits."

I asked the bishop if he thought the road to the Pacific had anything to do with Chico's death and the air of impunity reigning in Acre. His reaction was stronger than I expected. "You see that?" he asked. "You see? Your question suddenly made the hair on my arm stand on end." And he continued, "You are telling me something that I had never thought of before. Look, someone who has a lot of land in this area of the Trans-Acreana is a man who detests me. He has spread lies about me in Brazil and abroad. They even went to [the national newspaper] *O Globo*, accusing me of having had a rancher assassinated. I'm suddenly reminded of this. They have spread lies of the most low and shameful kind about me and other bishops. It could be that they think that eliminating me would facilitate the path to very big business. And they are the kind of people who would say, 'I didn't kill a priest, I killed a Communist.' They are bandits. You know, it is something I hadn't thought about before, but there could be large interests beneath all of this."

That week, I spoke to various figures of authority in Rio Branco, all of them involved in some way with the case, either in investigating or prosecuting it. None of the visits were very fruitful. The federal police chief was a recent replacement, for example, as was the public prosecutor, only a temporary one at that.

I also went to talk to Lourival Marques, the new director of public security in Rio Branco who had replaced Castelo Branco. Marques was an old man with a large mustache and curling white hair. Shortly after he arrived in Rio Branco, his son, Roberto, was killed during an argument, stabbed to death on the street.

Marques suggested that Chico's murder was Chico's fault, for he had not left Xapuri after receiving the threats. "But that's ridiculous," I said. "Was it your son's fault that he was killed, when all sorts of people are being given gun licenses even though the police know they are hired gunmen? Look," I said, "just tell me what you would do if you found out that there were very important and influential people behind the whole thing. Will you present that information to a judge?"

Marques burst into laughter. "You want to know what would happen?" he asked. He picked up the telephone as if he were receiving a call. "Hello, hello, yes? This is Dr. Marques. Oh, I am fired, am I? Okay. Bye-bye," and he put the receiver down. "You see?" he said, "Unfortunately, that is the way things are in Brazil."

A conversation with a man who had once been vice-governor of Acre — a colleague of Elizete's friend, Reginaldo — also provided some interesting information about the state's political machinery. According to José Augusto, there was an effective intelligence system in the region, not at all surprising considering that Acre was a border state. He said he remembered once in the seventies when a governor got wind of a plot by landowners to kill someone and forbade them from carrying it out. When they paid no attention to him, he had the ringleader's land expropriated without compensation.

Currently, he said, there was a split forming in the PMDB between young, progressive members, who sought modern methods for development in the state, and those of the old guard, landowners who wanted to maintain the status quo of power based on land. A complicated system of allegiances and family rivalry was another facet in the party, which had suffered greatly during the recent municipal elections, losing several municipalities to other parties. While the whole party seemed to be moving to the right, the old guard was doing so more rapidly than the bulk of the PMDB.

I felt that some of these events may have had a bearing on the ease with which Chico's assassination had been carried out, and the air of menace that pervaded the region, in spite of heavier media attention than it had ever received before.

It seemed quite possible that a group of powerful landowners, backed by certain politicians and members of the security forces may have acted to kill Chico Mendes, either in revenge or to prevent the rubber tappers' movement from growing. It was probably a combination of both. Perhaps they were indeed concerned that his presence would have deleterious effects on the project to build a new highway, and their own plans to profit from it.

It was out of curiosity more than anything else that I phoned the office of lawyer Ruben Torres to request an interview with his client, Darli Alves, in jail. My request was agreed to, and I took a taxi out of the city, along a wet, rutted dirt track, past isolated groups of miserable shacks and several sawmills, to the penitentiary. A couple of soldiers lounged at a small table outside the low, rambling building, listening to the radio. I had to wait almost an hour for Torres to arrive, so I too sat by the table, sheltered by the porch roof, the achromatic afternoon sky lit by a feeble sun. From what I could make out, the prison was built in a large square with an ample grassy yard inside. A series of small rooms led from the open doorway beside the table, then there was a covered driveway closed with a barred gate, with a row of offices on the opposite side. While I sat there, I was surprised to notice a cow's head, unexpectedly protruding through the open doorway. Then its body appeared, followed by another head. About five cows came through the doorway while the barred gate opened, and a dozen more made their exit. Shortly afterwards, Torres arrived, accompanied by a tall man with a Paraná accent, driving a small gray truck.

I was taken to a visitor's room with the two men. Both Darli and Darci were brought in. We sat at a large table, Darli beside me, then his son, and across from me Torres and the man from Paraná. Darci had changed his story and now claimed that he had had nothing to do with the murder of Chico Mendes and did not know who did. He had nothing more to say. When I asked him, "So why did you turn yourself in then?" Torres interrupted and told him not to answer.

Darli did most of the talking. A nervous little man, always rattling a paper or jogging his foot up and down, he spoke rapidly, poorly, constantly proclaiming his innocence. "Here, locked up, I am the same as Christ crucified," he said, "except that Christ was born for that. He was a saint, right?" He said that he had turned himself in because he was going to face the authorities in Paraná, and that everything said about him was lies. Indeed, "lies" was the word he used most frequently during the conversation. He said that the rubber tappers all liked him. "In three or four years, they will all be my friends again," he said, but it was people like Gomercindo, Osmarino and Gilson Pescador, whom he incorrectly assumed to be mayor of Xapuri, who caused all the problems. "They just wanted to be the chiefs," he said. "I think that in the investigation, the first thing the police, I mean the justice, should do is arrest those persons who already killed — the chiefs, the big chiefs, who are the real criminals, and who say that I killed thirty people, this Gomercindo Rodrigues, there in Xapuri, who is a criminal before the justice of the earth and of God, and Osmarino in Brasiléia also is another big crook, who just lives for politics. Certain people from the Church and from that party, too, who never work and spend all their time having meetings, so that they can grow. The authorities should arrive there and arrest those men. Because an innocent person like myself, in my case, I think that these humiliations I am suffering here are without justification."

On he went for about half an hour. Coffee was served, but he didn't want any. He was certainly not shy about talking, but he spoke so quickly and dropped so many syllables that it was difficult to understand him. Darci kept quiet. When I finished my interview and everyone got up to leave, Darli kept talking, like a machine that had yet to wind down. In the corridor on the way back to his cell, Darci finally spoke. "Canada," he said. "That is very far away, isn't it?" He seemed to be pleased that he might be heard of in a place so far away. I chatted to him, but not about anything important. Yes, he liked living on the farm. No, he hadn't gone to school for long, only about two years, and his mother had come once already from Paraná to visit him. It was as though he were in camp rather than jail.

Torres brought in a large cardboard box full of groceries for Darli, spoke with his client a while longer, and then offered me a ride back to the city. As I was looking at the door of the small truck, a Pampa, I noticed a bullet hole in the driver's door. I realized then that it was the truck Darli's son, Oloci, had been driving when the police went after him and shot him in the arm. In fact, Oloci was away that day because he was having the wound checked.

At the end of their preliminary hearings a few months later, Judge Adair Longhini found enough evidence to put both men on trial for Chico's murder, Darli for ordering it and Darci for carrying it out. The decision means the two will have to face a jury trial.

All the time I was running around talking to people about the past, the rubber tappers were trickling in to Rio Branco from all over the Amazon to talk about the future of the movement. Delegates were showing up for a general meeting of the National Council of Rubber Tappers, and for joint meetings with the Union of Indigenous Nations. Their presence in Rio Banco linked the causes of the rubber tappers and the Indians of Amazonia ever more strongly. This was the first council meeting since the death of Chico Mendes, and the city was also filling up with journalists, photographers and various interested groups. Luis Ignacio da Silva, presidential candidate and president of the Workers' Party, was expected to attend, as were members of the Green Party from Italy, Germany and Brazil. José Genuino, a former guerrilla and now a Workers' Party deputy, gave a speech at the opening rally.

There were two familiar faces from Seringal Cachoeira: Antonio Mendes, in a neat plaid shirt and jeans, and Manoel Custodio, who was wearing, as usual, his big cowboy hat. They had walked all the way from the forest to the highway, where they were picked up in a truck. They both told me that in spite of the great sadness and shock everyone was feeling because of the murder of Chico, life in the *seringal* went on. Everyone was well, and free of the fear of expulsion now that Cachoeira had been officially designated an extractive reserve. It was strange to see them in such circumstances. Those brief hot days in July, when I had stayed with the Mendes family on the rubber estate, seemed so long ago. I told them I was planning to get into Cachoeira again, even if only for a day, but could not find the words to say why exactly I wanted to go. The visit might provide, I felt, some kind of assurance that, as Antonio had said, life did indeed go on.

The convention went ahead exactly as it had been planned. I met Chico's cousin, Raimundo Barros, a tall, rangy man with dark skin and protruding eyes, and asked him how things were going now that Chico was gone. He told me that they were all very conscious of the loss. "Chico was really our spokesman," he said, "our greatest spokesman, and with his death, there has opened up a great gap inside the movement. We are working hard to fill it. We know that it will take two people, or three, or five to substitute for Chico, to fill this space. Even so, the space will still be there because of his loss, but his ideas, his dedication are still alive, and still working."

He said that once the conference was over, "We are going to have a program of work where, with the return of the comrades to the rank and file in the union, we will get back to the work we always did with Chico."

Raimundo was running for president of the council, as was Julio Barbosa, who had been chosen to replace Chico as president of the Xapuri Rural Workers Union. Julio was a small man with a squarish head, short, curly hair, and a wide mouth filled with spaced-out teeth. He had been the union delegate in Seringal Dois Irmaõs, a rubber estate some four hours from Xapuri. He told me of the union's plans to visit all the area's rubber estates, to speak with the tappers in the forest, who were now busy with the annual collection of Brazil nuts. With all the turmoil, Julio admitted that "it has been a while since we have had contact with the rubber tapper there in the forest. It is the first thing that we have to do now."

They told me that the strong relations the rubber tappers' movement was building with the nation's Indians were increasingly important. If the two groups worked together to demand that their rights be respected and their environment left intact for their use, their case would be much stronger. "We have to evolve policies that will benefit both the rubber tapper and the Indian," said Julio. "We need to work out something on the question of economic development in the lives of both so that one thing becomes the same as the other."

I asked the two men about the death threats they had received. Raimundo told me that the threats came in a variety of ways, an indication of how confident the men who had killed Chico Mendes still were. "There are people constantly coming to us," said Raimundo, "some in the movement, some outside of it, some from people who are in between, sitting on the wall. They hear the conversations of these people, know about their meetings, and always tell us about it. At times, I have to admire these sources. Some are from inside the courts, or even the police. What care they have to take to pass this information on to us." But, by describing where some of the information came from, Raimundo was indicating how deeply imbedded the corruption was in the state apparatus.

Later that day, I went to call on Ilza, who had just returned from a trip to the United States, where she had gone to pick up an award for her late husband. When I first met her, a year before, I had asked if she too was involved in the movement. She had quietly replied, "Oh, no, I have enough to do looking after the house and my family." The idea of this shy young woman, who had grown up in the jungle and never journeyed farther than Rio Branco, traveling to Washington and New York made me realize how totally and suddenly her life had changed.

But with her immeasurable grief had come a strong desire to work for the cause and take part in the struggle. A widow at the age of twenty-five, with two young children to look after and no education, Ilza had decided to be more than just a tragic icon to the movement. I found her that afternoon in the house of some friends, an ordinary little wooden house, shaded by trees, where Elenira was sleeping on a cushion on the floor and Sandino in a hammock. "I can't talk to you for long, *companheira*," she said to me, "because I've been traveling and have a ton of clothes to wash." "We'll do the laundry together," I said, "and that way it will go faster."

We went across the street to the house of her brother-in-law, Francisco de Assis, a bulky young man in his early twenties, Chico's youngest brother. Unlike Chico and Zuza, Assis I found to be rather quiet, almost uncommunicative; he seemed to prefer to keep to himself. He was a soldier in Xapuri with the rank of private, but had recently been accused by the police of killing a gunman, Zezão, who had been found murdered several weeks after being released by the special investigator, Delegado Nilson. Assis said he had not been in Xapuri at the time of Zezão's death, but had been staying with Joaquim and Cecília in Seringal Cachoeira.

Ilza and I sat outside on a bench in the garden and talked for quite a while. She told me that she had never expected the gunmen threatening Chico to come right to their house, and especially not over Christmas. Describing the night of the murder, she admitted, "After I saw Chico dying, my life ended also. For me, there would never be any more pleasure, any more happiness. I began to think, My God, what am I going to do? What is the way out? And the way out I found was this."

By "this," Ilza meant throwing herself into the fight. She had long wanted to join a women's group, she told me, and now she had. "We, the women of Xapuri," she said, "are getting together, working with the men. We are going to get involved, have meetings, visit the areas and participate in the union." And while she recognized that she had a lot to learn, she would learn with "the other people of the rubber estates, and continue the struggle of Chico. I know it is going to be difficult," she added, "but after they killed Chico, this came into my head. I am not going to run away. I am going to stay and fight, defend the forest together with the comrades in the union, really talk about what is happening to us, about our suffering, about the persecutions. That won't be so hard because it is just telling the truth. It is a just cause."

I asked her what she thought about the police investigations into her husband's death, the constant assertions from the authorities that they had the Alveses, so all was well. "That's just empty talk," she said. "For us, all is not well just because Darli and Darci are in jail. Where are the others? Where are the real instigators who plotted the death of Chico? All loose out there. And doing what? Plotting the death of more comrades." She herself, she told me, had received a death threat, a phone call, just before leaving for the United States, but she did not care. "I really don't," she affirmed. "No one is going to make me run away, stop me from being with the other rubber tappers, and denouncing the injustices that happen to us."

I turned the conversation toward the newly formed Chico Mendes Foundation, of which she was honorary president. I asked her what she hoped it would achieve with the funds gathered, and her reply was immediate and firm. "Create new union leaders, new unions," she replied. "Create new Chico Mendeses."

After the interview, we gathered up the clothes that needed to be laundered. Ilza washed and I rinsed, then hung them up to dry on the line in the backyard. Referring to the interview, Ilza asked me, "Was that okay? Did I answer your questions all right?"

That night I ran into Osmarino, the Brasiléia union president, at the Casarão Restaurant, where I usually went to have dinner. I had not met him during my previous trips, but we had chatted several times in the past few days. I told him about my conversation with Martinello, the editor of A Gazeta, but he didn't seem surprised. "It's true," he said, "being a leader in the rubber tappers' movement today is the quickest path to the cemetery." Then he invited me to sit down and eat with him and his two bodyguards.

Osmarino was a fiery, pint-sized young man with a thick, dark beard, hooked nose and a boundless energy that kept him going all the time. Followed by the two young bodyguards — who cost him a lot of money, since he was responsible for their meals — he was always working, talking, stopping to consult or chat with people here and there. A tireless little dynamo of a man, I could see why he might be the next on the list.

Osmarino had entered the movement when its first union was formed in Brasiléia, with Wilson Pinheiro as its leader. He had known Pinheiro well, and respected him greatly. It was through Pinheiro that he had found himself gradually devoting more and more of his time to the union. This involvement had transformed his life and had impelled him to learn, when he was already an adult, how to read and write, so that he could take notes at union meetings and bring them to the *seringal* to discuss with the other rubber tappers. "I always thought to myself," he told me jokingly, "there's no way I'm going to involve myself entirely. I'm only going to do what I can. Then there came a moment where I realized that I'd involved myself so much that I was living only for this. I was into it right out to the ends of my hair." Now he felt the need to dedicate himself to the movement was greater than ever. "Every day I learn something," he said, "from the discussions and meetings with the rubber tappers. And these days, that means that one has little chance to stay alive in Acre. But there is no going back now."

The atmosphere of threats and violence had deep roots, said Osmarino. "After they killed Wilson Pinheiro, the massacre spread. They killed Jesus Mathias, Ivair Higino, Raimundo Callado, then Chico, a whole series of our comrades who were union leaders. They thought that by killing Chico Mendes, they would manage to put the brakes on our movement. But exactly the opposite happened. The movement gained a much greater dimension. Before I was elected president of the union, for example, there were only 211 members in the union. Now there are more than 2000. Even people in town — this has been really impressive in Brasiléia — have been giving us, and me personally, so much support." That was how he had found out about the past four attempts on his life, he said, through tip-offs from people in Brasiléia, even the police. Behind the threats, he insisted, was "a group that is led and financed by the UDR," and he listed a number of influential politicians and businessmen, "who support the UDR."

Of the police investigation into the murder of Chico Mendes, Osmarino said, "I don't believe in justice anymore. We know that more of our comrades will die, because we question the policies being applied in the region. We ask why they are giving titles for large properties to certain people, big landowners, why they do not have a policy of defending the environment. There has never been a policy in this region that benefits the majority."

We also talked about the problem of the Trans-Acreana, the road to the Pacific. According to Osmarino, the rubber tappers living in the region through which it would pass had no titles to their land. "It will be very easy to expel them," he said. "And we know that farmers are already buying huge pieces of land up there." He was also worried about the depletion of timber resources. While many people had pointed out that Japan and other Pacific Rim countries would be very interested in buying cheap wood from the Amazon, logging was already common all over the region, without any kinds of controls or quotas. Osmarino was matter-of-fact about it. "The state has no way of confronting all the middlemen, exporters and smugglers of the natural resources of our region," he said. "They can totally destroy the forest without bringing any benefits to the people of Acre."

On Sunday morning, I got a whiff of what that menacing sensation of threat must be like for Osmarino and the others. At the time, I was trying to find one of the mysterious witnesses to the Rio Branco Club card game. The witness was a doctor whose identity and working hours I had found out, but not his address. I went early that morning to look for him at the hospital, unsure of what to say to him or what his reaction in such a public place might be. It turned out, however, that he had just finished his shift and gone home. I decided to ask the bishop for the man's address, but found the residence closed. A priest in the cathedral asked me what I was doing and, from the sidewalk, I explained that I was trying to track down a certain doctor. The priest went to find out the man's telephone number and the name of the district in which he lived. While I waited, I noticed a truck drive in and turn in the parking lot between the cathedral and the bishop's office. A few minutes later the truck was back again, driving straight through this time to Benjamin Constant Street. While I was standing beneath the window beside the cathedral, I saw it a third time, then a fourth, just circling the block over and over again. I found it odd and slightly menacing.

As soon as I had the information I needed, I left, but crossing over to the main square, suddenly realized that I had to get the truck's license plate number. I sat in the park for a minute, partially camouflaged by a palm tree, sure the truck would come around again. It did. As it stopped at the light, I could see that it was a Ford F1000, the kind of truck the landowners liked to use, painted an anonymous gray. But there were no license plates. For just a moment, I was frightened. Could the truck's occupant be after the bishop? Could they be after snoopy journalists? Did someone know I was trying to track down the mysterious witness? That night, I phoned the elusive doctor. But when I told him I was a journalist, his tone of voice changed dramatically. He denied all knowledge of any card game or gambling club. He sounded terror-stricken, so much so that I decided then and there to drop the matter.

All that remained for me to do was to travel to Xapuri and from there to Cachoeira to see Dona Cecília and Seu Joaquim and their family. Because it was still raining frequently and quite heavily, I was worried that I might not even make it to Xapuri, but predictions of impassable roads and canceled trips turned out to be false.

At the bus station, I ran into Genesio, the Church lawyer, and another young lawyer, Luis Marques. Both were on their way to talk to Delegado Nilson about the investigations. There was only one delay during the trip, when the bus in front of us broke one of its wheels and had to use our bus's jack to fix it. Otherwise, there were just the same wide strips of pasture — green, now, thanks to the rains — dotted with burned trees and invading palms, visible through the mudspattered windows that I remembered from previous trips. As we arrived in the town and I stepped down from the bus into the open station, Genesio voiced my feelings exactly when he said, "Xapuri without Chico."

It was a pleasant surprise to find Gilson Pescador waiting for us. He had come to the main square, he said, for the Saint's Day celebrations, and I realized it was St. Sebastian's Day, exactly a year to the day since my first arrival in Xapuri. As we walked across the grassy park to the union hall, Gilson invited all three of us to stay that night with him and his family. He had not been successful in his run for the mayor's office in November, losing to the PMDB candidate by about two hundred votes. He told me that he had found several instances of fraud, but the local judge, Adair Longhini, who was now presiding over the murder trial of Darli and Darci Alves, had refused to declare the balloting spoiled.

Gilson told me he felt that the rubber tappers had suffered a major blow with the loss of Chico and were in danger of becoming disheartened. Nor did it help when their leaders were so frequently absent — they had rarely spent more than eight days at a time in Xapuri or in the rubber estates since the beginning of the year. Nonetheless, a new period of growth was beginning, and new leaders were coming forward to pick up where others had left off. Courses were going to be set up with industrial workers from the south, to help them organize more effectively. Gilson himself was busy as temporary vice-president of the Chico Mendes Foundation. All kinds of people were phoning him and insisting that they had the best plan for a film of Chico's life. Differences of opinion over which direction the foundation's work should take were already cropping up, he said. Some felt it should become an apolitical, international organization, like Greenpeace or the World Wildlife Fund. The union, however, wanted it to carry out the political work Chico had begun, with education programs, small projects and support for existing and new unions to keep fighting the devastation of the forest. They did not want to have decisions and programs imposed on them; but rather they wanted to keep on directing the struggle for rights and land on their own terms.

We stopped at the union hall, now swathed in a large black banner with the single word *Basta!* ("Enough!") written across it. Chico's rangy assistant, Saba, sat as usual behind the desk. "I knew you were here," he said to me right away. "I read it the other day in the *Gazeta*." There was also the driver who had taken me to Cachoeira on my two previous visits and an older man, small and wiry, whom I had seen before, named Vilela. After the greetings, it was hard to know what to say. There was nothing to say.

I asked about getting to Cachoeira, and Saba told me that he did not think I would make it. The road was a veritable sea of mud, the Toyota was broken and in need of a new part. No other vehicle would make it through, and it would take me too long to go on foot. I spent most of the following afternoon pestering poor Saba with new ideas for getting to Cachoeira, but in the end, none of them worked, and I never did so.

We left the union office to continue to Gilson's house, which happened to be on the same street as Chico's. Walking past the church, around the corner and up the street toward Chico's house, I was again filled with a powerful feeling of uselessness and loss. It felt like something heavy and impending, dragging me down. I knew that Chico's house had been turned into some kind of museum, and the thought, the idea of this man and his struggle, somehow petrified, bothered me. I kept wondering what it would be like to go into that house again, remembering the last time I had been there, the lunch of paca, little Sandino sitting on a bicycle that was too high for him, all the talk about building the union.

The house began to emerge among the trees, the rickety picket fence, the familiar faded pink boards, the blue trim with small diamonds of wood tacked to the eaves. A long sign ran across it now, saying "Fundação Chico Mendes" in large, uneven letters. The last time I had seen the house, I remembered, Chico had been sitting at a table in the front yard, playing cards.

It turned out that the house was not empty, not a place to display the past, but was full of people. Raimundo's wife, Mariazinha, was making lunch in the kitchen. Young men from the union were hanging around, just as they had been in July. Children were playing in the front yard, skipping rope and playing tag with loud screams. The place was as alive as ever, just like the movement Chico had helped to build.

The four of us stopped for a moment and looked at it from the street. Seeing the sign nailed across the fence, I began to realize that, while it would never be possible to come to terms with Chico's death, the death of the movement to which he had devoted his life would be even worse. Certainly little had changed since his death. The decisions over the future of Brazil and its people were still being made in the boardrooms of São Paulo, and in bankers' offices abroad. There was still a crushing debt to be paid, and there were still profits to be made in a country now the eighth-largest economic power in the world. But I couldn't help but hope that the massive outpouring of attention suddenly focused on the Amazon would have a positive result, that rural workers all over the region might find the strength and support to carry on the struggle for their forest and their rights. I thought about all the people I had met during the months of travel, the river dwellers, peasants and Indians, and realized how much they could achieve with just a little help from the Chico Mendes Foundation, their foundation, created in the Amazon, in memory of one of their own, who had fought and died for the ideals they, too, believed in. There were bits of Chico Mendes everywhere, wherever the people of the region organized themselves to take control of their lives. I remembered Chico himself saying to me, the last time I saw him, "*A luta continua*" — the struggle continues. "They can kill me, but they can't kill this movement." It was a consolation, a memory that had become reality, which almost made me feel that Chico was still alive.

GLOSSARY

Cachaça
Cheap sugar cane liquor

Colocação
One unit within a rubber estate, clearing where one or two families live, each with an area of forest to use

Companheiro,-a
Comrade, companion, or sometimes refers to the person one lives with

Curandeiro
One who cures sickness or bad luck through herbal remedies or charms

Dona
A feminine form of address, common in Brazil, connoting respect

Farinha
Cassava meal

Garimpeiro
An independent prospector, a worker who pans, or runs simple machinery, to mine surface gold

Maloca
A Yanomami word, denoting the large palm thatch house in which the entire population of a village lives

Marreteiro
A merchant or trader, who travels from place to place

Mateiro
A professional guide or woodsman, one who know the forest

Palafitte
A wooden house on stilts

Pistoleiro
A hired gunman

Posseiro
A squatter, a peasant who occupies land without legal title

Seringal
A natural rubber estate, an area of forest containing widely dispersed wild rubber trees

Seringueiro
A rubber tapper, one who gathers the latex of the rubber tree

Seu
Like Dona, above, a masculine form of address

A word on pronunciation
The letter "x" in Portuguese is pronounced as "sh," so that Xapuri, for example, is pronounced "Shapoori," and not "Zapoori." The letter "h" after an "n" or an "l", as in the word *farinha* is pronounced like a "y," as in "fareenya," and *velho* (old), which is pronounced "velyo." The letter "ç" is pronounced like an "s." The dipthong "ao," as in São Paulo or the name Chicão, is pronounced "ow."

ABOUT THE AUTHOR

AUGUSTA DWYER is a Canadian writer and journalist. She has contributed to the *Globe and Mail*, Toronto *Star*, *Maclean's* magazine and the San Francisco *Examiner*. She has been a free-lance journalist in Haiti, the Dominican Republic, and Central America, a translator (Spanish to English) and a social worker in London, England. *Into the Amazon* is her first book.